BASILDON

THROUGH TIME

Lisa Horner

AMBERLEY PUBLISHING

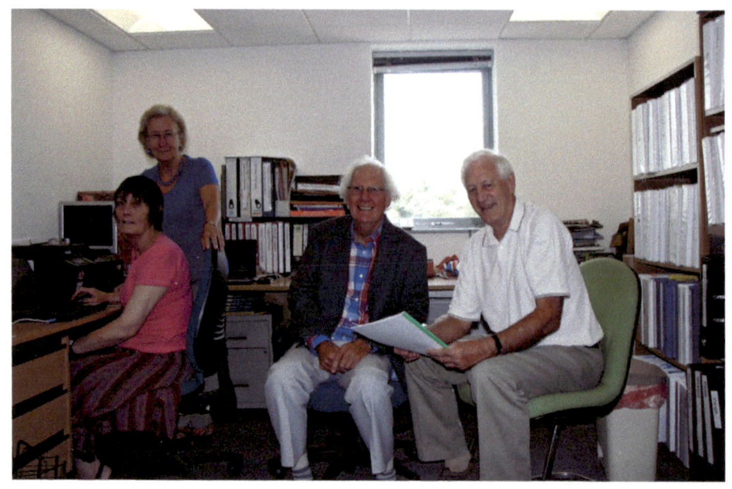

I dedicate this book to the Basildon Borough Heritage Group (www. basildonheritage.org.uk). From left to right: Denise Rowling, Jo Cullen, former member Vin Harrop, and Ken Porter. Many thanks.

First published 2014

Amberley Publishing
The Hill, Stroud
Gloucestershire, GL5 4EP

www.amberley-books.com

ISBN 978 1 4456 3494 4 (print)
ISBN 978 1 4456 3515 6 (ebook)

British Library Cataloguing in Publication Data.
A catalogue record for this book is available from
the British Library.

Typeset in 9.5pt on 12pt Celeste.
Typesetting by Amberley Publishing.
Printed in the UK.

Appointed GPSR EU Representative: Easy Access
System Europe Oü, 16879218
Address: Mustamäe tee 50, 10621, Tallinn, Estonia
Contact Details: gpsr.requests@easproject.com,
+358 40 500 3575

Introduction

Basildon New Town was created to accommodate the overspill of the population of London after the devastation of the Second World War. With 7,834 acres of land formed from a collection of villages, namely Laindon, Langdon Hills, Lee Chapel, Basildon, Vange and Pitsea; taking the name Basildon, as this was the central village.

Go back to ancient times and Basildon was home to roaming hunters. Many tribes occupied Britain, each with its own king, capital and territory. The tribe of the Kingdom of Essex was the Trinovantes. Evidence of their activities have been found in the tools and weapons that have been discovered, such as a flint toolmaking industry that was found at Langdon Hills, and the Bronze Age 'Vange Hoard' that was found when workmen were digging the foundations of Basildon New Town's first school.

In AD 43, Emperor Claudius and his army of some 40,000 Romans crossed the Thames, probably marching through this area on their way to capture Colchester. Roman tiles have been found in Vange, proving the Roman occupation of Basildon. The Saxon raiders invaded the Essex coast again in the fourth century. The villages as we know them today began to take shape during the early Saxon period; clusters of wattle and daub huts set around tiny wooden churches were built.

The *Domesday Book* came into existence in 1086. Basildon is mentioned several times under the entry for Hundred of Barstable. Barstable had seven households, including one villager, three small holders, two and a half lord's plough teams, and one and a half men's plough teams. All Saints church was built at Vange around this time, as its nave dates back to the eleventh century. Essex was abundant with clay, so the production of pottery and bricks was a significant industry, together with farming and salt extraction.

Beorhtel was a Saxon who owned the hilly land to the north of the Holy Cross church, which became known as Beorhtel's Dun ('dun' was the Saxon word for 'hill'). This is where the name of Basildon is derived from; it has changed over time, some variations are Berdlesdon, Batlesdon and Belesduna. It is believed that the Holy Cross church, which dates back to 1230, was at the centre of the village of Basildon.

In 1620, the floods in Vange were so disastrous that Dutch engineer, Cornelius Vandenanker, was employed to reclaim land. Around this time John Puckle remembered the poor children of the Parish of St Nicholas, Laindon in his will, leaving his 62 acres of land so that a schoolmaster's wages could be afforded. Beer was a normal drink for all the family in the early 1600s as water was often impure – tea was unheard of.

In 1821, the village of Basildon had 142 inhabitants while Laindon had a populous of 402. Around 1891, farmers sold thousands of acres of land to The Land Company due to the agricultural depression. The Land Company, in alliance with the railway, organised cheap trips to Laindon, Pitsea and Wickford. Posters went up in London advertising the benefits of country living. Plots were offered for as little as £10.

Weekend residences sprung up all around the area. Lots of specialist shops and some small cinemas began to line the High Roads. After the First World War, there was an influx of east-enders, the majority of weekend residences became permanent after the Second World War.

In 1946, the New Towns Act was introduced. The proposed new towns would accommodate the overspill from cities such as London after the Second World War. West Ham alone had 20,000 people on its housing waiting list. Harlow and the Basildon area were designated to be new towns in Essex. Despite a lot of opposition, The Basildon Development Corporation was established; Basildon New Town came into existence in 1949. With a plan to build a town for 80,000 people, the vast majority of plotlands were obtained through compulsory purchase with the intention to build housing estates, provide industry and the necessary amenities.

The population of the Basildon district as of 2010 was around 172,000, with plans for further regeneration in the area. It is predominantly a centre of industry, although many residents commute to London for work.

The purpose of this book is to give an insight into how Basildon has changed through time. Our journey stretches from west to east, with each area covered from further periods in time to more modern. I hope you enjoy your time travel as much as I have.

Lisa Horner, BA (Hons)
16 July 2014

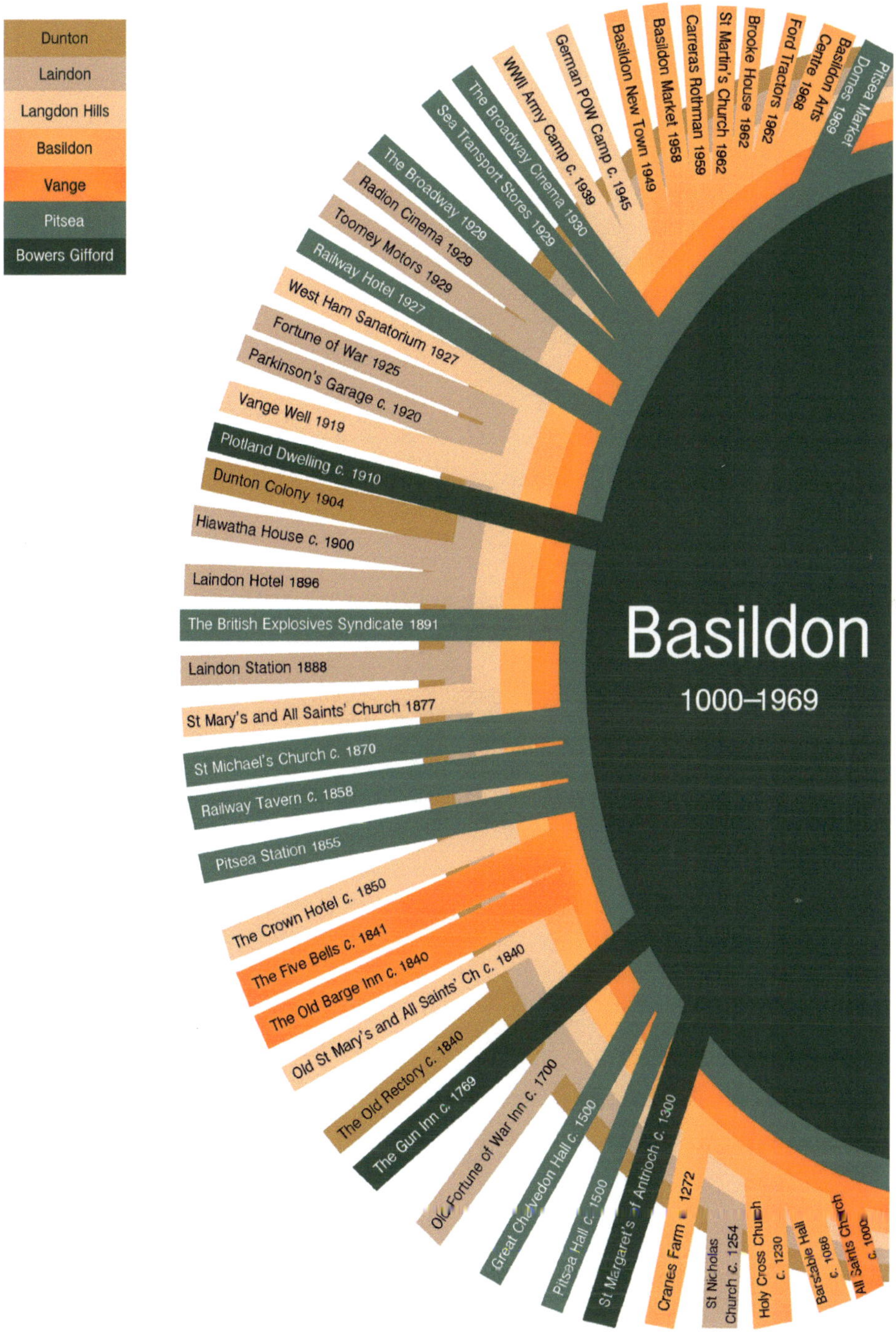

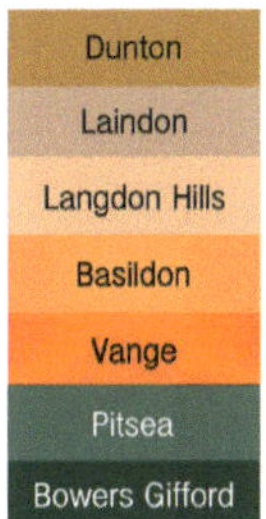

Basildon
1000–1969

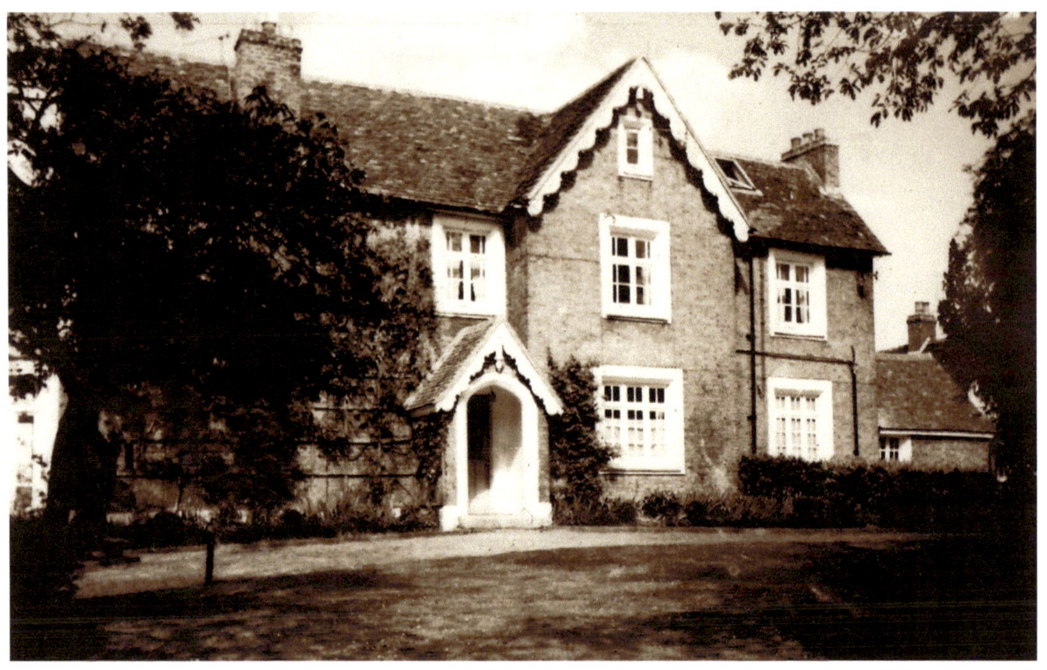

The original rectory, built in the seventeenth century, burnt down. Then the present rectory was built *c.* 1840s. It served St Mary's church, which became a private residence in the 1970s. Lord Charles Edward Leatherland bought the property in 1934, living there until 1951. After serving in the First World War, he was a journalist for a leading Labour newspaper, the *Daily Herald*. He was later a Labour councilor and long term member of the House of Lords. Today, the Old Rectory is a wedding ceremony and reception venue.

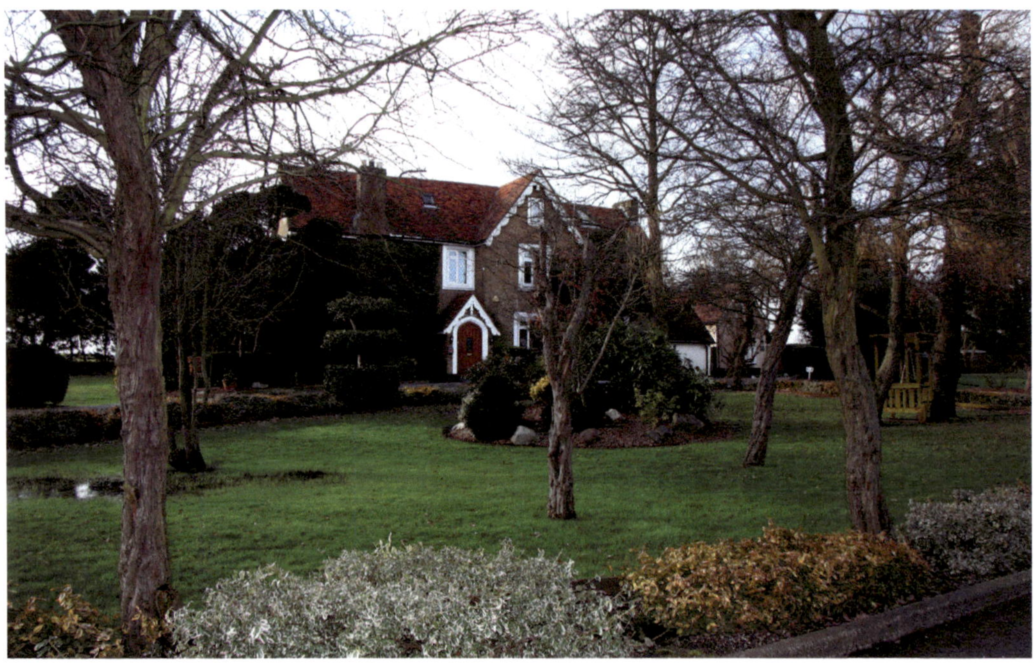

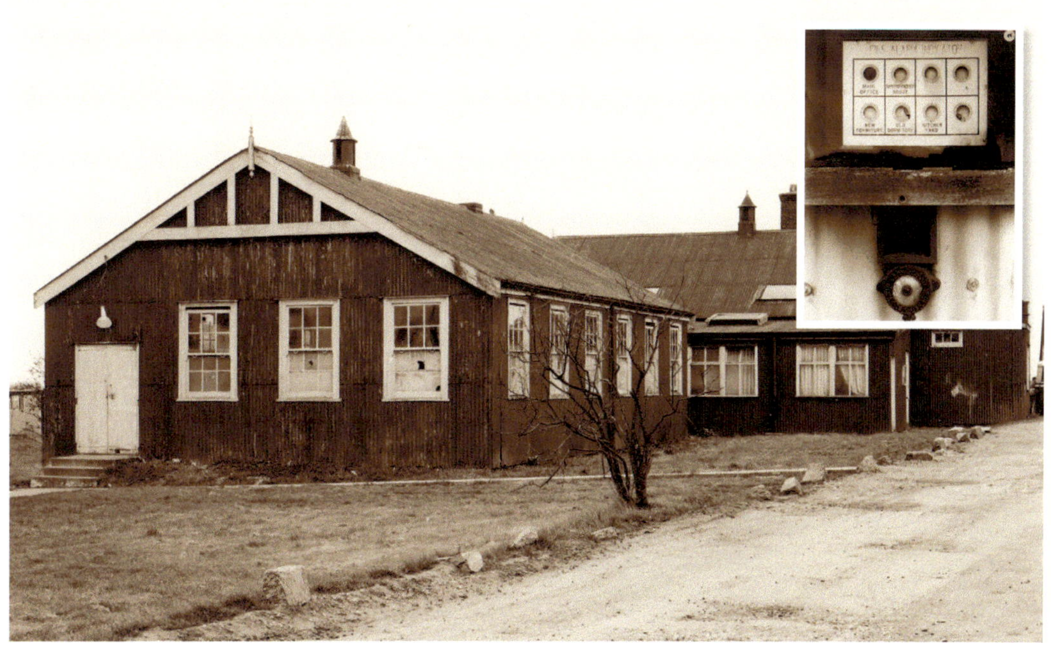

Dunton Colony

Supported by Poor Law administrator George Lansbury, Joseph Fels purchased Sumpers Farm in 1904. Becoming the first Poor Law Labour Colony in England, it was run by the Poplar Board of Guardians and aimed to equip unemployed London men with agricultural skills so that they could build new lives. The building above was previously a large dormitory and gymnasium. In the inset image we see a fire alarm indicator. In 1928, London County Council took over the property and ran a self-contained community until 1941. It's now the site of the Dunton Residential Caravan Park.

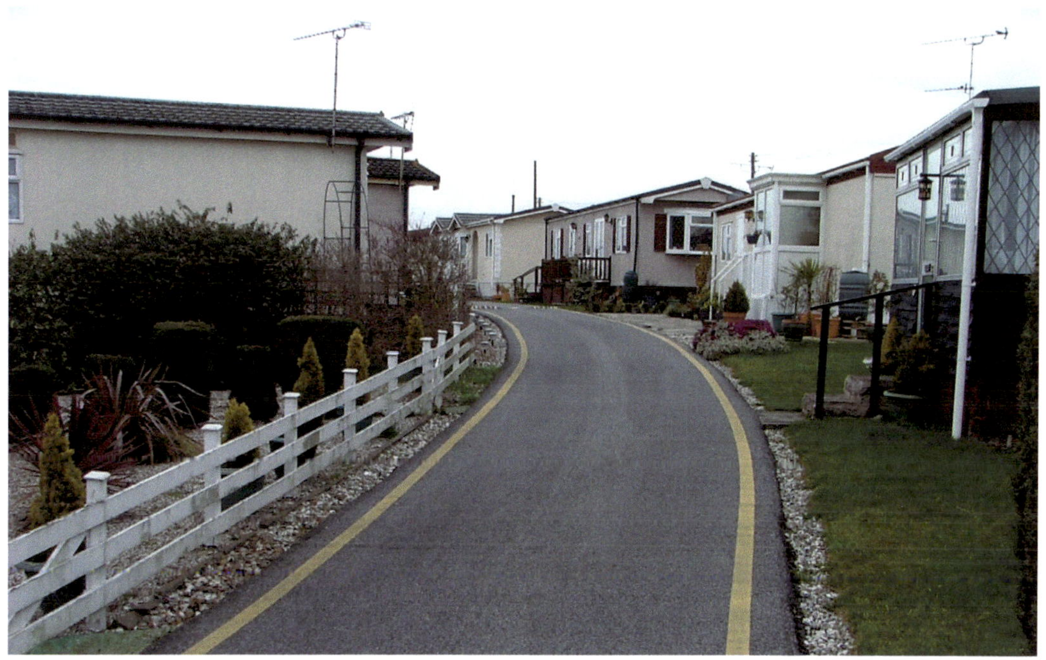

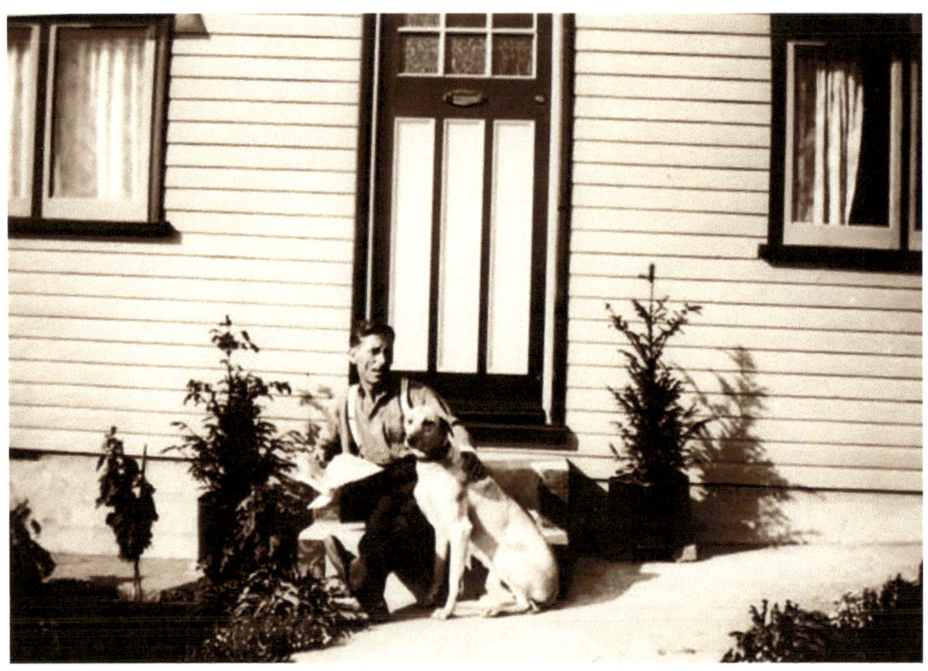

Dunton – The Haven, Third Avenue, Dunton Hills Estate

The Mills family built the property in 1934 and lived there until 1983. Most homes were basically built, warmed by paraffin-filled heaters and lit by oil lamps. The families depended on shared wells or standpipes for water. The Haven was made a museum when the Essex Wildlife Trust took over the reserve in the 1980s. Members of the community play *Beorhtel's Hill* posed in front of The Haven in 1989; they were getting the feel of being a plotlander. Some are from the Thalian Theatre Group, formed in Basildon in 1972 (*see page 65*).

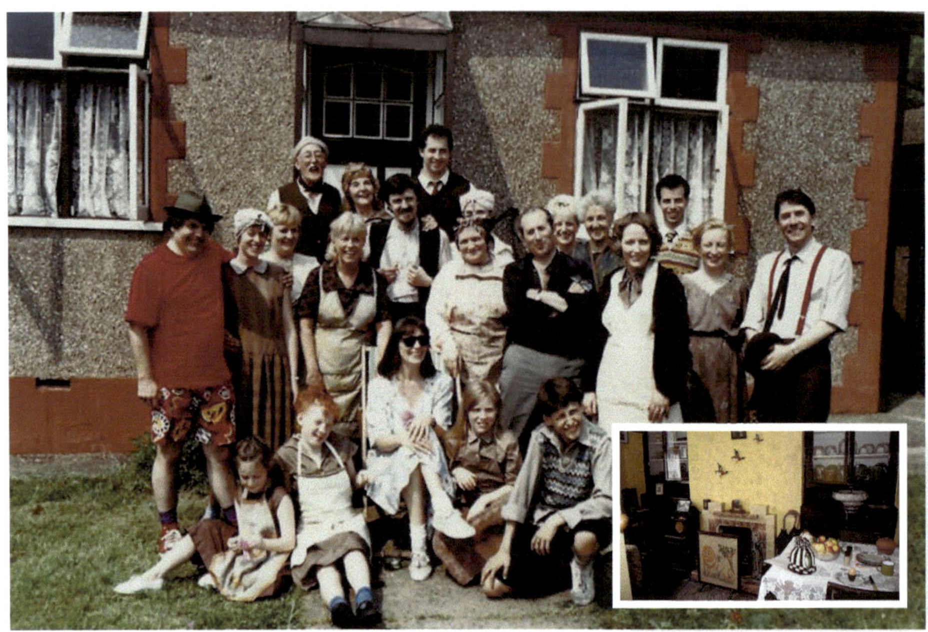

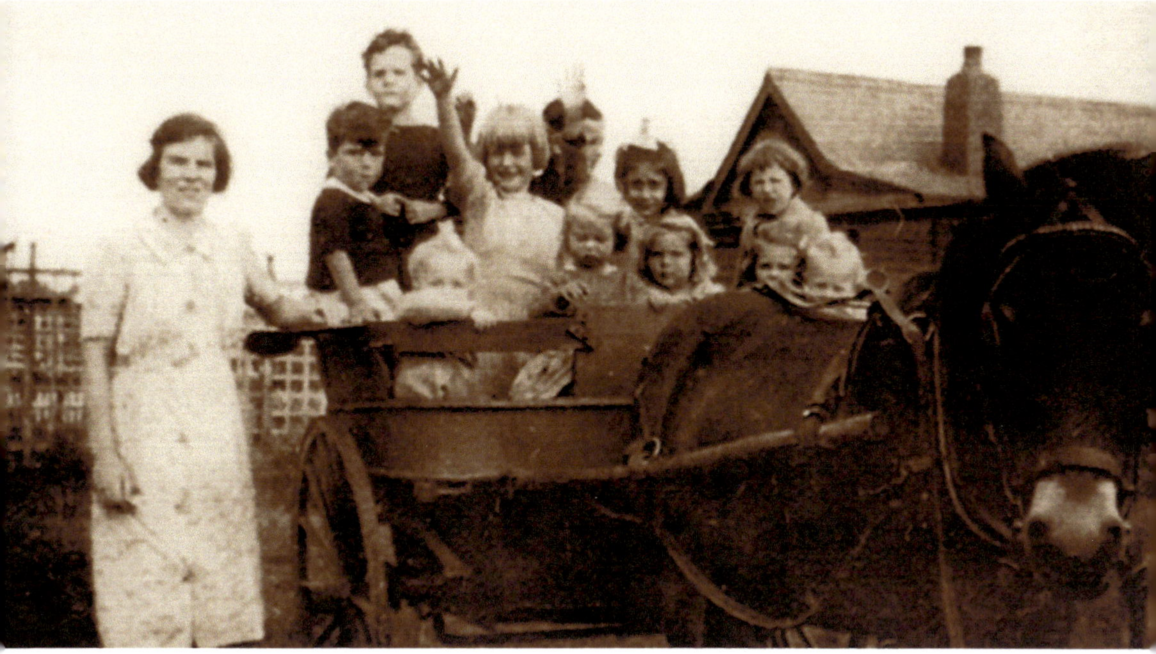

Dunton – Joe Goodman: 'King of the One Liners'

In 1939, a six-week-old Joe Goodman was found in a shop doorway, in Laindon High Street, in a wet pram. He went on to live in several Dunton plotland bungalows with his foster mother, Ethel Thomas. (*boy furthest left, above*). From winning *Opportunity Knocks* in 1970, he starred in several royal variety shows and received prestigious awards. Joe was a member of the Grand Order of the Water Rats. He also regularly attended the annual Dunton Reunion. Sadly, he passed away at the age of seventy-five on 28 April 2014. He will be sadly missed by many from all walks of life.

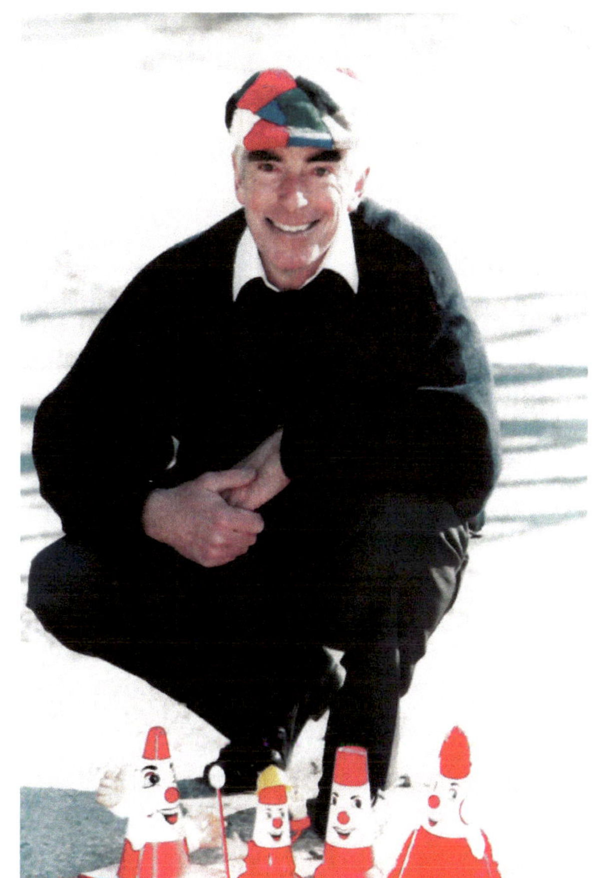

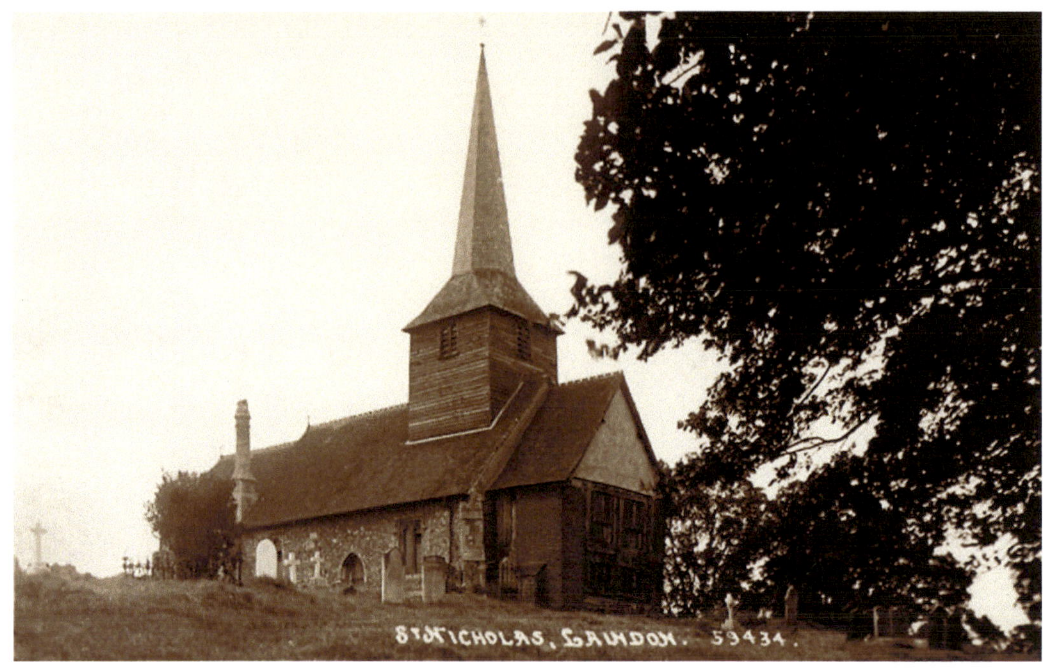

Laindon – St Nicholas Church

Believed to have been built in the thirteenth century, St Nicholas church (a Grade I listed building with a fine timber-frame bell tower) has a panoramic view over Laindon, south towards the New Town, and north to the A127. It is said that on a clear day you can see Canary Wharf. The first recorded rector was Richard de List in 1254. Recently, Revd Diane Ricketts, who was the minister of the church, retired.

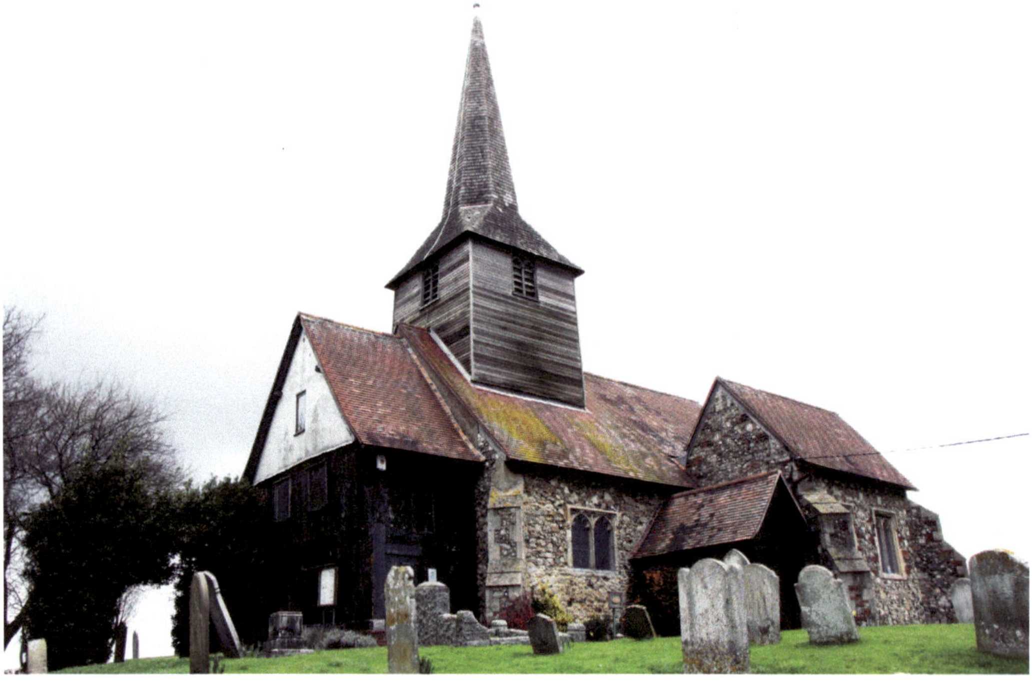

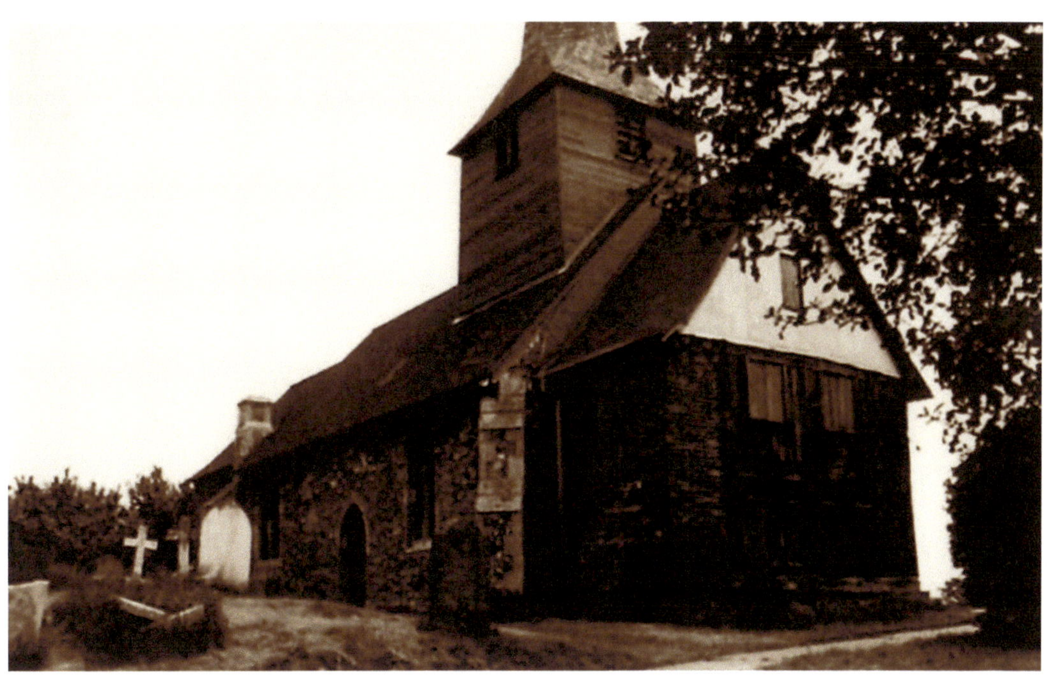

Laindon – Puckle's School

Attached to St Nicholas is what once was once a sixteenth-century priest's house, later becoming a school for over 250 years. It was named Puckle's School after John Puckle left his seventeenth-century farmhouse and 62 acres of land to the church as long as they promised the endowment would pay for an Oxford or Cambridge graduate teacher's wages. Inside the church hangs a tablet commemorating the landowner. He is also remembered by a special sermon on St John's Day. The last teacher who worked and lived there was James Hornsby. A local secondary school was named in his honour.

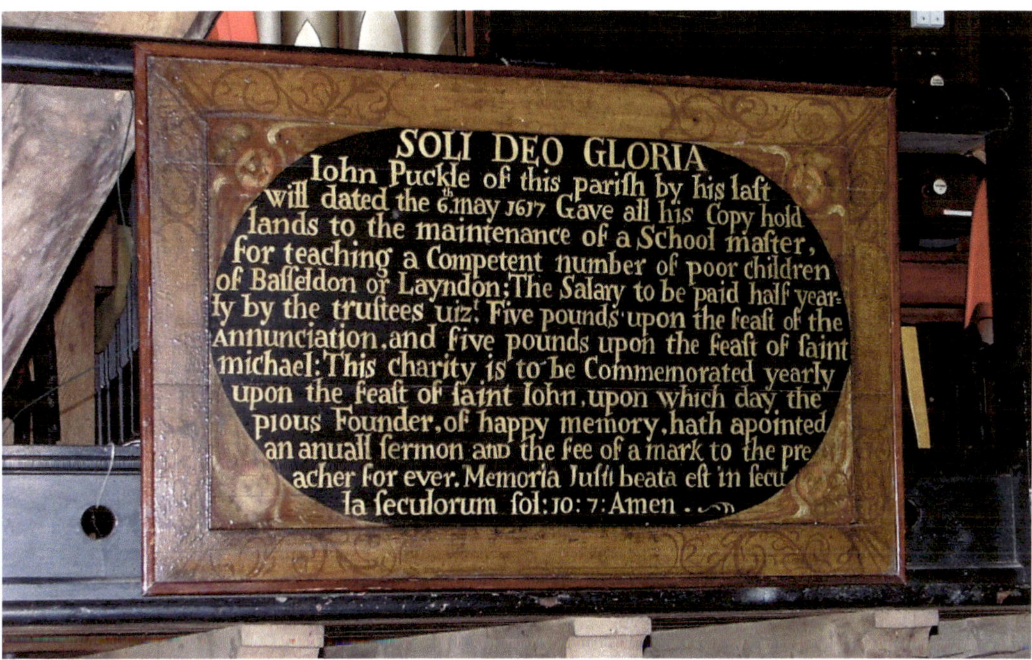

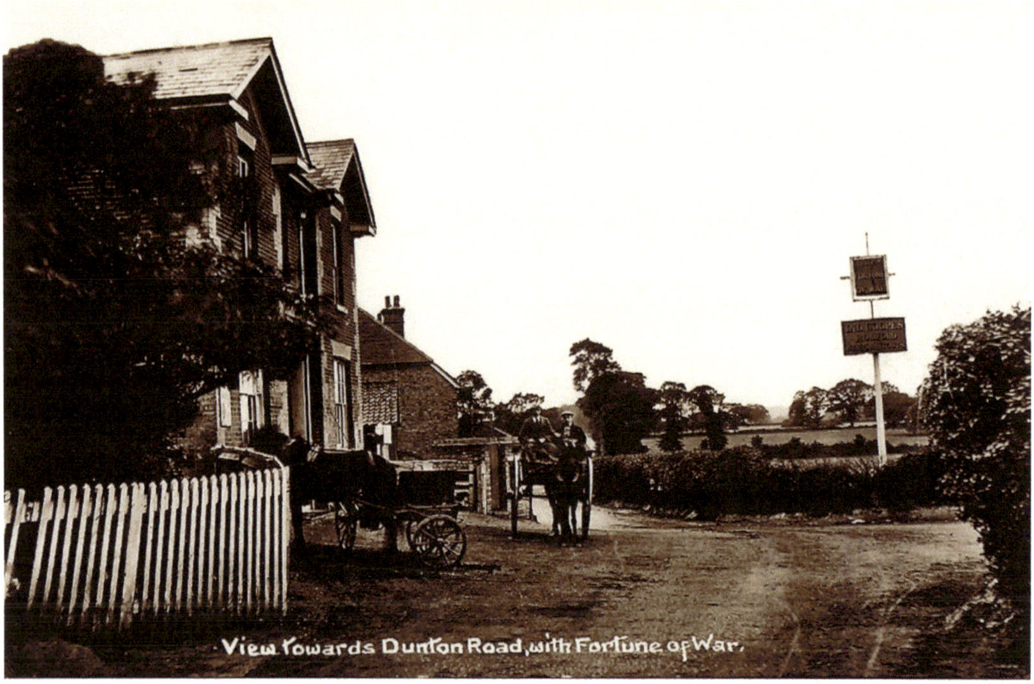

Laindon – The Old Fortune of War

Before the realignment of the roads, the Fortune of War was situated at the historic Laindon Cross, where four roads met. It was possibly built around the 1700s and rebuilt around the 1900s. It is said that it was named and founded by a soldier returning from the Napoleonic Wars. DGT Alloy Wheels & Tyres occupies the building on the corner of Wash Road and Noak Hill Road.

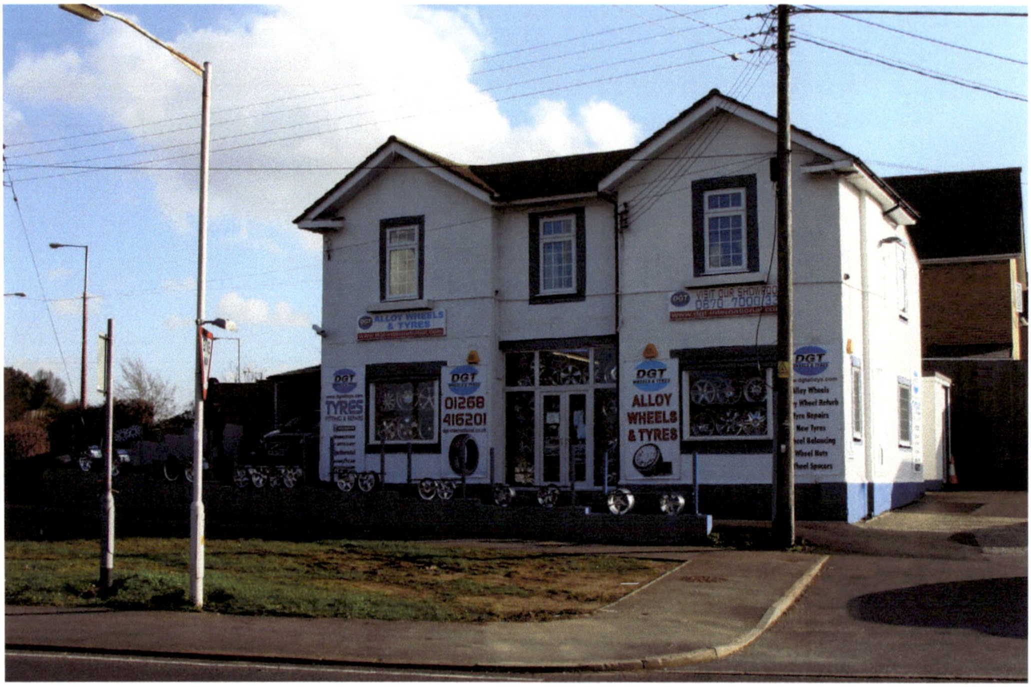

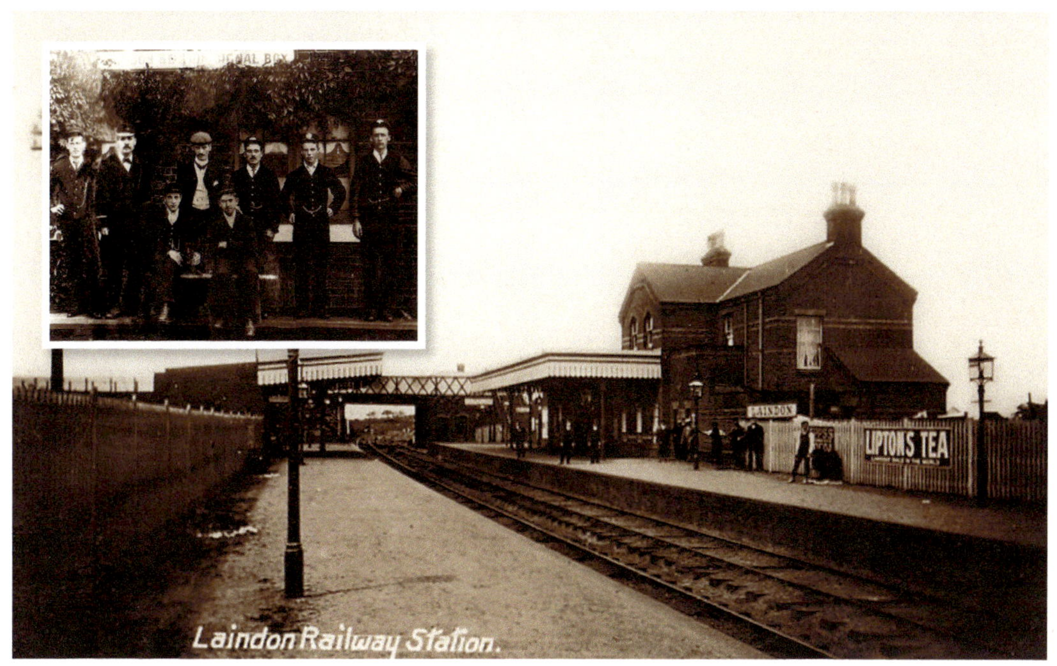

Laindon Station

Laindon Railway Station came into service in June 1888, which gradually changed Laindon from a remote area to a busy commuter town. Seen above is the station in the 1920s. Steam trains were used then, and the last one left Fenchurch Street in 1962. On 18 June 1962 the electric service commenced. Here we see staff at Laindon Station around the 1910s. Today, the station staff work on a station that has CCTV coverage and many modern amenities.

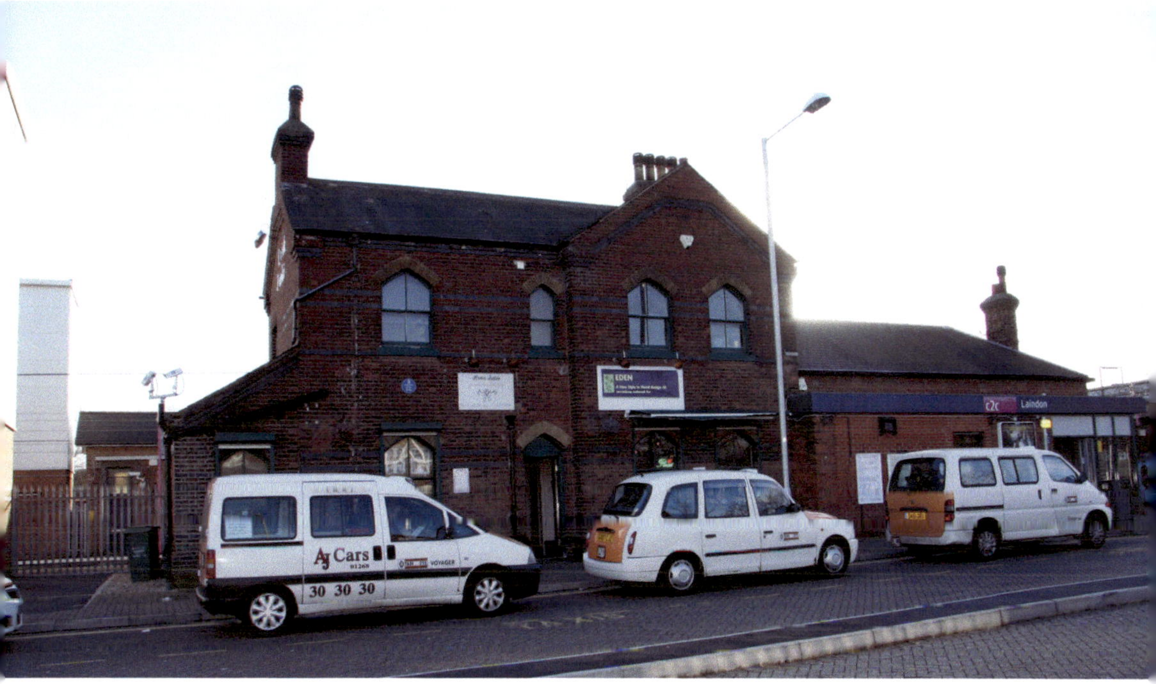

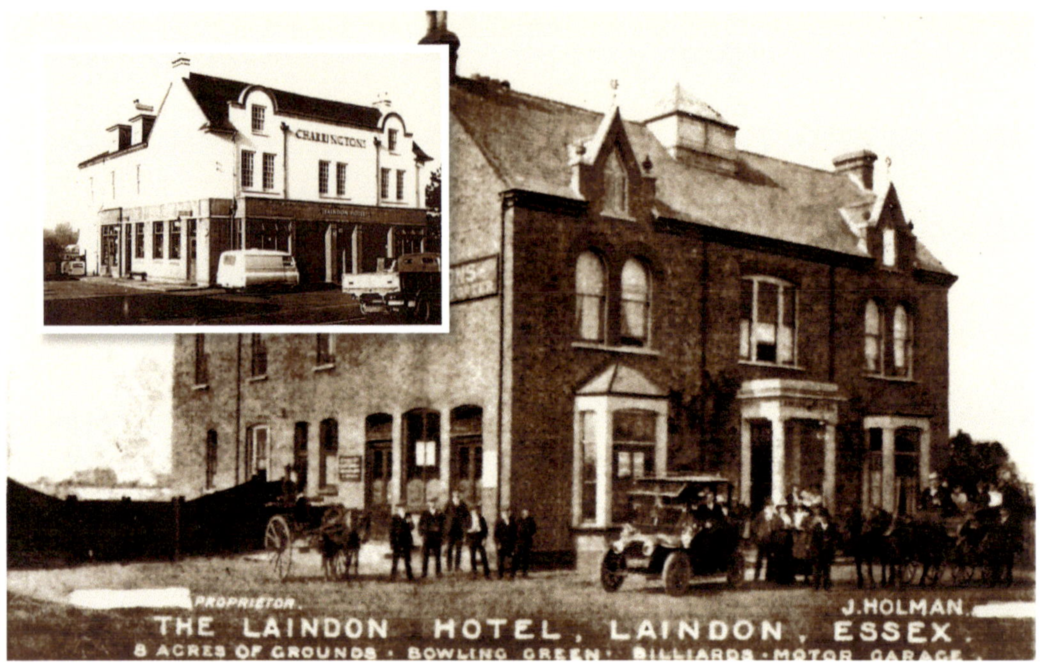

Laindon Hotel

The Laindon Hotel was built in 1896, along with plans for a Laindon Racecourse that failed after a few races. Located on the High Road between Durham Road and Aston Road, it was made famous in 1966 when British Pathe filmed a palomino horse playing a game of football with Billy Foyle, then presented him with a pint in the Laindon Hotel. It closed in the late 1980s and was later demolished in 1991. Laindon Holdings Group of Companies owns the land.

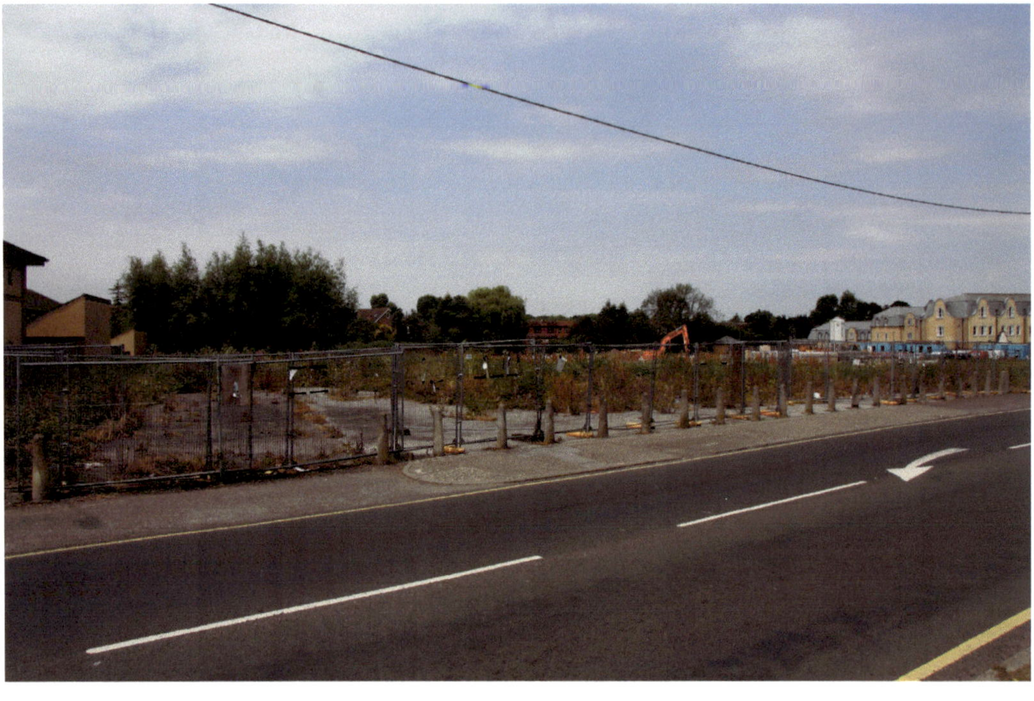

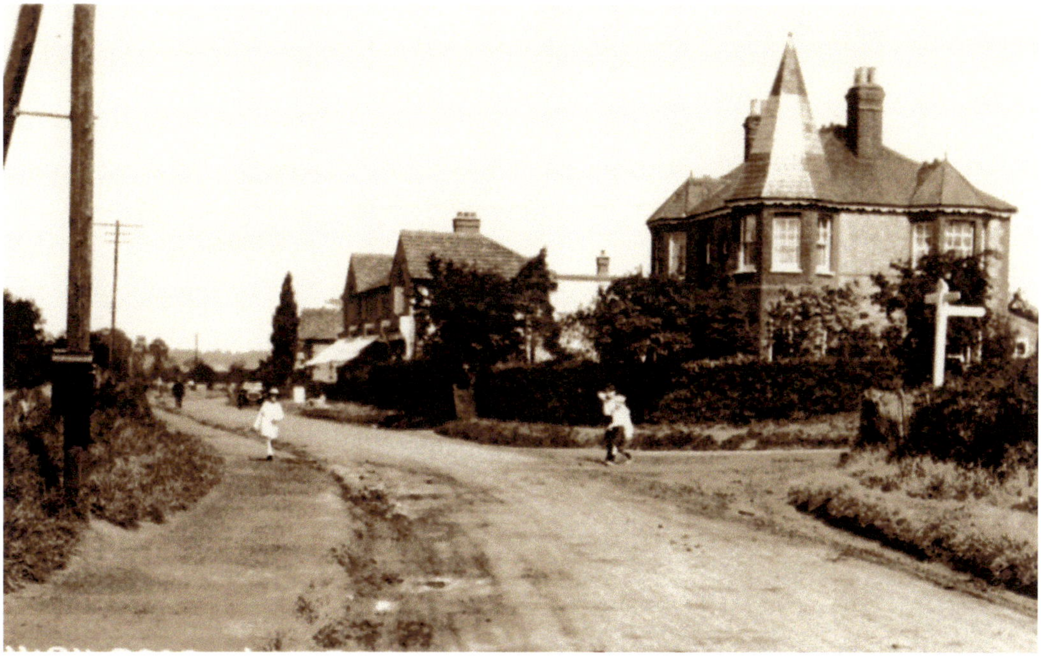

Laindon – Hiawatha House, 1920s

Greenhaugh was built around 1900 where St Nicholas Lane meets the High Road. Its tower inspired locals to rename it Hiawatha House, Hiawatha (*Hári Wáta* in Ioway language) meaning 'I am looking far away'. It was a doctor's surgery from the 1930s and, in 1947, a young Ann Bullimore had her head stitched by Dr. Long, and her mum mistakenly paid a florin instead of a half-crown. Mrs. Long followed her up the hill for the missing sixpence. In 2012, Century Place, a row of terraced houses, was built in its place.

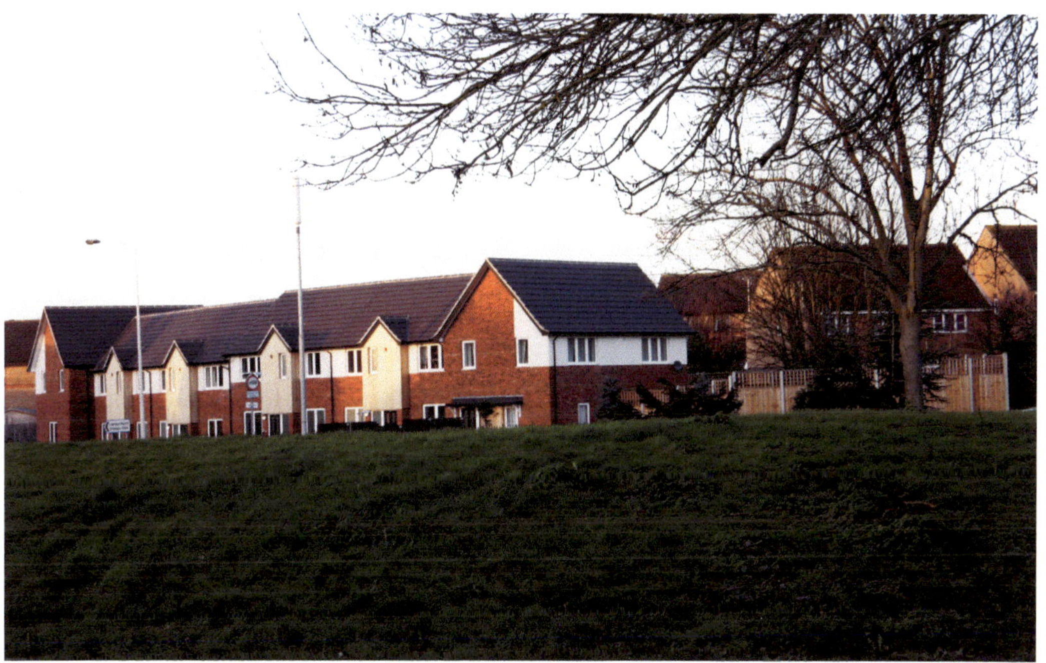

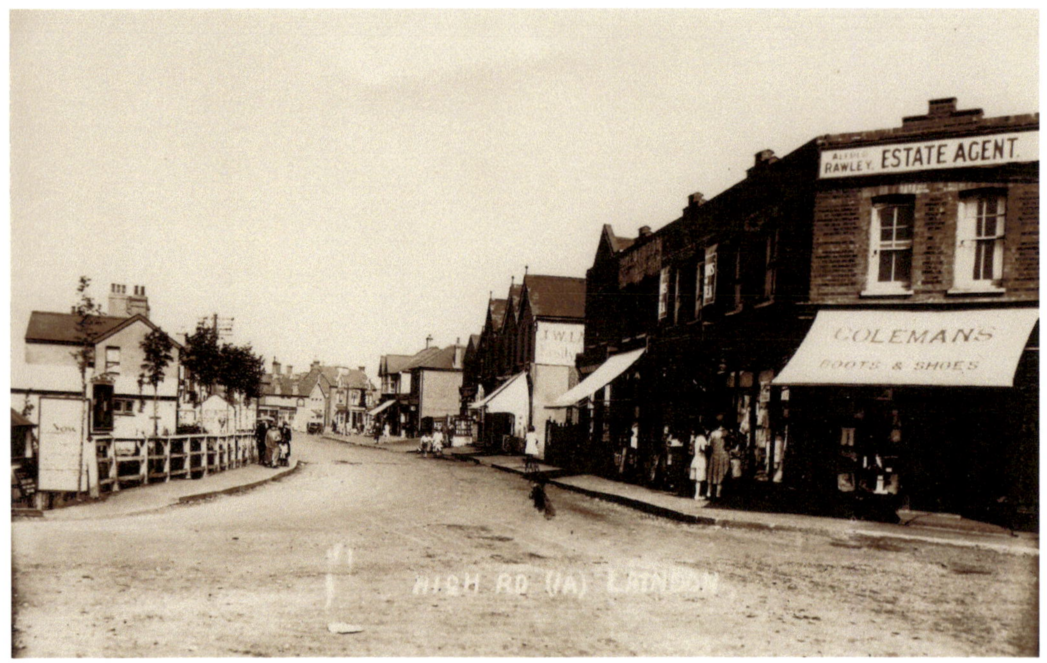

Laindon High Road

Due to the influx to the area because of the opening of Laindon Station, the High Road expanded to a street of 120 shops between Laindon Station and past the Fortune of War during the 1920s and 1930s. Businesses began to close due to the development of Basildon New Town in the 1950s and the Laindon Shopping Centre in the late 1960s. Most of the shops have gone now, replaced by residential buildings.

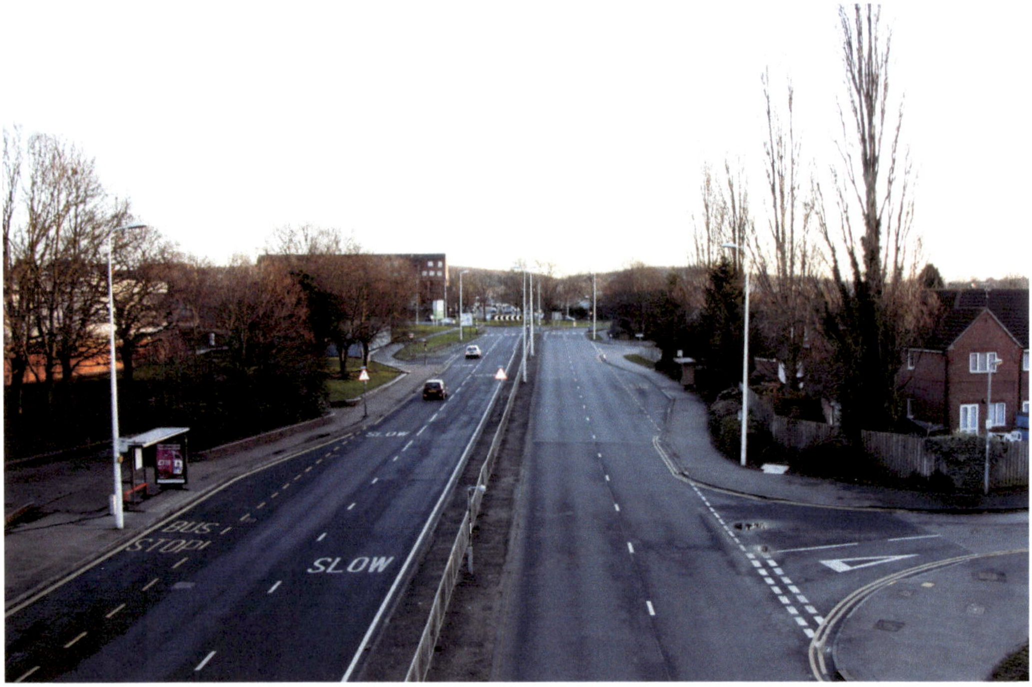

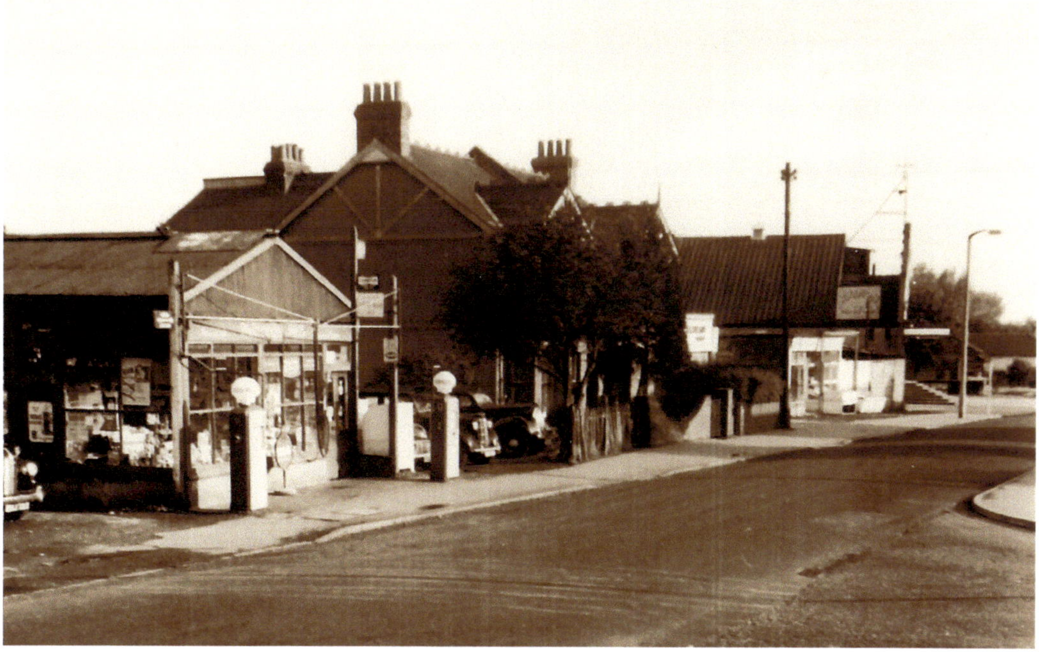

Laindon – Parkinson's Garage, 1960s

Cliff, Bert and Cyril Parkinson ran a garage on the High Road at the corner of Somerset Road. Their father started the business after the First World War, selling petrol, paraffin and running a taxi service. In 1957, a teenager called Peter Robinson worked for Cliff Parkinson. He remembers that Parkinson 'kept an octopus in formaldehyde in his shop window for years, used a draw for a till and never threw anything away - he kept piles of stuff'. Houses and back gardens stand on the site today.

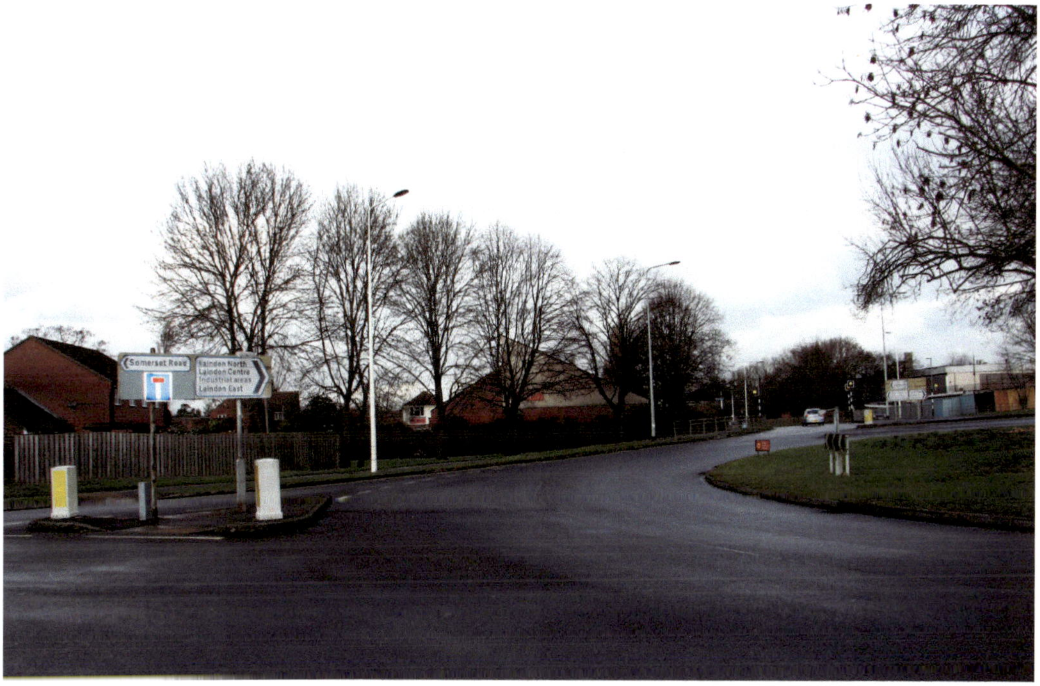

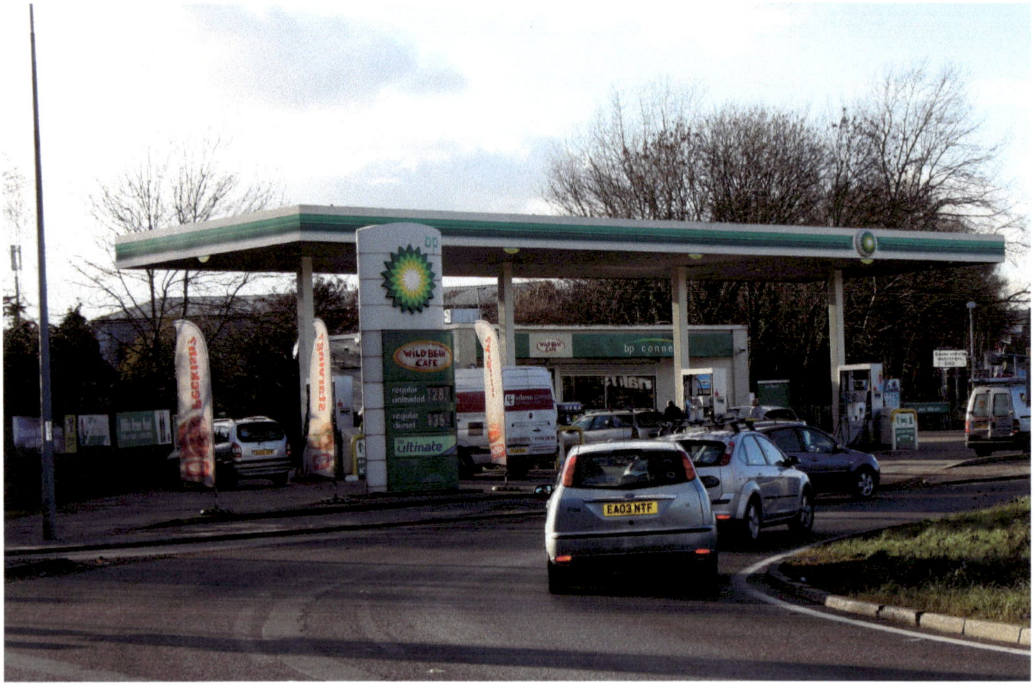

Laindon – Parkinson's Garage

Bert opened a garage on the Southend Arterial Road at the Fortune of War crossroads, remaining there until the business was forced to move to Durham Road when they were compulsorily purchased in 1960. Now a BP petrol station is in its place. The corner shops at Durham Road are called Parkinson's Corner in honour of Cliff Parkinson, a well-loved character of the area.

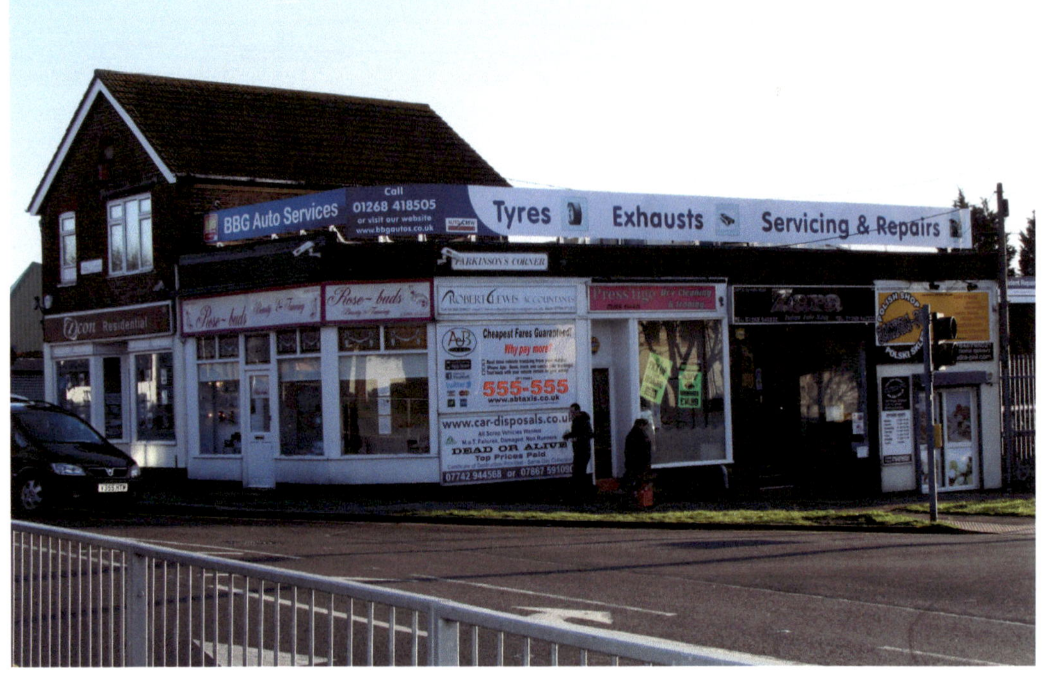

Laindon – Henbest

'Henbest for Honesty' was established in 1924, near to Aston Road, west side of Laindon High Road. It was run by Maud Henbest. Its business was in drapery and hosiery, soft furnishings and haberdashery, offering dry-cleaning, alterations and repairs. The building is owned by the Laindon Holdings Group of Companies and was once rented by the NHS. It is situated next to Laindon Community Centre.

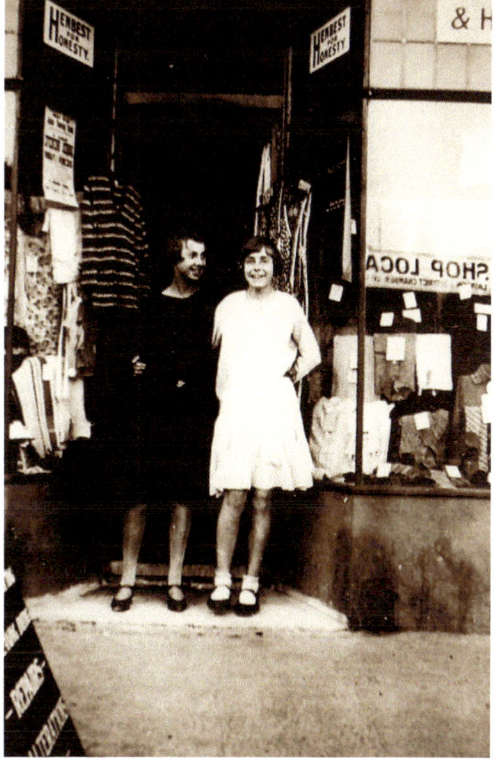

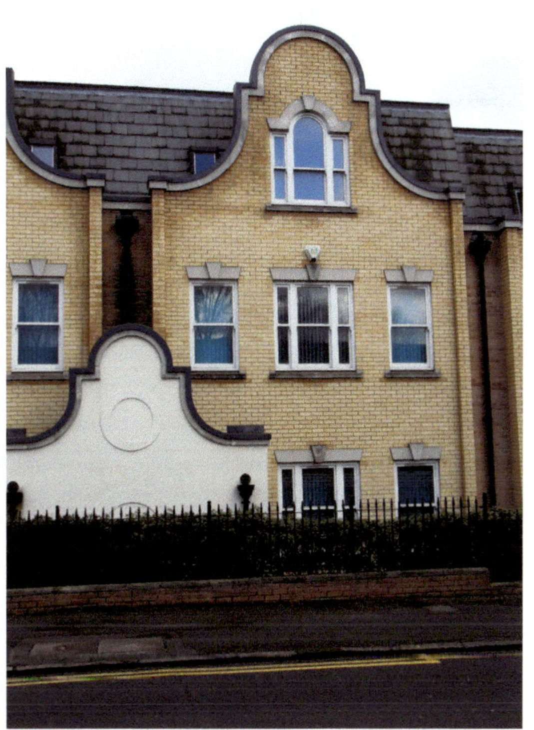

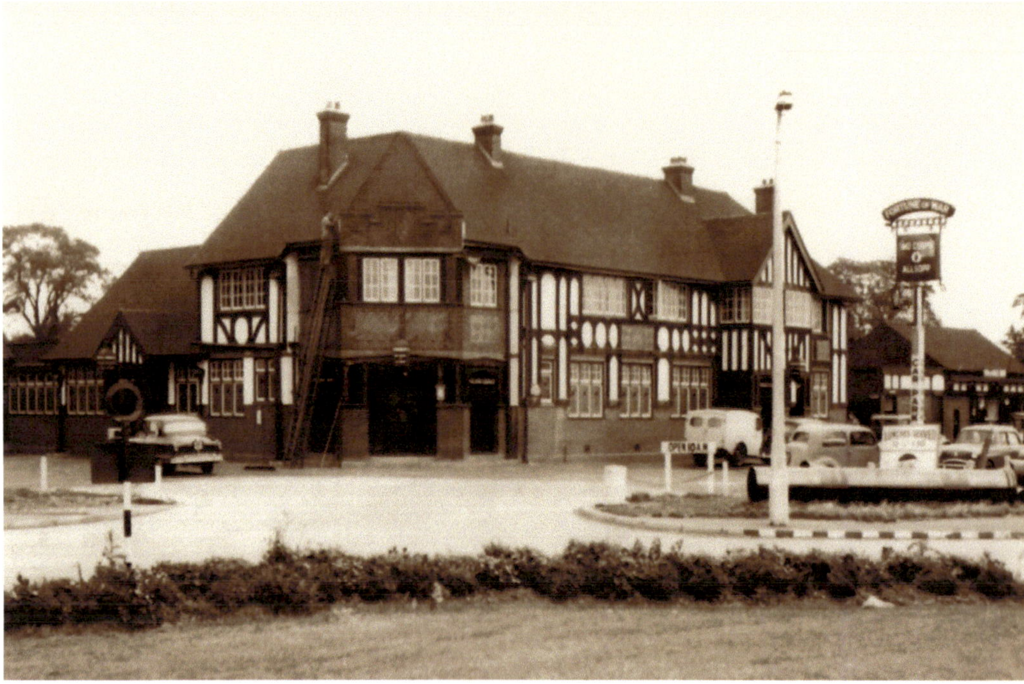

The Fortune of War on the A127 opened to the public around 1925, by the brewers Ind Coope, taking its name from the public house in Wash Road. For a brief spell it was called The Hustlers. It was popular for a *Beano* and pit stops by coach day-trippers on the way to Southend. After closing for business in 2003, the site was redeveloped by Barratt Homes.

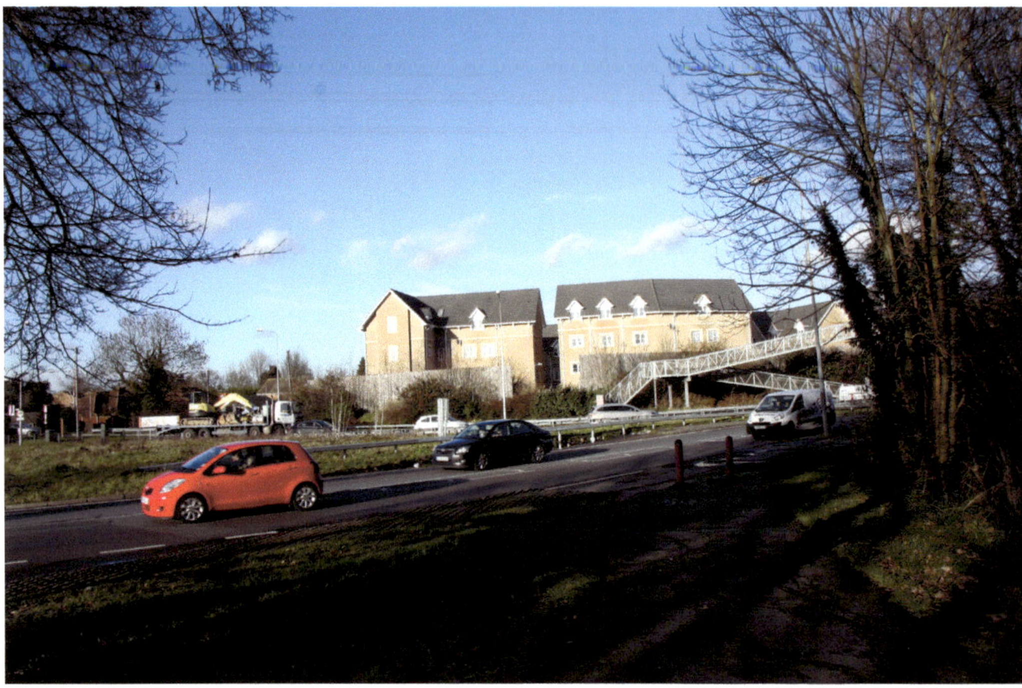

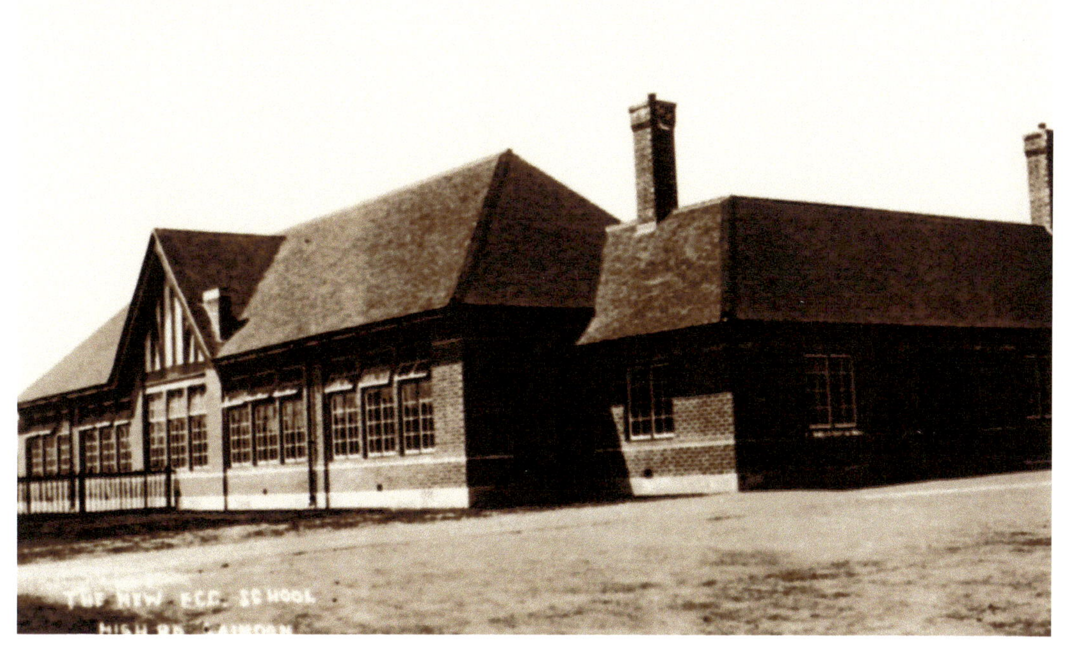

Laindon High Road School

The Laindon High Road School was opened in 1928. The Rt Hon. Lewis Silken, Minister of Town and Country Planning in Clement Attlee's post-war Labour government, attended a crowded public meeting and made his famous speech here on 7 October 1948. Parents were very worried about the imminent school closing, wondering where their children would go. When it closed in 2000 it was a sad day for the generations who went to school there. It's now the Radford Park Development, built by Bellway Homes.

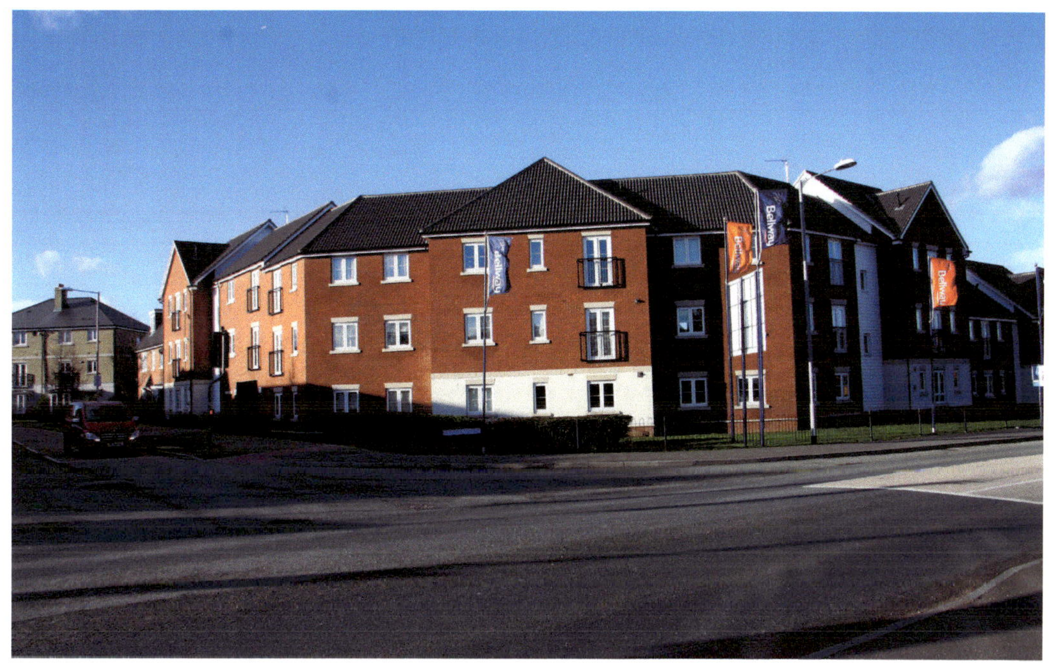

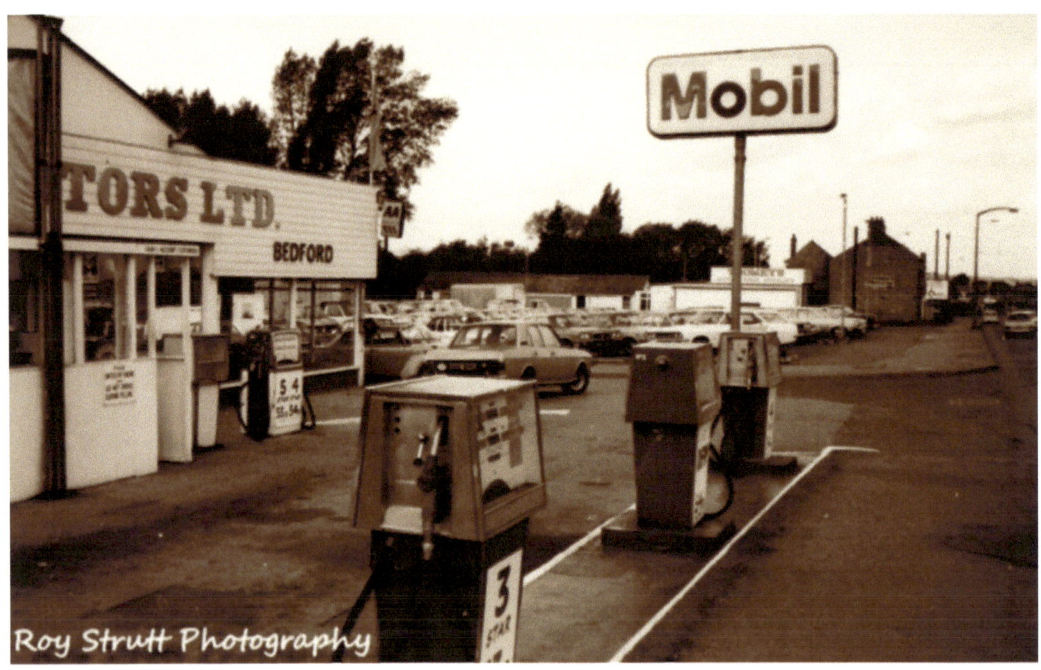

Laindon – Toomey's

J Toomey Motors Ltd stood between Service House and Toomey's Garage, at the corner of Aston Road on Laindon High Road. Penny Betteridge remembers filling up her Mini for 50p here in the 1960s. Toomey's is one of the great success stories of Laindon. Joseph Toomey started his business with Laindon Accumulators in 1929, selling batteries for the wireless and motorised vehicles. The present-day company is Laindon Holdings Group of Companies, a major force in the local commercial vehicle market. Today, the land is fenced around for redevelopment.

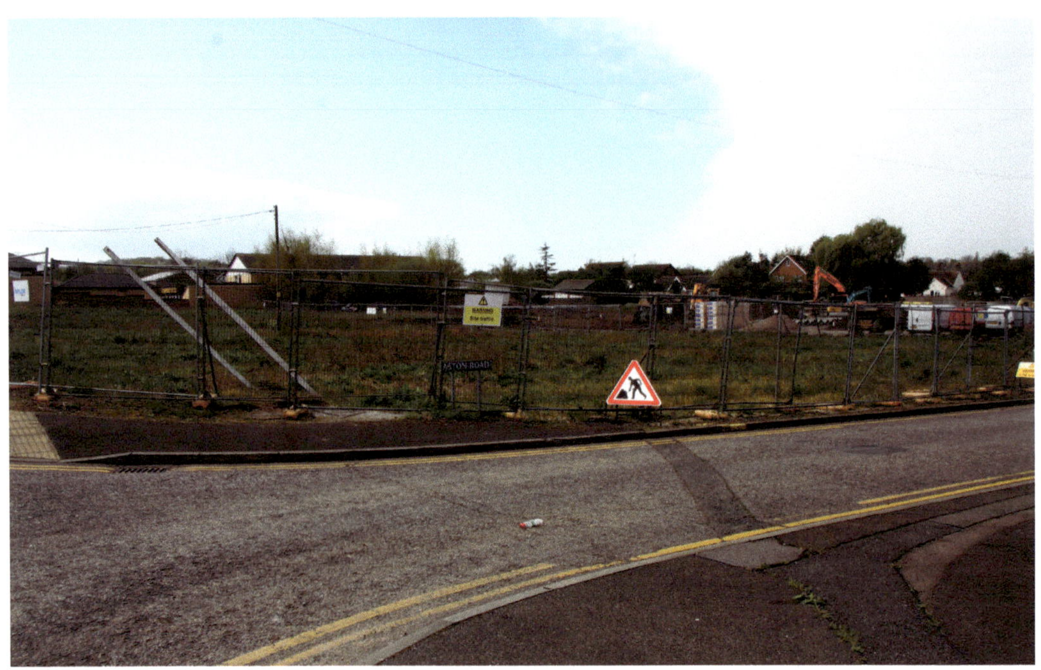

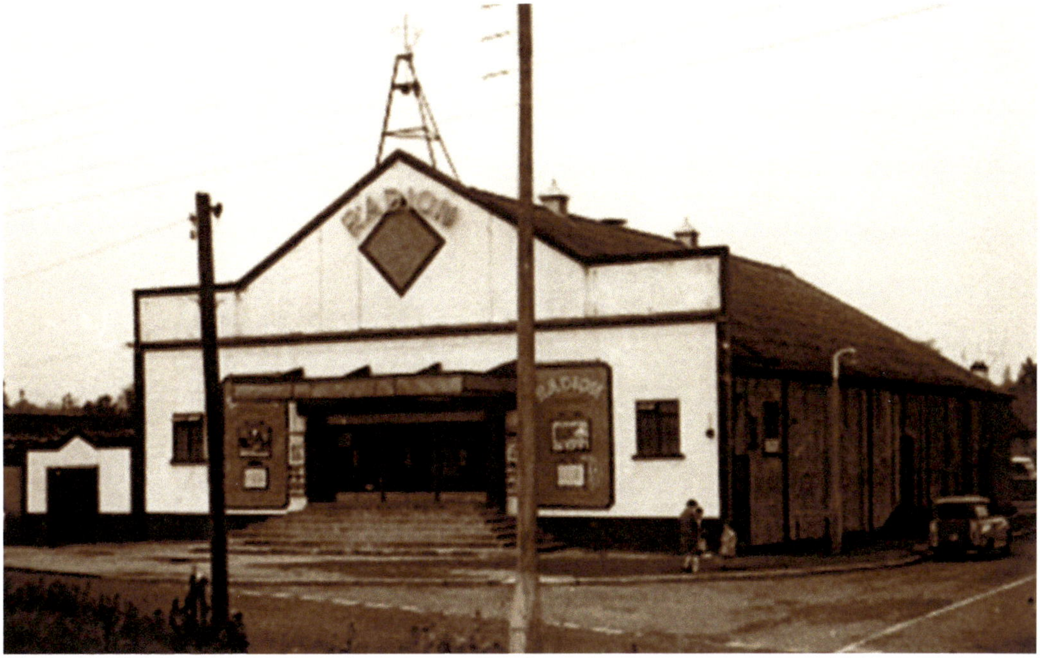

Laindon Picture Theatre/Radion Cinema, High Road, 1950s

Laindon Picture Theatre opened in 1929, becoming Radion Cinema later when it changed ownership. Michael Marchant joined the Radion Cinema as a projectionist on January 2 1957, earning £5 for a six-day week. His main duty was changing the film every twenty minutes. They built a dressing room for Joan Sims, who was in regular variety shows before her film fame. *Carry On* films, John Wayne and Audrey Hepburn were popular. The cinema closed in 1969, and some of its 680 seats went to Basildon Arts Centre. Laindon Library was built on the site in 2001.

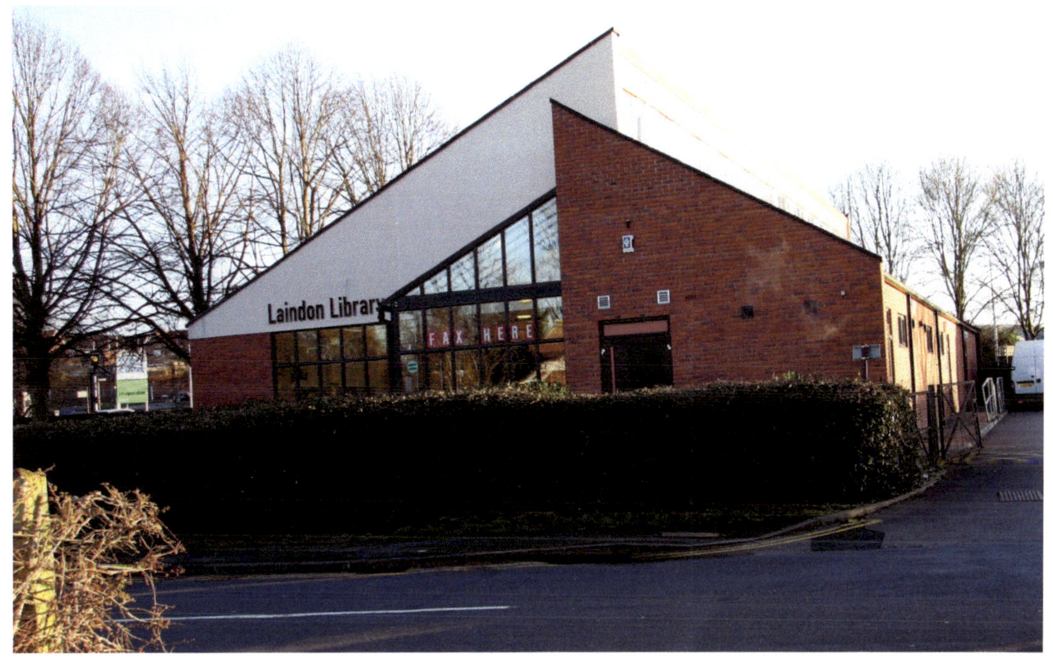

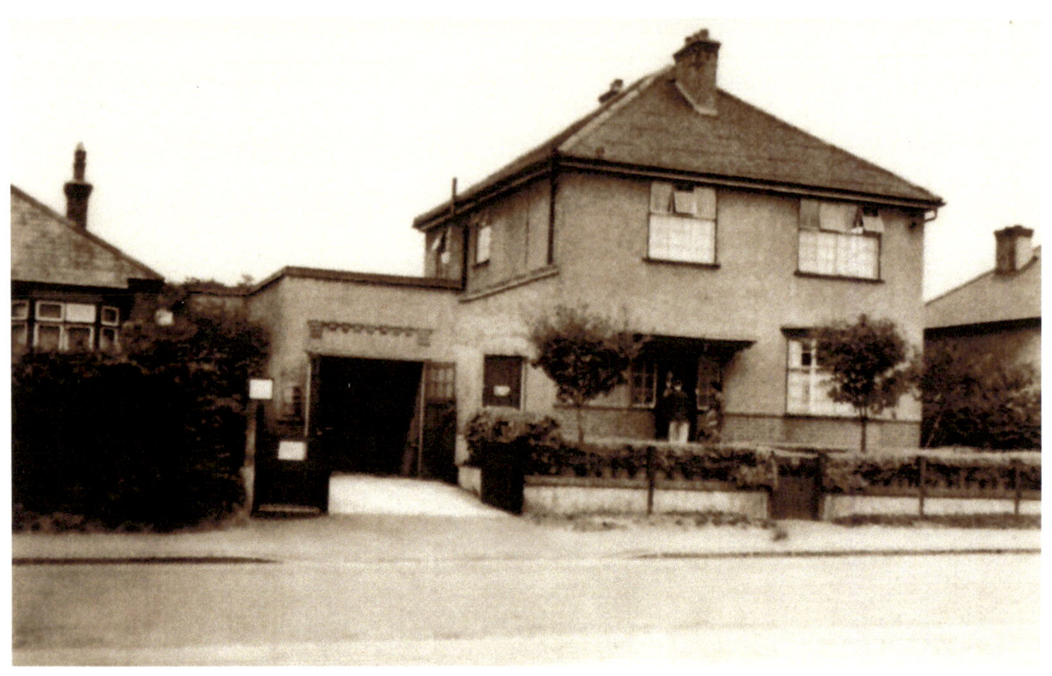

Doctor Chowdhary and family moved to Daisybank on the High Road in the 1930s. Penny Betteridge remembers the good-humoured, hard-working doctor well. When she was six-years-old she got bitten on the arm by next-door's dog. When presented to Doctor Chowdhary, he commented, 'And why didn't you bite him back?' He died suddenly in 1959. Such was the community's loss that crowds stood on the High Road pavement watching the funeral procession. Laindon Shopping Centre stands near to where Daisybank once was.

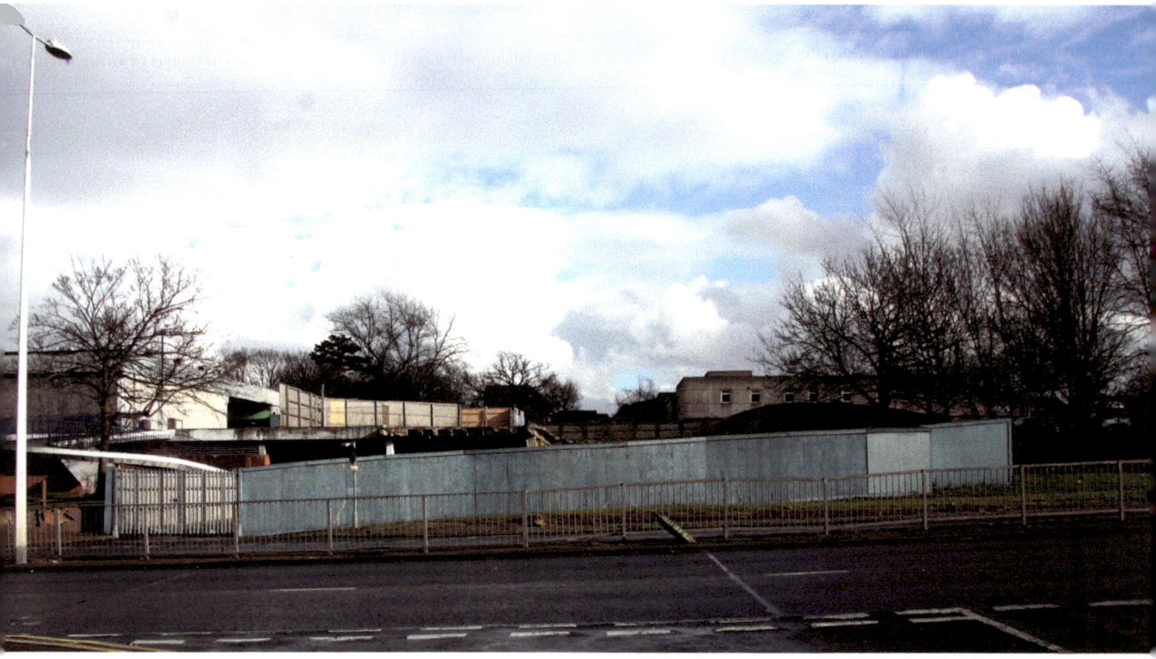

Laindon – Joan Sims

In 1930, the stationmaster's daughter, Joan Sims, entered the world. She lived at Station House and often put on impromptu performances for waiting passengers. Later, she appeared in many amateur productions with the Glee Club, Laindon Operatic Society (now BasOp) and Langdon Players. She was famous for her appearances in twenty-four *Carry On* films. She died in 2001 at the age of seventy-one. A plaque was placed in her memory on the Station House by the Joan Sims Appreciation Society on 9 May 2005 (which would have been her birthday).

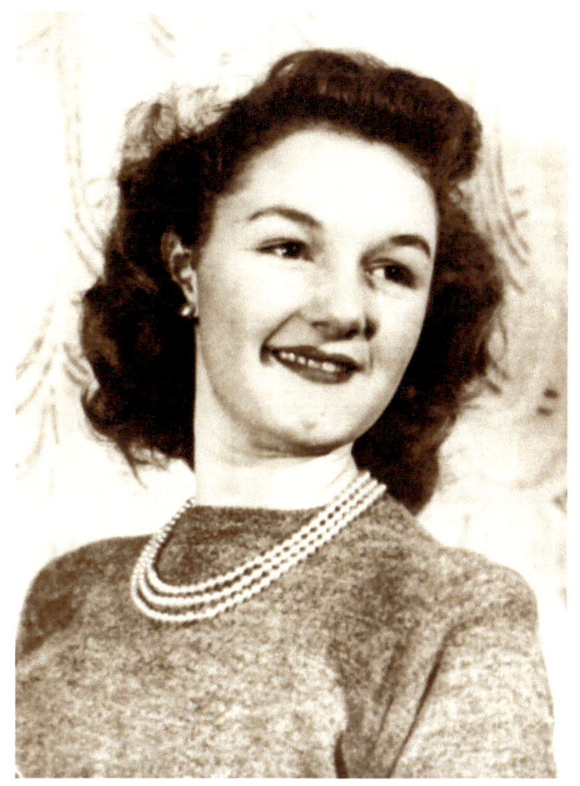

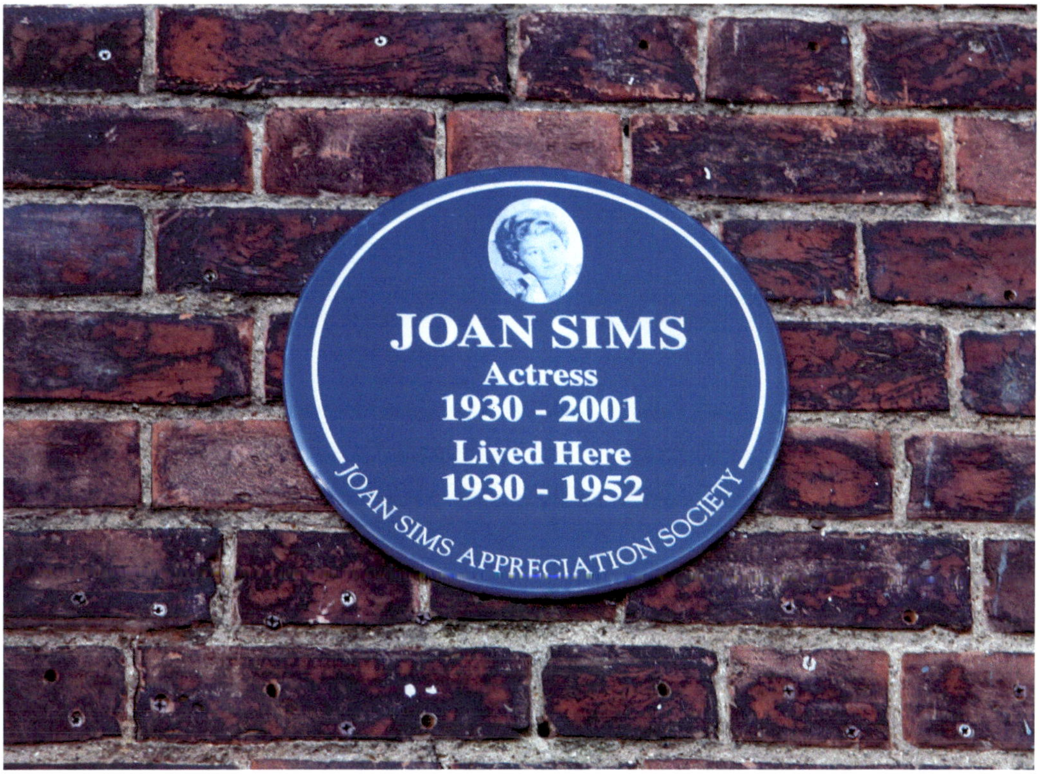

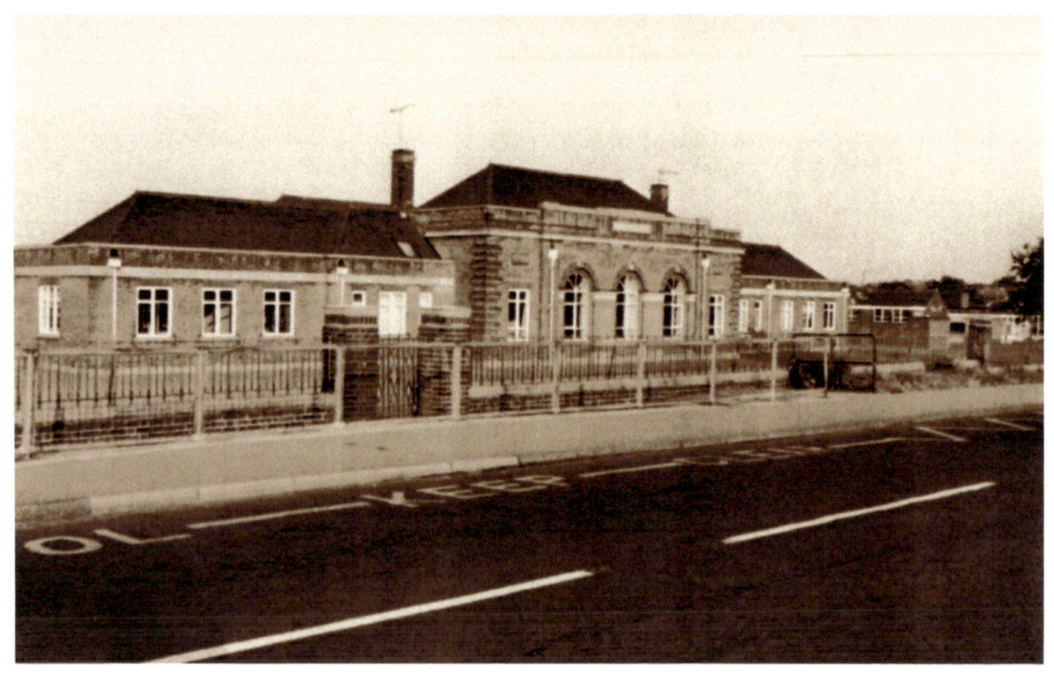

Laindon Area – Janet Duke School (Lee Chapel North)

On 2 November 1933, Markhams Chase Primary School was opened to the public. Janet Duke was appointed Headmistress at the age of twenty-nine. She was previously a teacher and Acting Head Mistress for the infants and juniors at Laindon High Road. On the year of her retirement, as a tribute, the school was renamed after her. Initially, there were 406 children in the school, there are now about 585 children, and the Headmistress is Harriet Phelps-Knights.

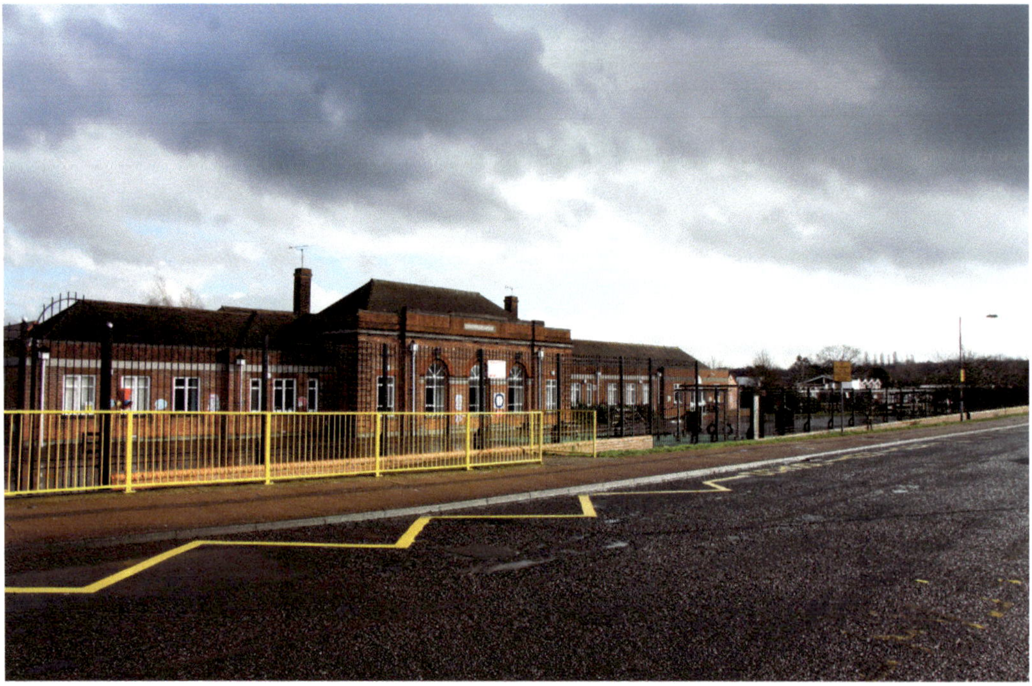

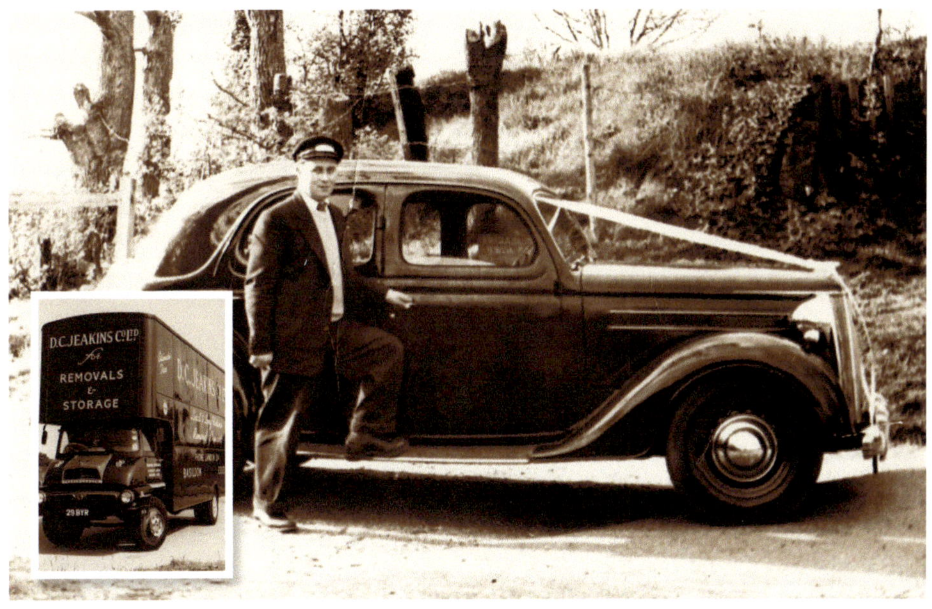

Laindon – D. C. Jeakins Co. Ltd.

Mr Derek Charles Jeakins and Mrs Myrna Doreen Jeakins started their removals taxi and car hire in 1953, from a small shop on the High Road. They lived above the shop with three of their six children. Derek acquired the removal and the taxi business from his grandfather. He then passed the business onto his father and brother, which became C & M Taxis. The company D. C. Jeakins & Co. Ltd continue to trade to a level of three depots throughout the UK. The operation of the company continued to be removals, car hire and haulage, operating over seventy-five articulates/trailers. Sadly, Mr. Jeakins passed away in 1987. The removals aspect of the company continues to operate successfully under the guidance of Derek Jeakins, Michelle Jeakins and Kevan Horton. It is one of the most successful removal and storage companies in Essex.

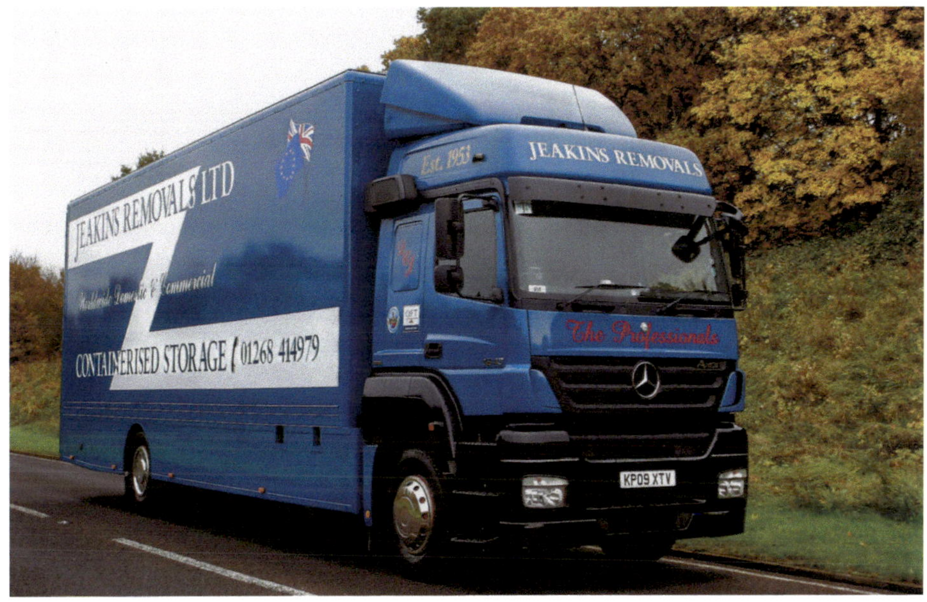

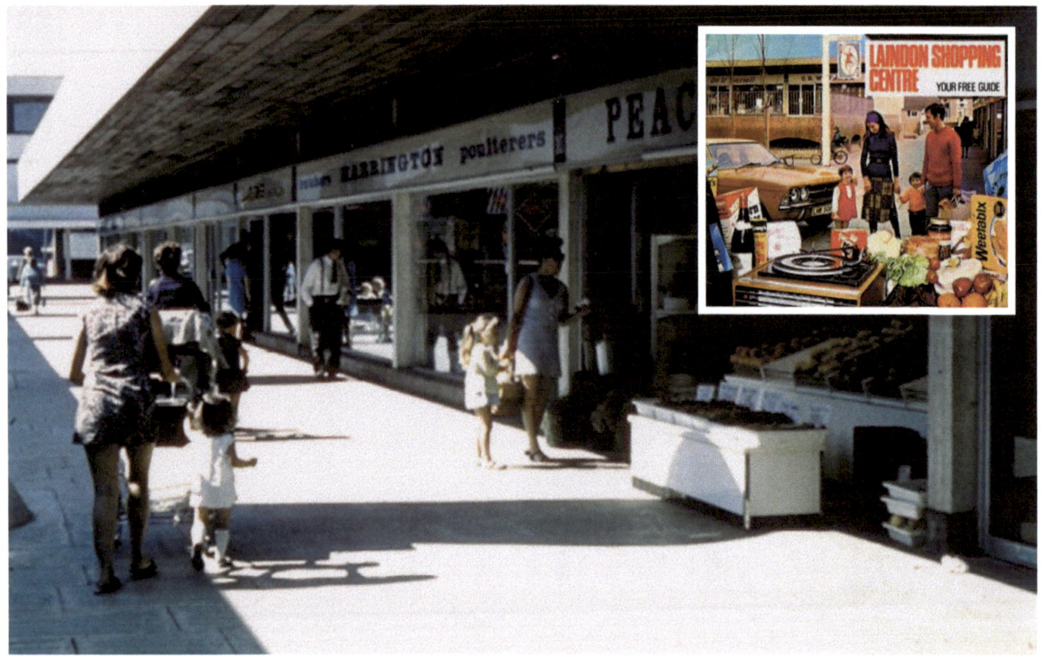

Laindon Shopping Centre

Laindon Shopping Centre opened in 1969. In the 1970s, Gary Clark, a Laindon High Road schoolboy, went there every week for his dinner. He recalls often terrible fights between his school and Nicholas School pupils. He said, 'It was great then, the betting shop was opened by Trevor Brooking!' He remembers queuing outside the sports shop when the West Ham goalkeeper, Mervyn Day, signed merchandise. Over time it fell into disrepair and a decision was made in 2008 to refurbish it.

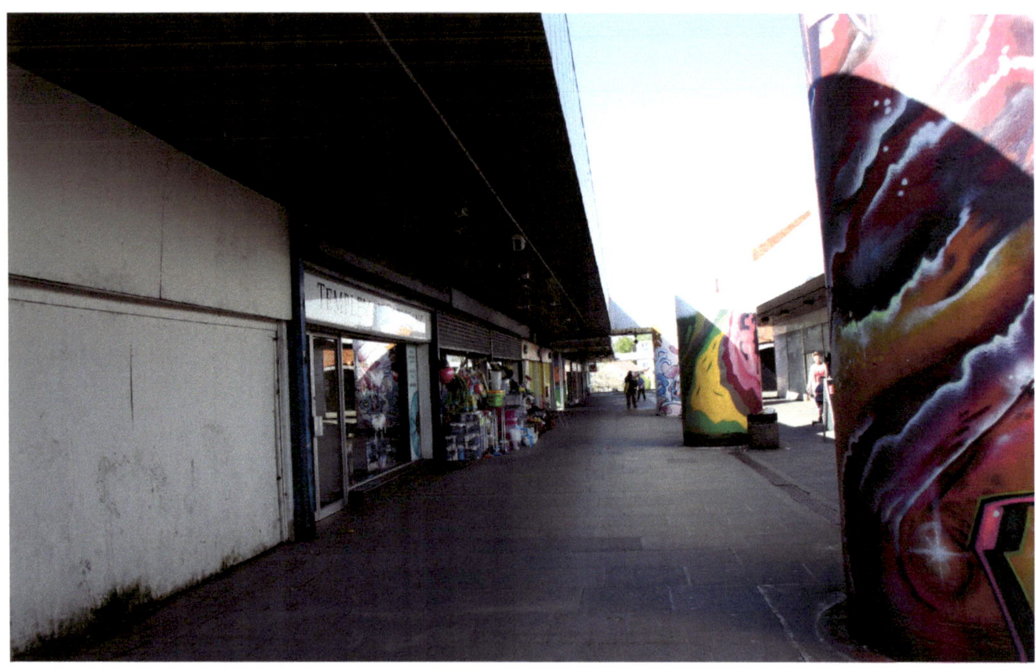

Langdon Hills – St Mary's and All Saints' Old Church

St Mary's and All Saints' old church stands in Old Church Hill. It is believed a church has stood on the site from the fourteenth century. This one was rebuilt around the 1840s. In 1877, a new church was built at the top of Crown Hill to replace the old church, which was considered too small and far away from the incoming population. The old church gradually slid into disrepair, and was then made redundant in the 1970s. It was sold as a private residence, but its churchyard still remains under control of the current church.

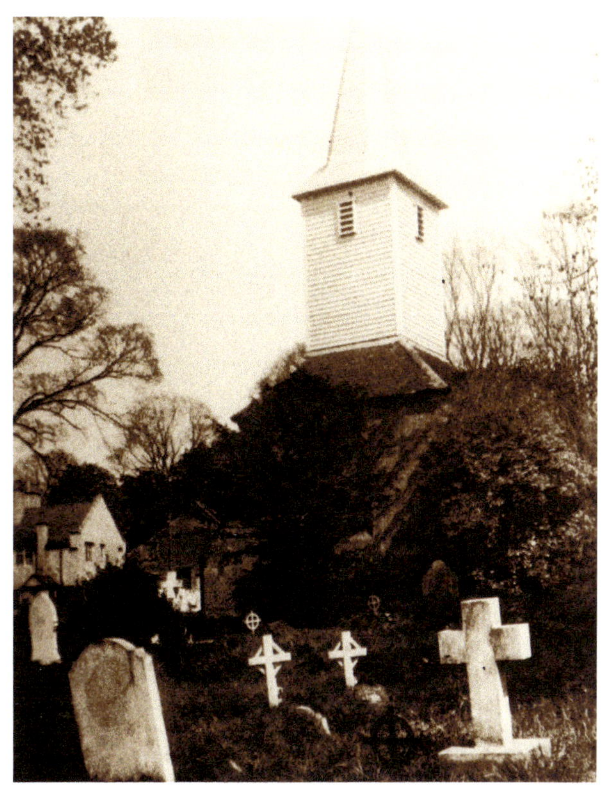

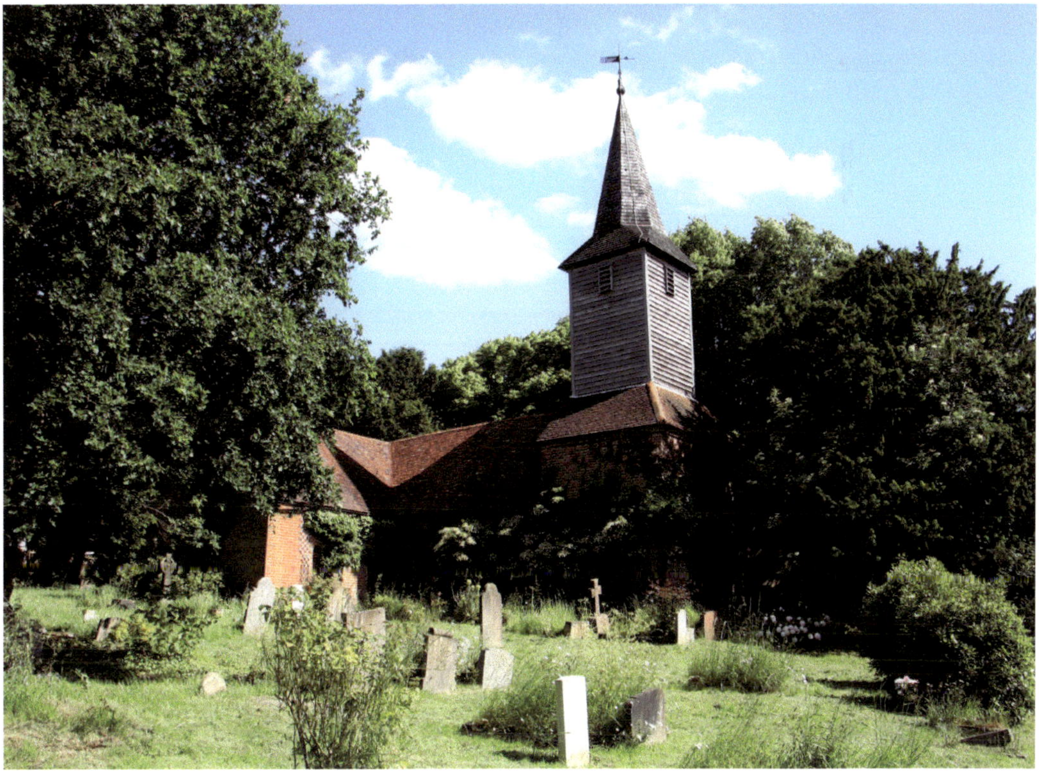

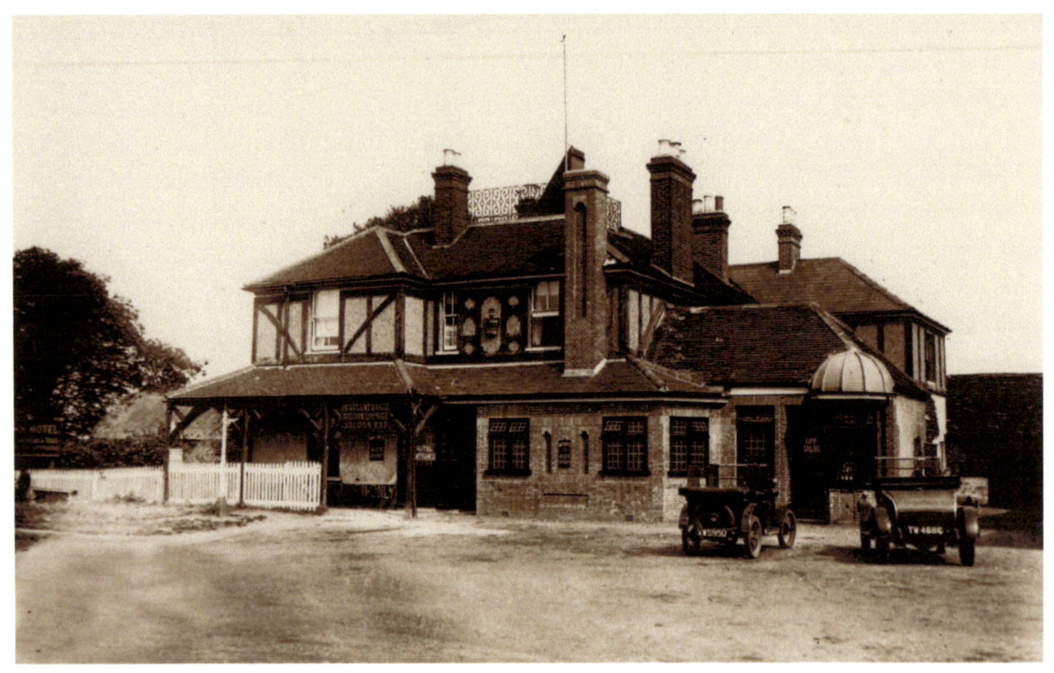

Langdon Hills – The Crown Hotel, 1930s

The Crown Hotel was built in the 1850s, but an inn has occupied this site for centuries. It once hosted smoking concerts – these were live performances, usually of music performed to an audience consisting only of men. Hunting parties often used to meet at the Crown Hotel too. The Crown is now a Harvester public house and restaurant. It stands on top of the High Road, Langdon Hills, otherwise known as Crown Hill.

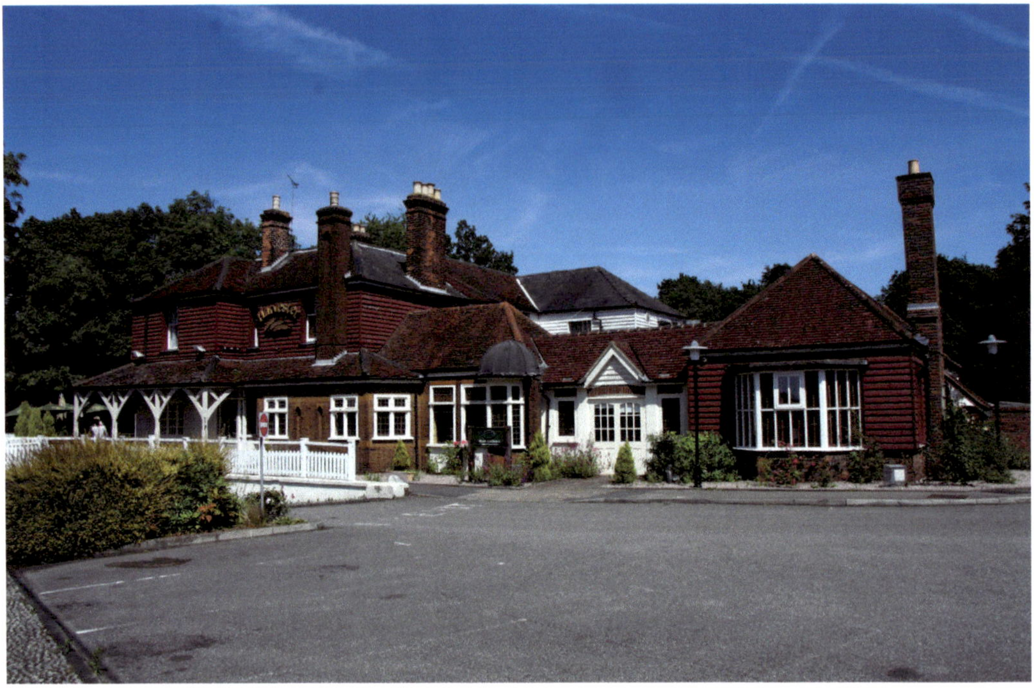

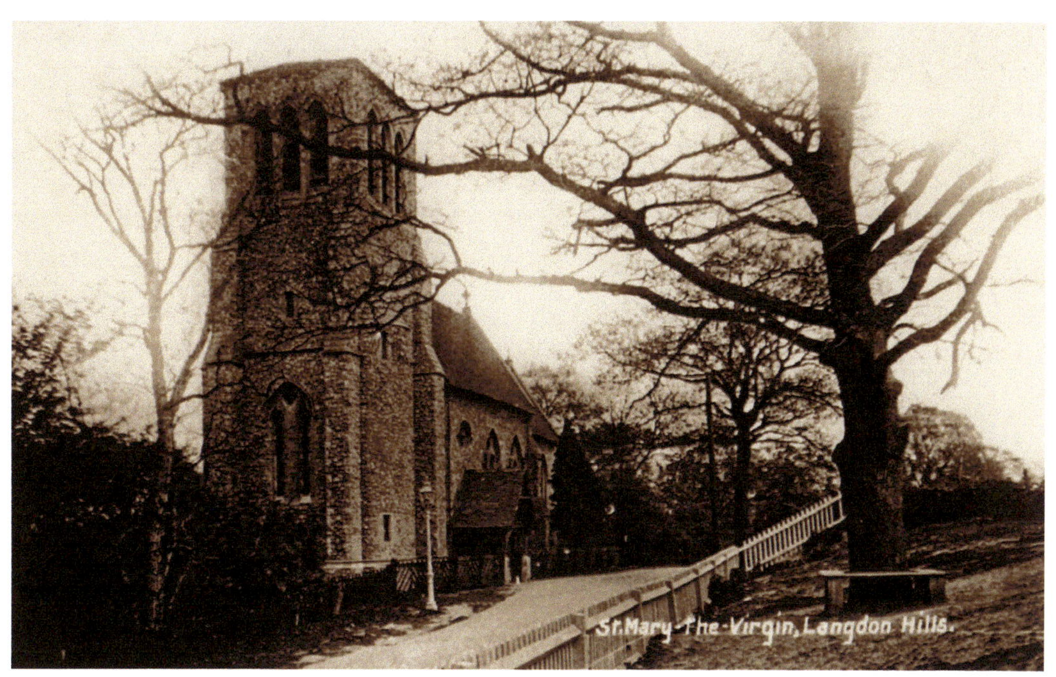

Langdon Hills – St Mary's and All Saints' Church

In 1877, a new church was built at the top of Crown Hill to replace the old church. It was paid for by the Rector, Revd Digby Cleaver. Penny, who had sung in the choir, married Mike Betteridge here in 1971; Reved Cooke married them. Amanda Farley remembers Minnie and Jack Bentley, who ran the Sunday school and Monday Club at St Mary's church hall in the late 1970s and early 1980s, with affection. They would arrange games of rounders and coach trips for the children.

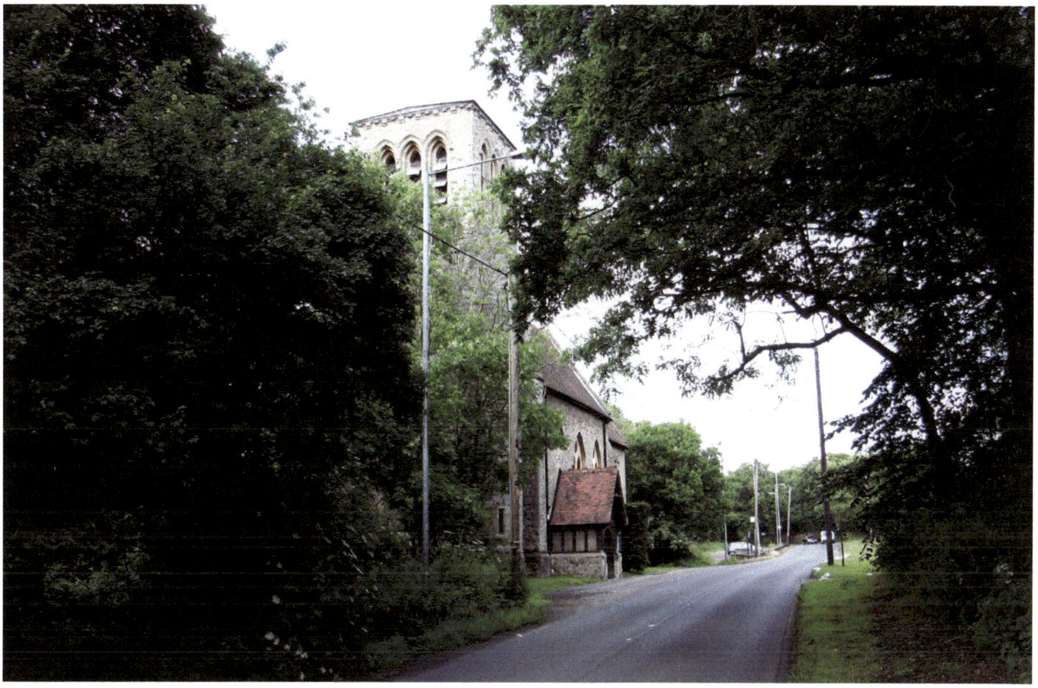

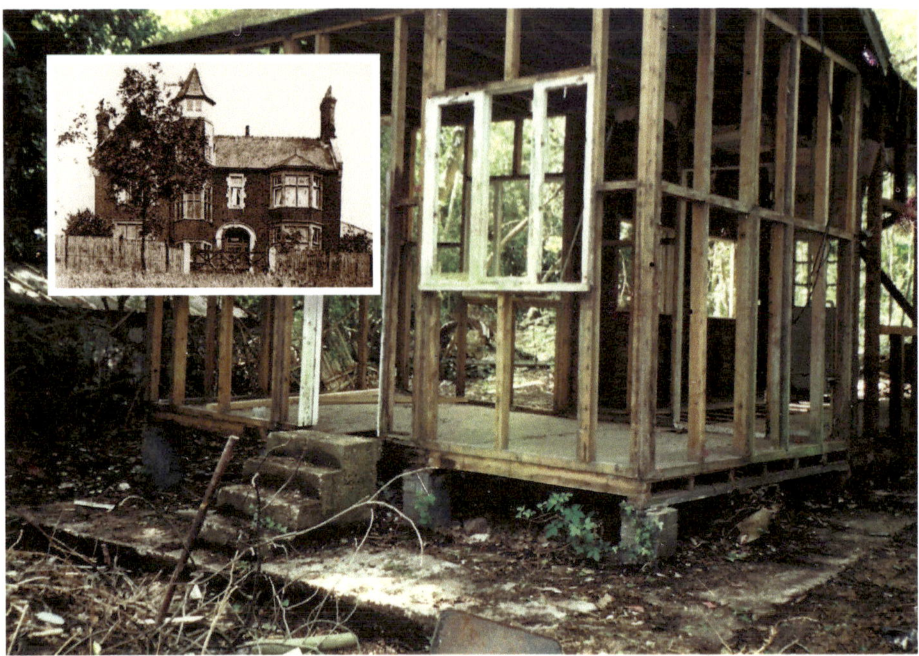

Langdon Hills – Nore View

Nore View was built by Mr Dolman around the 1890s, when land was cheap after the agricultural depression. It was his family home until 1924, when Mrs Mary Ellen Chataway took ownership. In 1938, it mysteriously burnt down when she was away visiting friends. Nore View was surrounded by a growing number of plotland dwellings, which were compulsorily purchased at a later date. The picture shows a plotland building being erected. The site is part of the Marks' Hill Wood Nature Reserve.

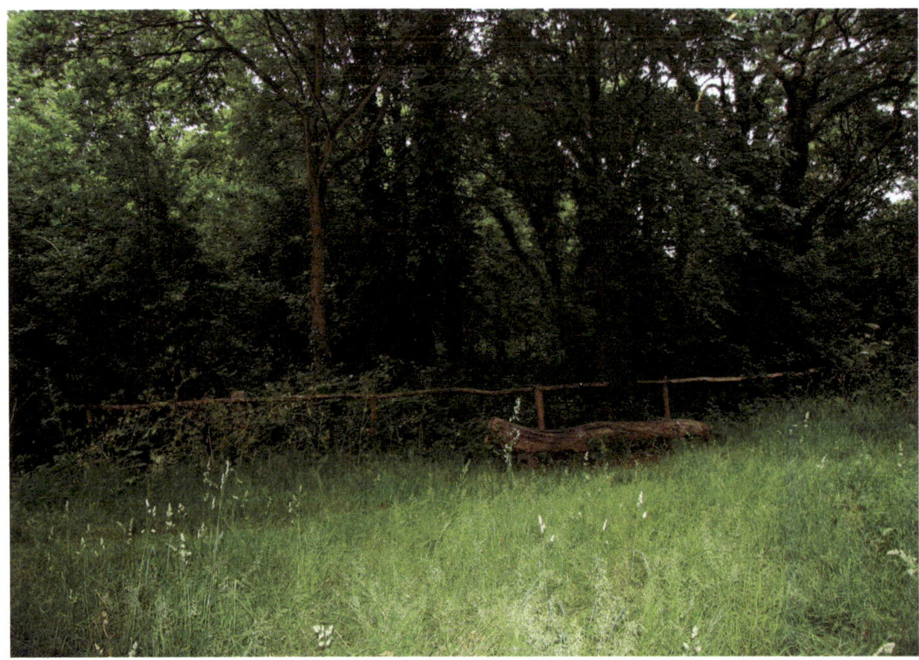

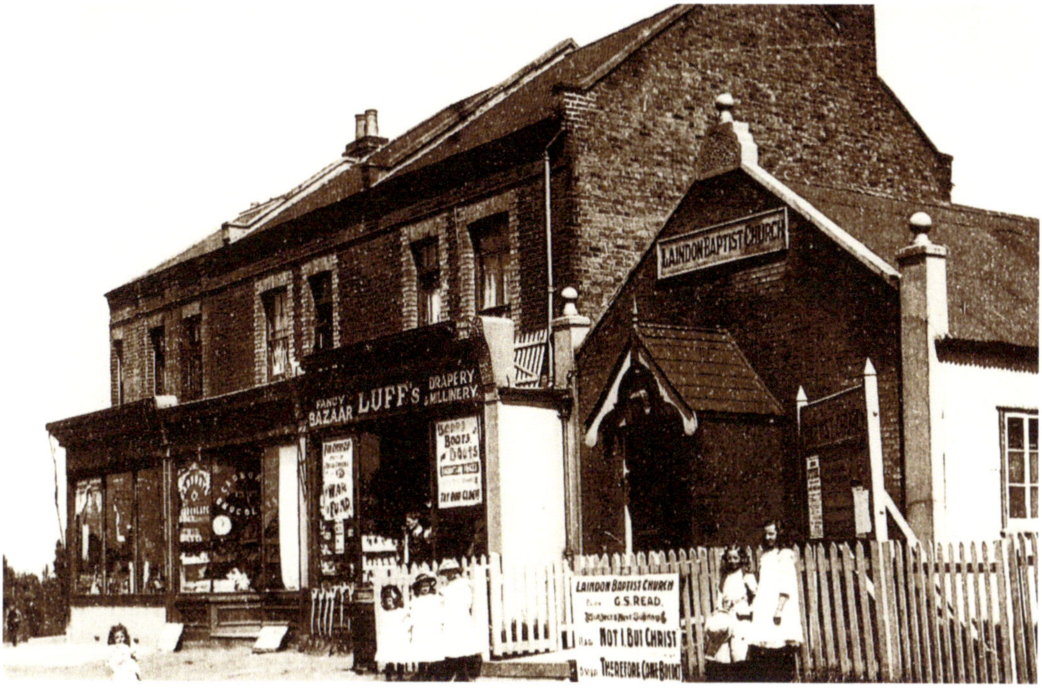

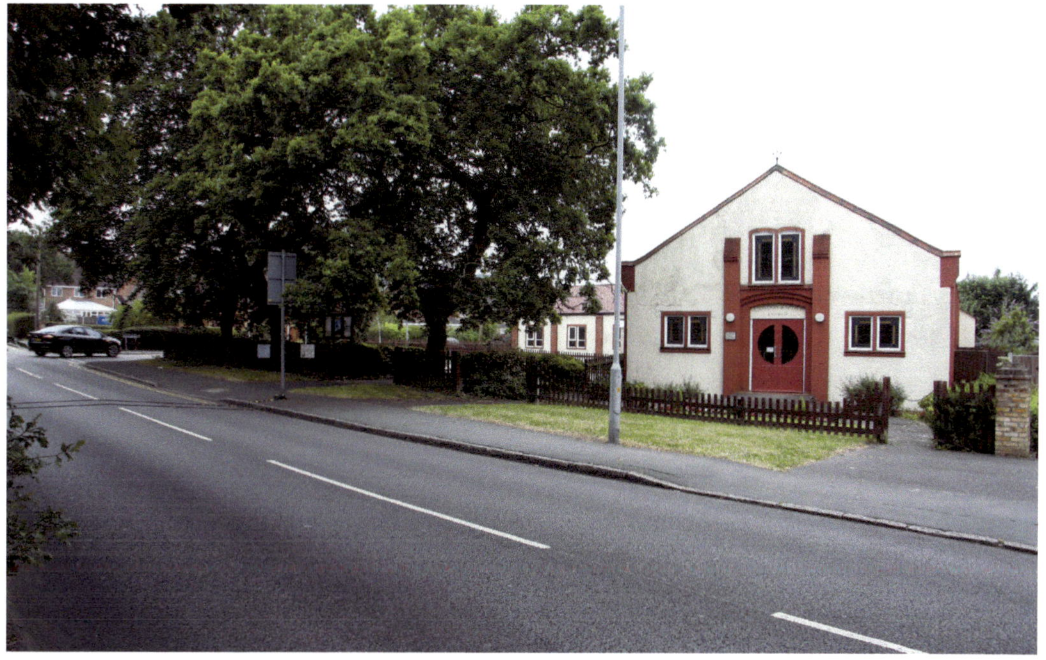

Langdon Hills – Nightingale Parade

Next to Laindon Baptist church is Luff's Woollen's, which dealt in drapery, millinery and shoe repairs. Beside that was a sweet shop/post office, next door was an off-licence. In 1909, Laindon Baptist Fellowship, began under the leadership of Mr G. S. Read who conducted their worship in Nightingale Hall. Today, the hall is still used for the same purpose, but the shops went a long time ago.

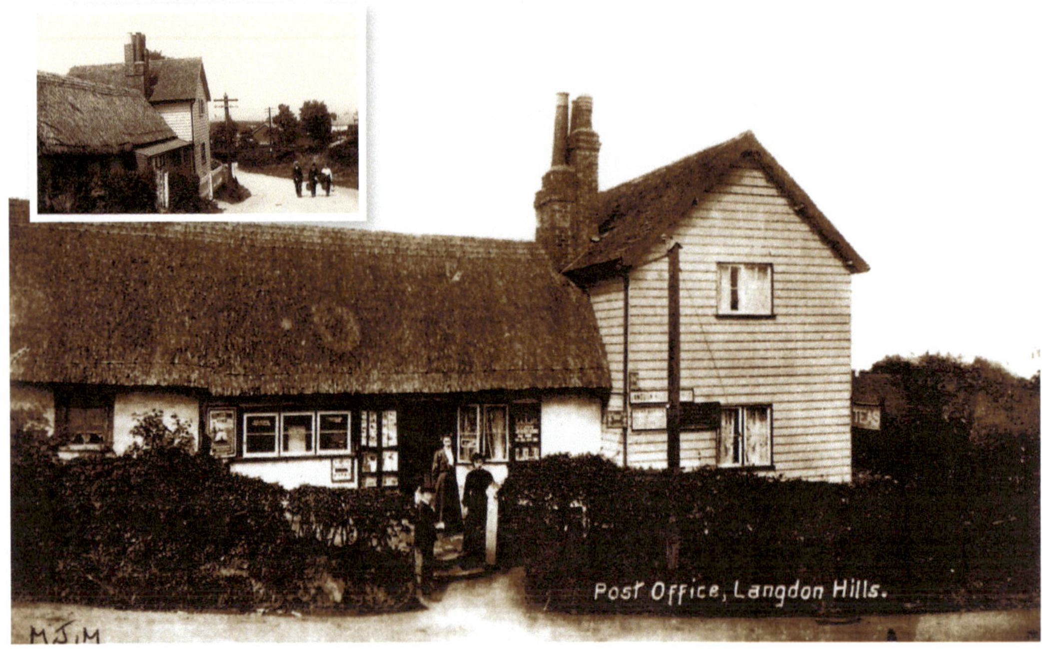

Langdon Hills – The Old Thatched Post Office

The old thatched roof post office and weather boarded house stood at the foot of Crown Hill *c.* 1920s. It is said that the Noakes family lived at the post office. They possessed a collection of boats in Leigh-on-Sea that were commissioned, in 1944, to go to Dunkirk and rescue the soldiers off the beaches. Unfortunately, these quaint buildings were demolished in the 1960s to make way for a dual carriageway.

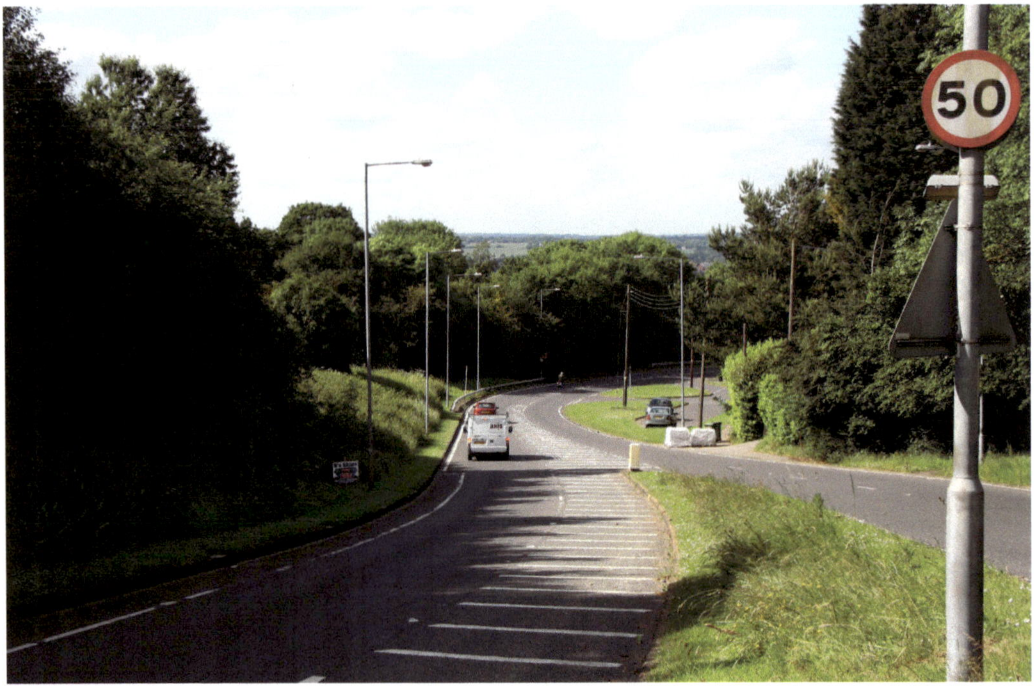

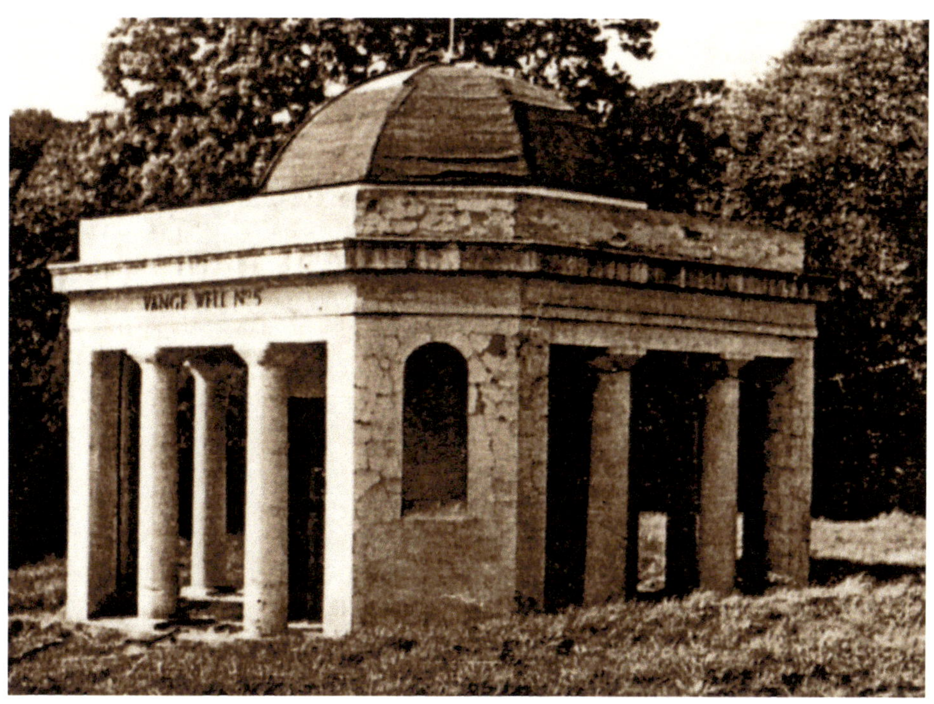

Langdon Hills – Vange Well No. 5

In 1919, Mr Edwin Cash developed a well from a natural spring that was originally found on his neighbour's land on the Vange Hall Estate. He formed the Vange Water Company. The highly sulphated, medicinal water contained seven ingredients. In 1920, a national newspaper did a front-page spread on the water, which boasted a cure to rickets and stomach disorders. This brought in the crowds. Interest eventually dwindled, but you can still see what remains of the well at Martinhole Wood, Langdon Hills.

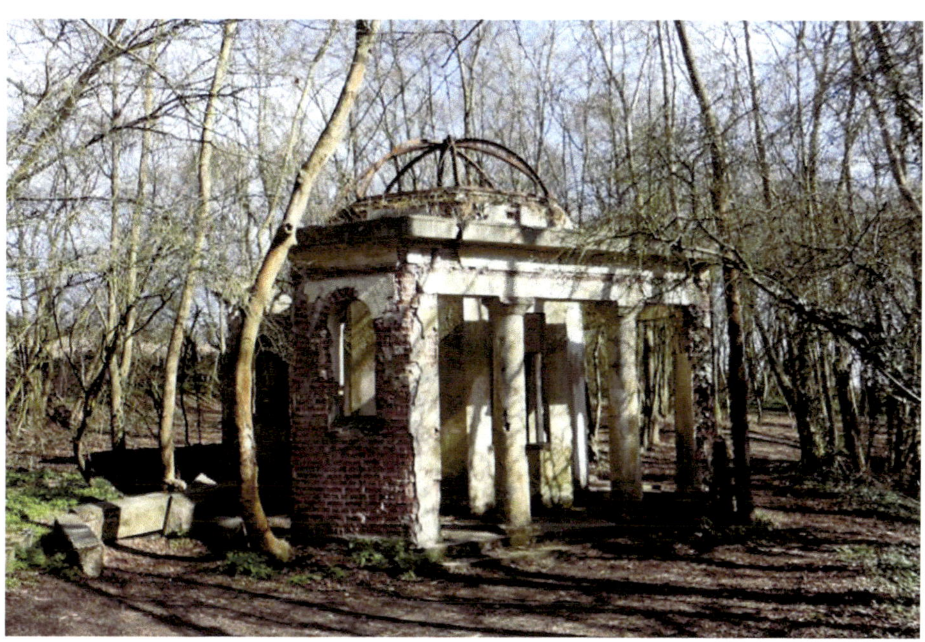

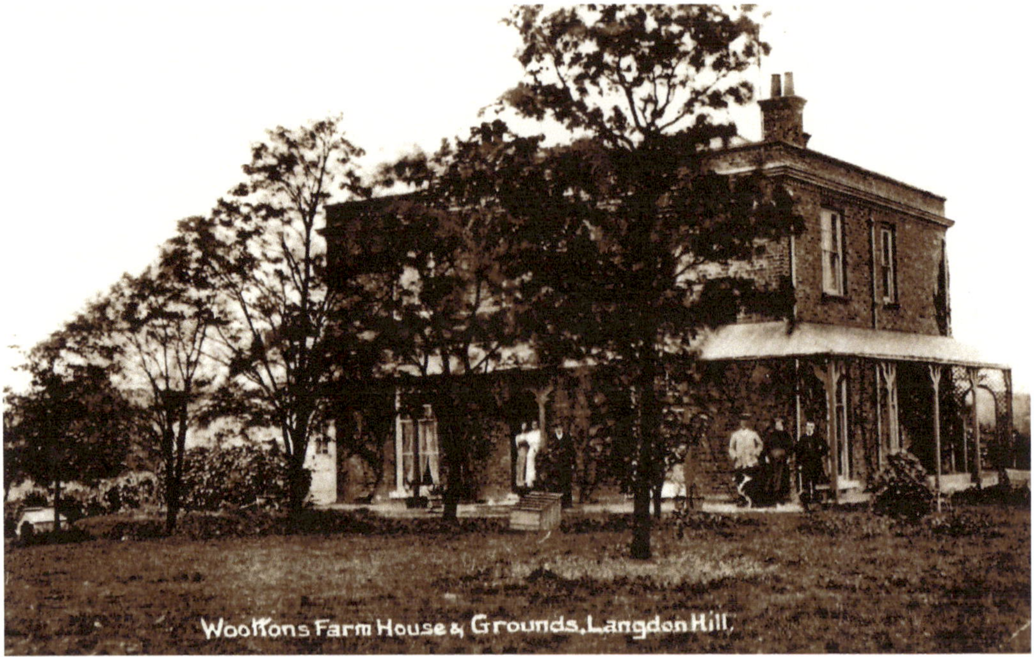

Wootons Farm House & Grounds, Langdon Hill.

Langdon Hills – West Ham Sanatorium, Wootton Farm, Dry Street

Wootton Farm House was built in 1890 on the site of a property that was historically important during the Civil War. There is apparently a tunnel, thought to be a priest hole, remaining from the previous house. West Ham Borough Council purchased Wootton Farm House and the 100-acre site for the West Ham Sanatorium for children with Tuberculosis, which was officially opened on 26 October 1927 by the Mayor of West Ham, Alderman Ernest Reed. TB generally affected the lungs, so the property, that was high above sea level, was an ideal location.

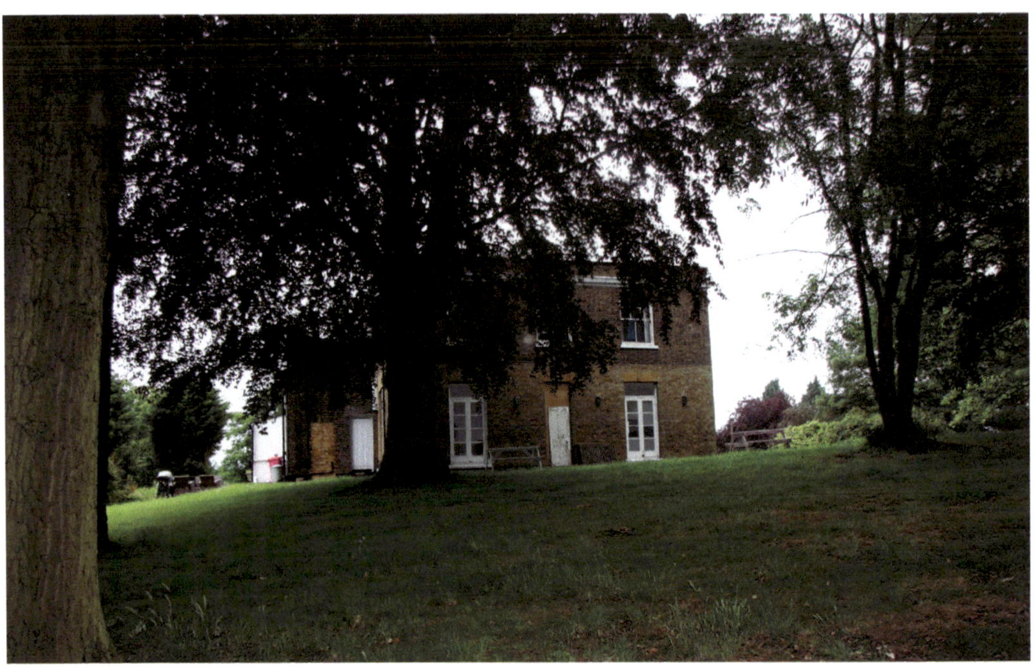

Langdon Hills – West Ham Sanatorium

A schoolroom and accommodation was built for up to forty children up to the age of sixteen, and the Matron and sisters lived in the large farmhouse. Below, we see one of the remaining single-storey buildings that was used as a ward. From 1950–57 it was converted into a TB hospital for adult males, and renamed Langdon Hills Hospital. In 1964, most of the grounds were purchased by Essex County Council and became part of Langdon Hills Country Park. Later, after its closure in the 1950s, it became Wootton House Boarding Kennels for many years, then a private residence in 2013.

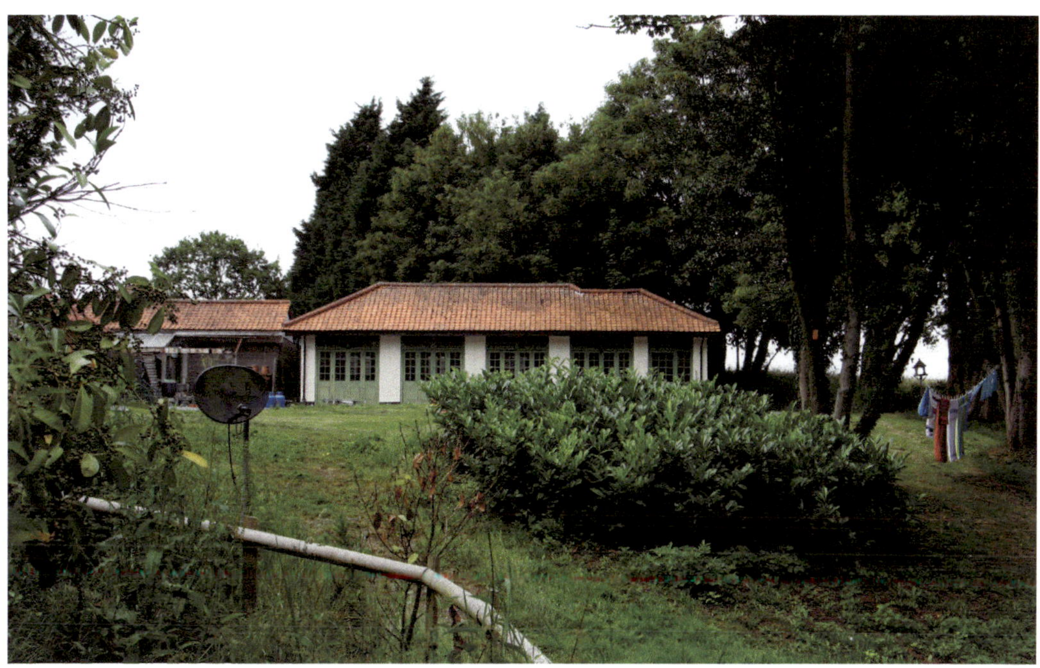

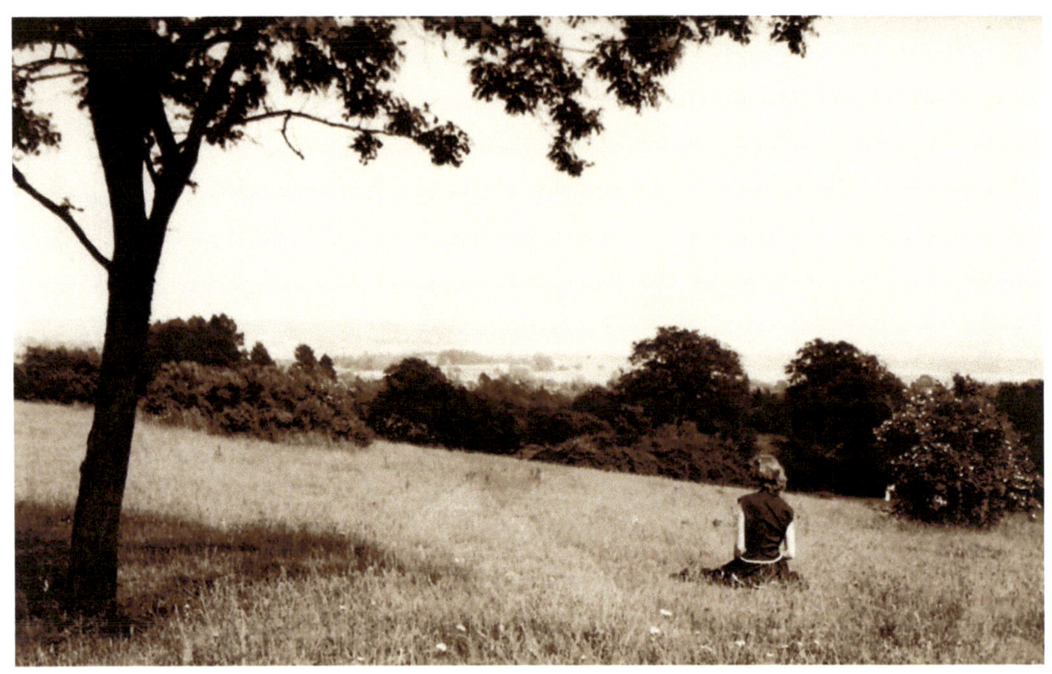

Langdon Hills Nature Reserve

In 1926, the Wheatons, a farming family, offered the parish council a field of sixteen acres. They accepted and paid £250 for the field. In the 1930s, land was saved from a major housing development when bought by the county council under the Greenbelt Scheme, purchasing further land around Westley Heights until 1964. In 1973, the Langdon Hills Open Spaces was declared as a country park. There is now 400 acres of nature reserve, home to many species of birds, butterflies and woodland creatures. Part of it is One Tree Hill in Corringham, Thurrock.

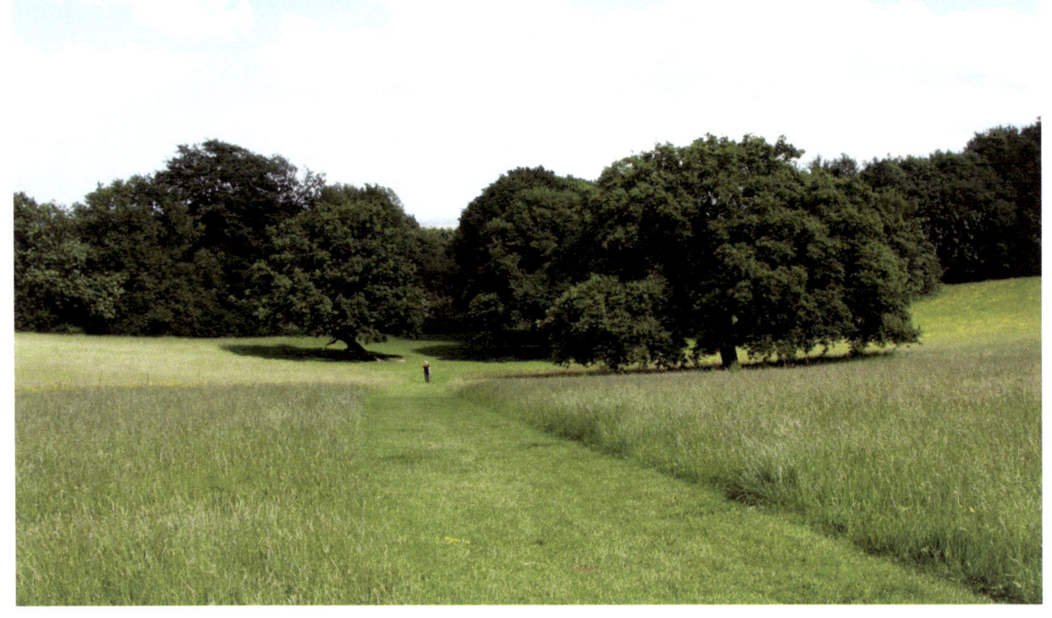

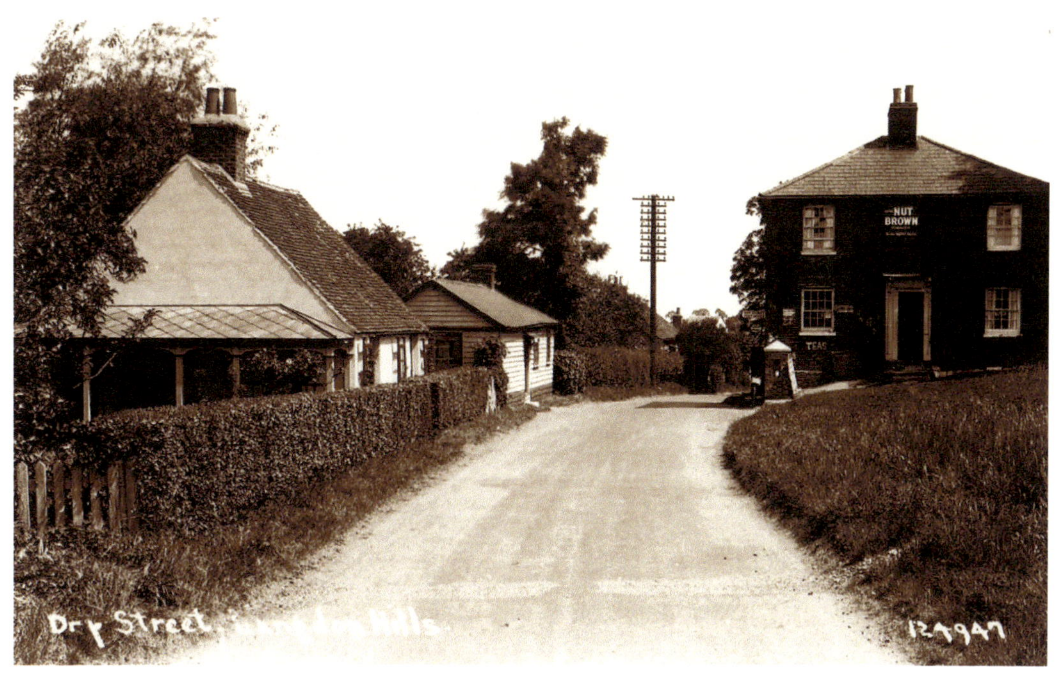

Langdon Hills – Post Office, Dry Street

The building to the right was used as Dry Street Post Office and Grocery Store between the 1930s and 1940s, but originally, it was the Red Cow Beer (Coach) House built in 1843 for that purpose. Because of the Beer Act of 1830, any householder, on the payment of 2 guineas to excise, could open up their front parlour and sell beer. The first Duke of Wellington pushed this through in order to encourage beer drinking and put a curb on gin drinking, which was thought of as ruinous to the nation. After the post office was robbed twice, it became a residential building.

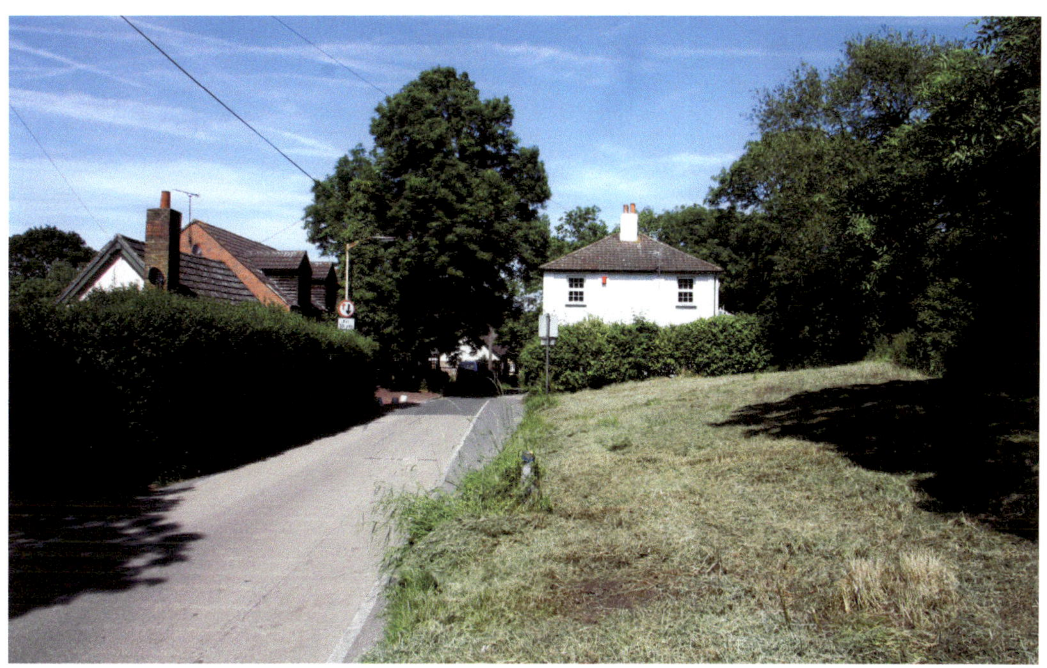

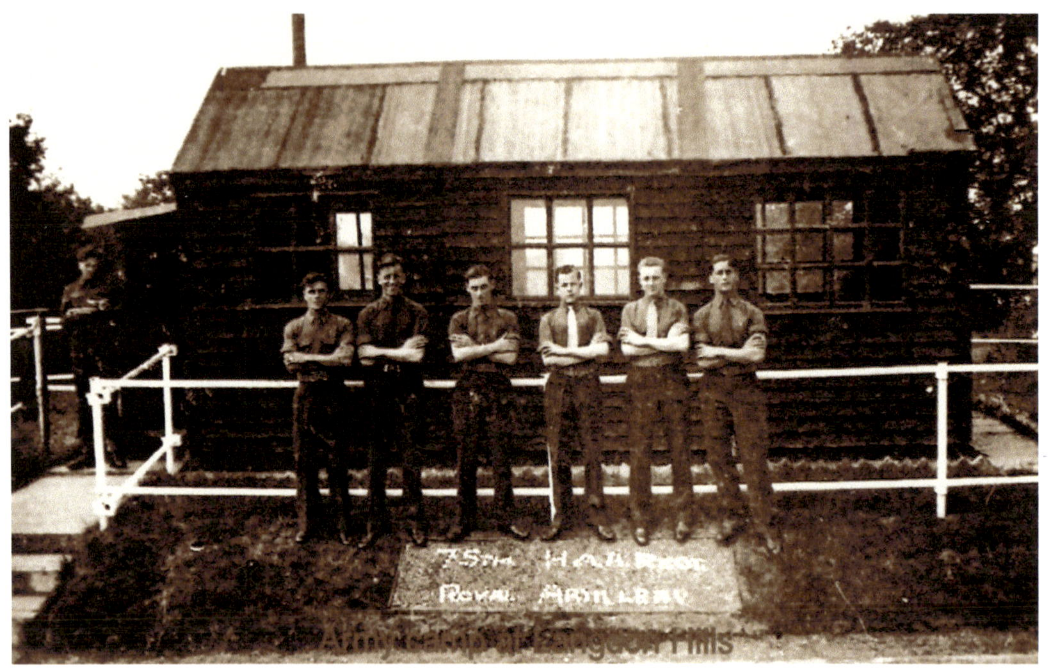

Langdon Hills Second World War Army Camp

Langdon Hills Second World War Army Camp was based at Bentley Farm off Old Church Road Hill, Langdon Hills. A sentry hut is all that remains; it is the hut with the door in the middle, to the right of the stables. This serves as a tiny remnant of the army camp that consisted of four blocks of barrack rooms, a washing and toilet block, a cookhouse and dining hall. A lot more is written by Ken Porter about the camp on www.laindonhistory.org.uk

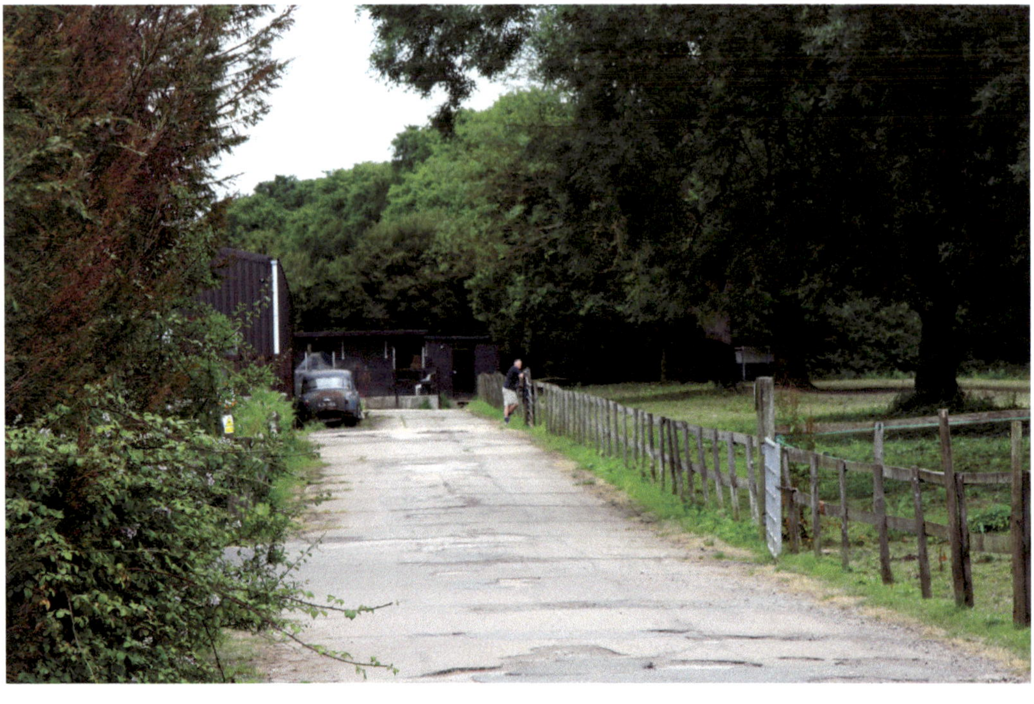

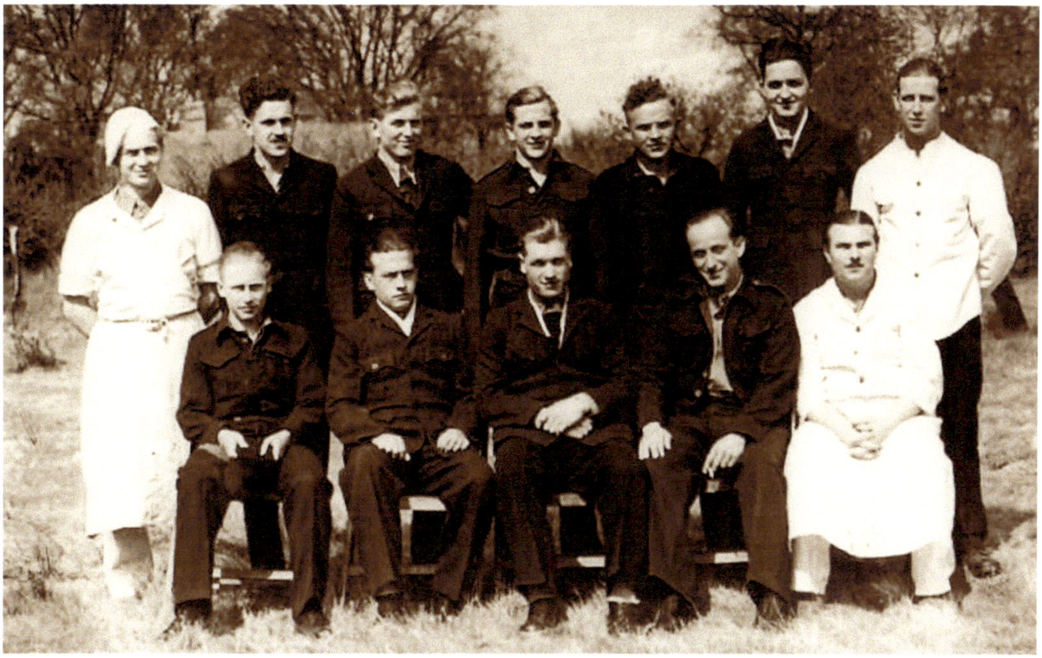

Langdon Hills – German P.O.W. Camp, 1940s

All that remains of Hutted Camp 266 is a concrete base in Beacon Field that is thought to be the base of the camp's cookhouse. It housed captured German adversaries from the end of the Second World War to 1948. Prisoners worked on the nearby fields. Some met and later married local girls. After it closed in 1948, it was used by Shell to house its workers at Coryton until the 1950s. Later, Westley Cricket Club used the remaining base for its pavilion. Now the space is used for recreation.

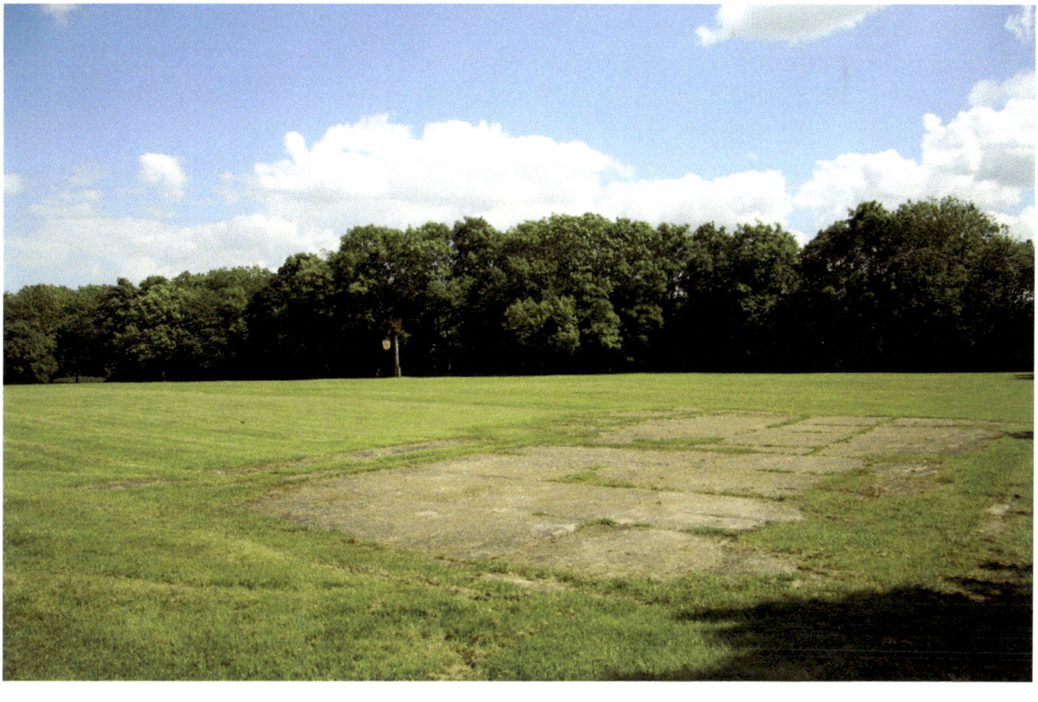

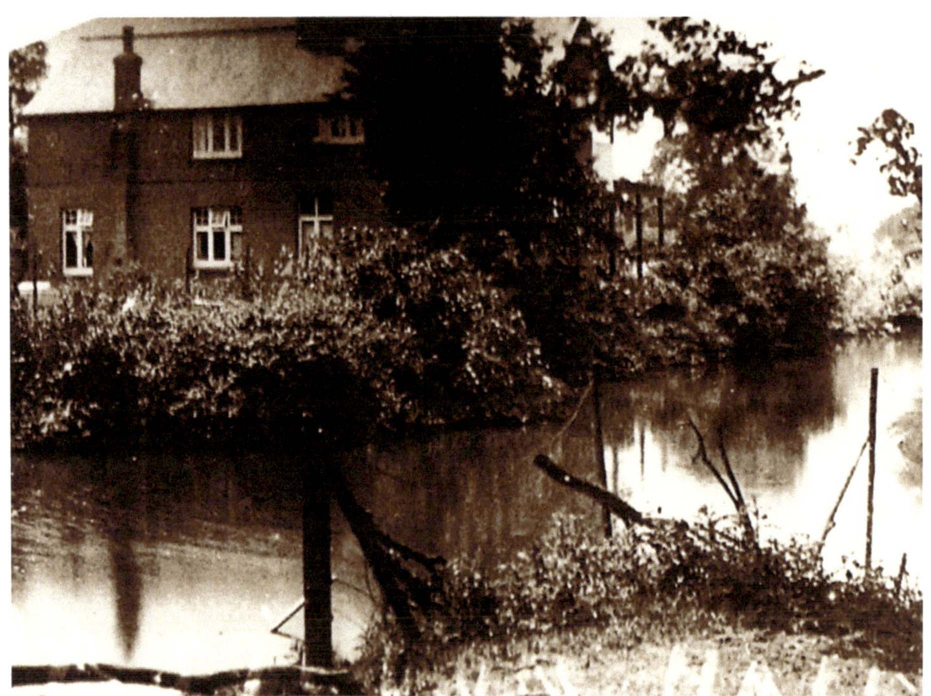

Basildon Hall

Basildon Hall (Barstable Hall) was an ancient, moated building that featured in the Domesday Book. This was a moot site, a place for important meetings in Saxon times. After burning down, it was rebuilt around 1830. In 1930 it was ransacked and set ablaze by locals when the German owner, Mr. Gliessner, was interned. He rebuilt it when out of prison. In 1961, Basildon Hall was demolished and the moat was drained by the Basildon Development Corporation. What remains now in East Thorpe is the circular dip of what was once a moat.

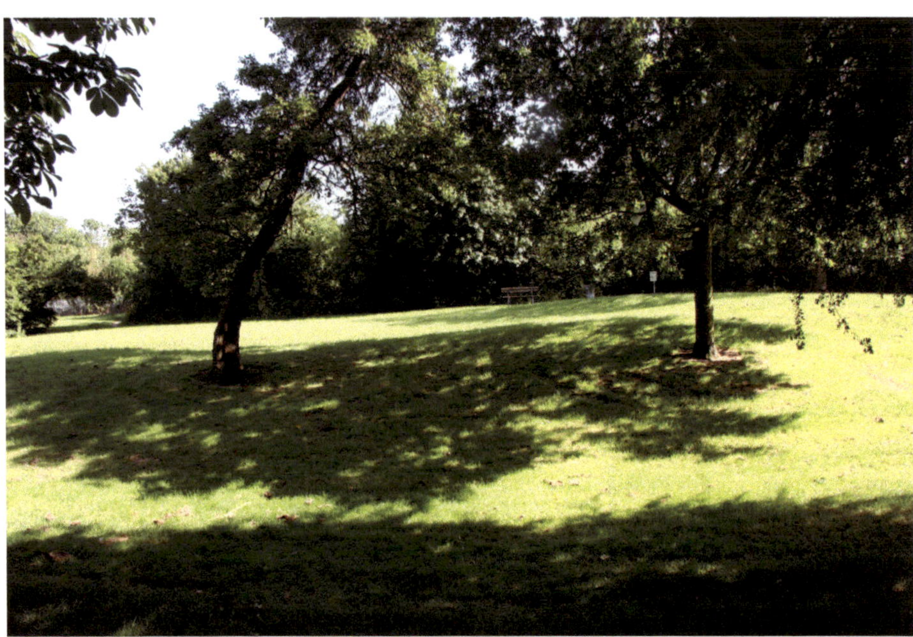

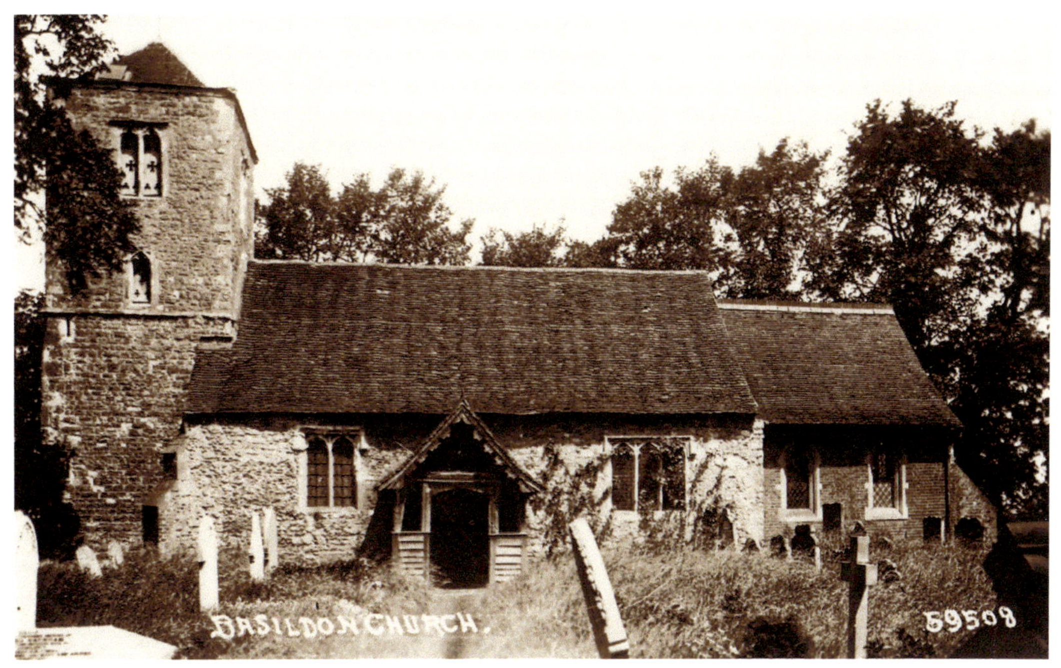

Basildon – Holy Cross Church, Church Road

Holy Cross chapel was first recorded in 1230. This early church probably stood at the site of today's building and part of the Manor of Botelers, which later became Moat House Farm. The nave of the church is fourteenth century. It is believed that Holy Cross church was at the centre of the village of Basildon. In the 1960s, Bryn Infant and Junior School, and Manor Infant and Junior school (now The Willows Primary School) were down Church Road.

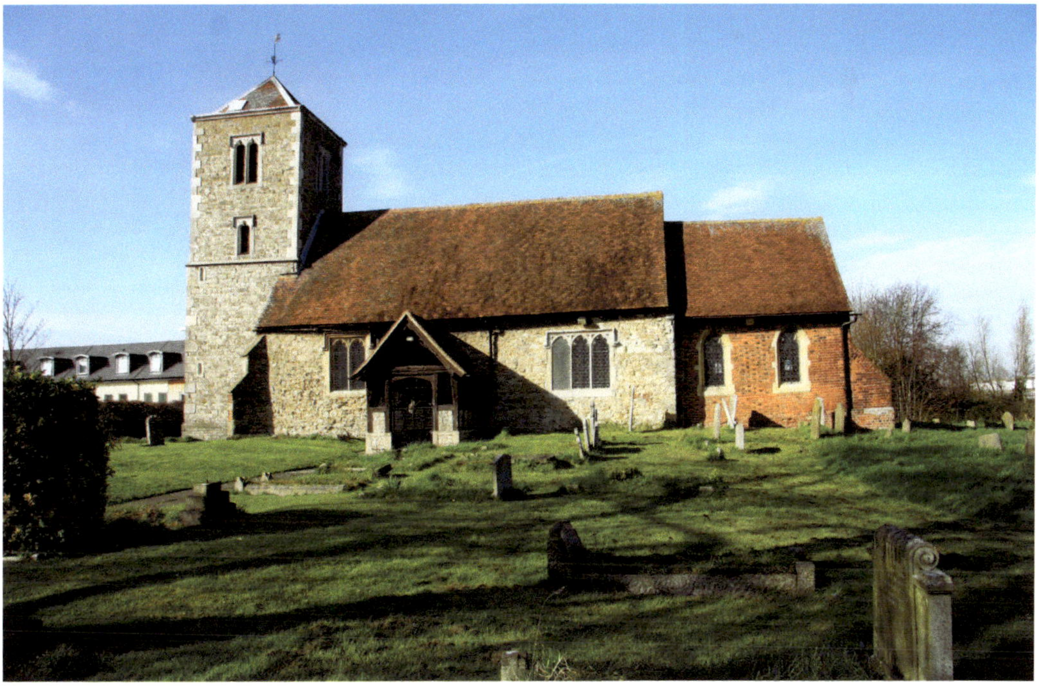

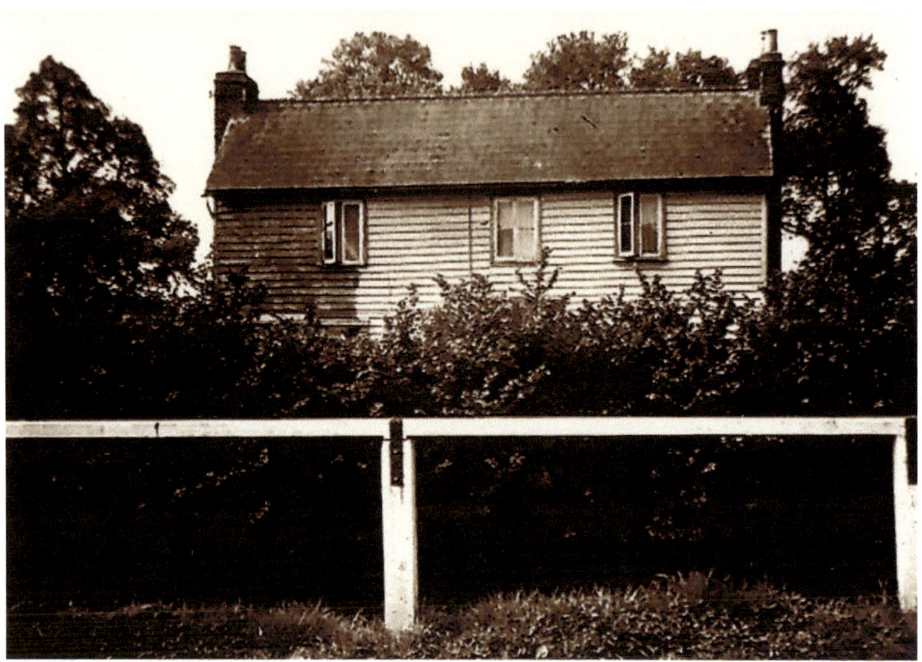

Basildon – Cranes Farm, Nevendon

Cranes Farm was one of the area's oldest farms. Cranes Farm Road is named after it as it replaced the narrow road that once ran past it. The family of Hugh le Crane gave the name to the farm in Nevendon in 1272. Although the area is known locally as Nevendon, local maps show the area as Basildon now. Quite recently, Oakwood Grange Development was constructed by Messrs. Bellway Homes has been built on the site of the farm.

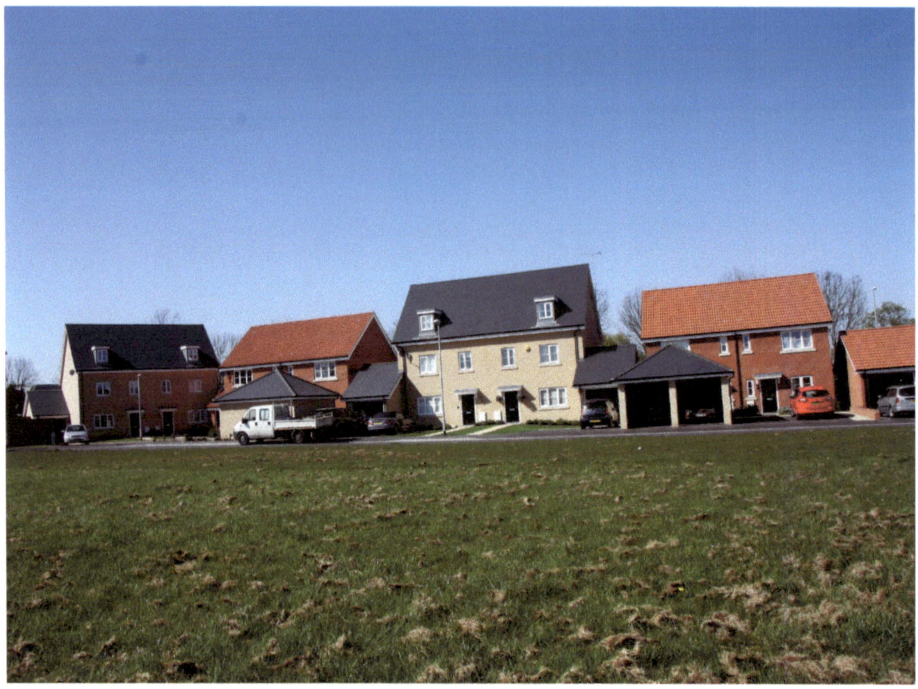

In the busy town square where Marks & Spencer is today, stood Barstable Cottage in Hotwater Lane. IIt was surrounded by a moat with its own pond. A former cottage on this site was mentioned in the Domesday Book. A Jessie Styles was born in the two up, two down cottage in 1889. In the 1950s, the James family were the last people to live there before it was compulsory purchased for £150 by the Basildon Development Corporation. Sadly on 21 April 2018 Marks & Spencer closed its Basildon store, which had been in the town for forty-seven years.

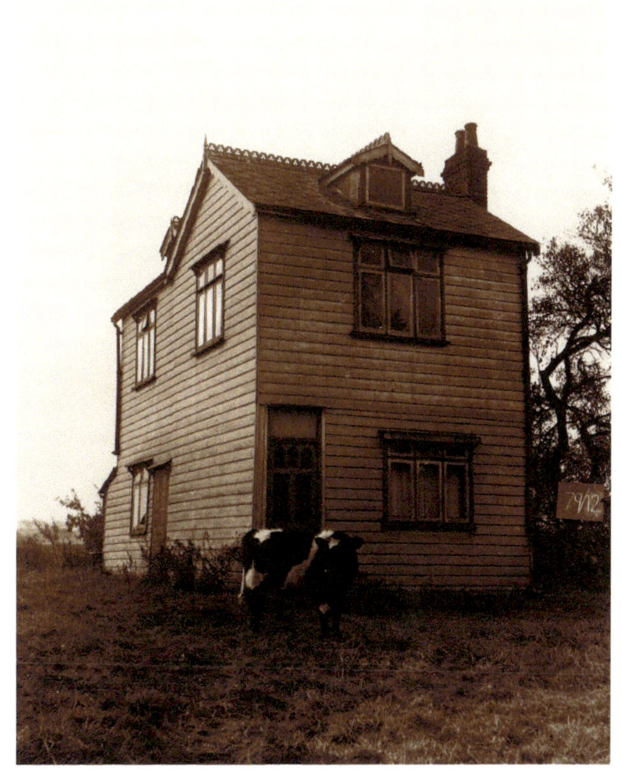

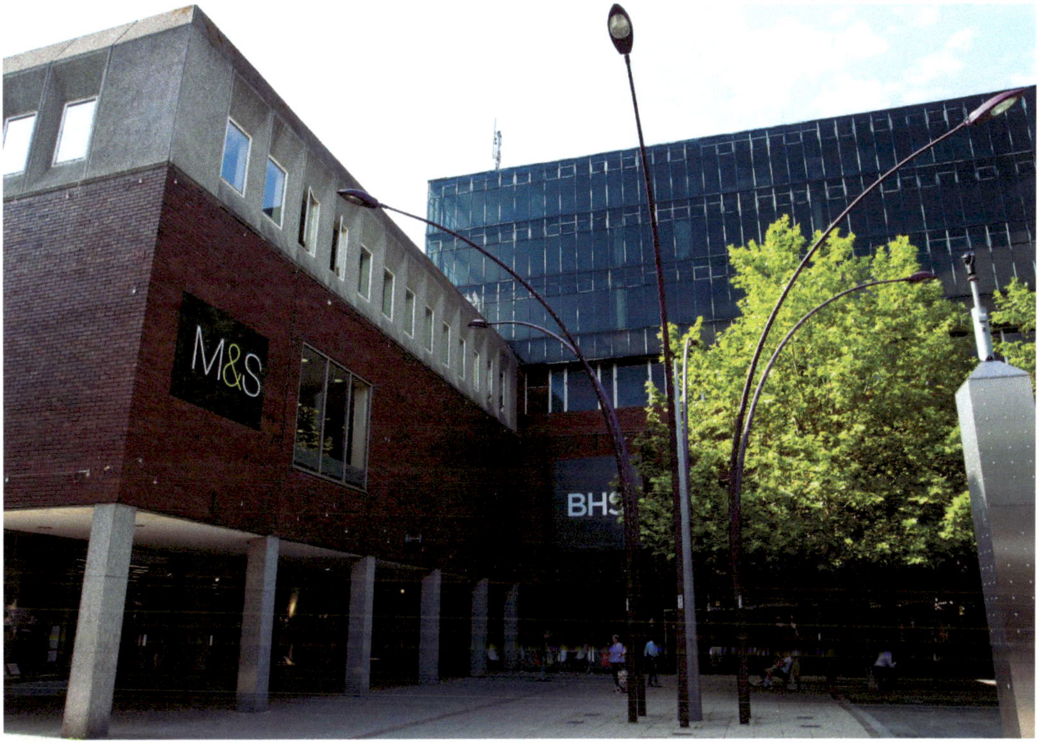

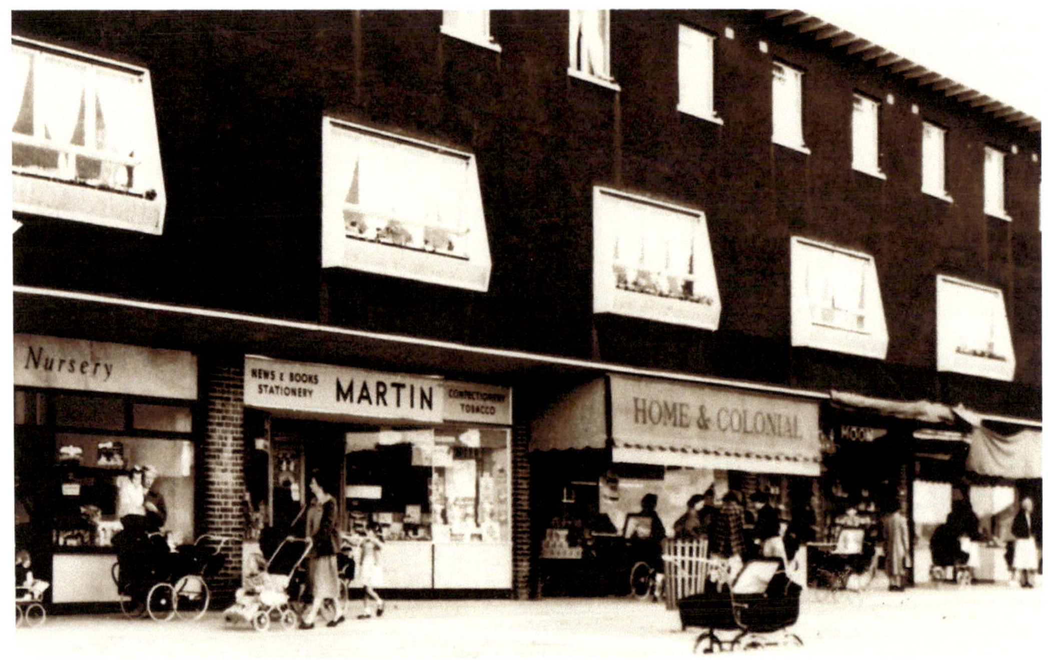

Basildon – Fryerns Sub-Centre, Whitmore Way

The first shopping parade in Basildon was Fryerns Sub-centre at Whitmore Way, with shops such as Martin's newsagents and a Home & Colonial store, which was once one of the United Kingdom's largest retail chains. Also a post office and Battleswick Fish Bar could be found. This was and still is an excellent fish and chip shop that has hardly changed. You can still see Martin's newsagent at the parade of shops today; it's near the Jolly Friar public house.

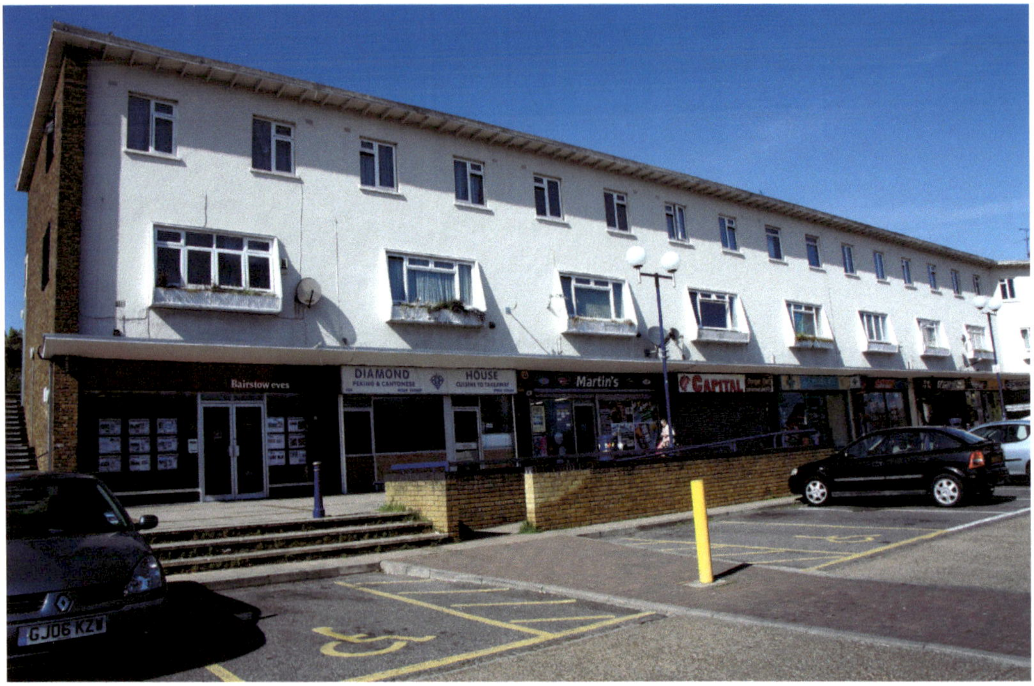

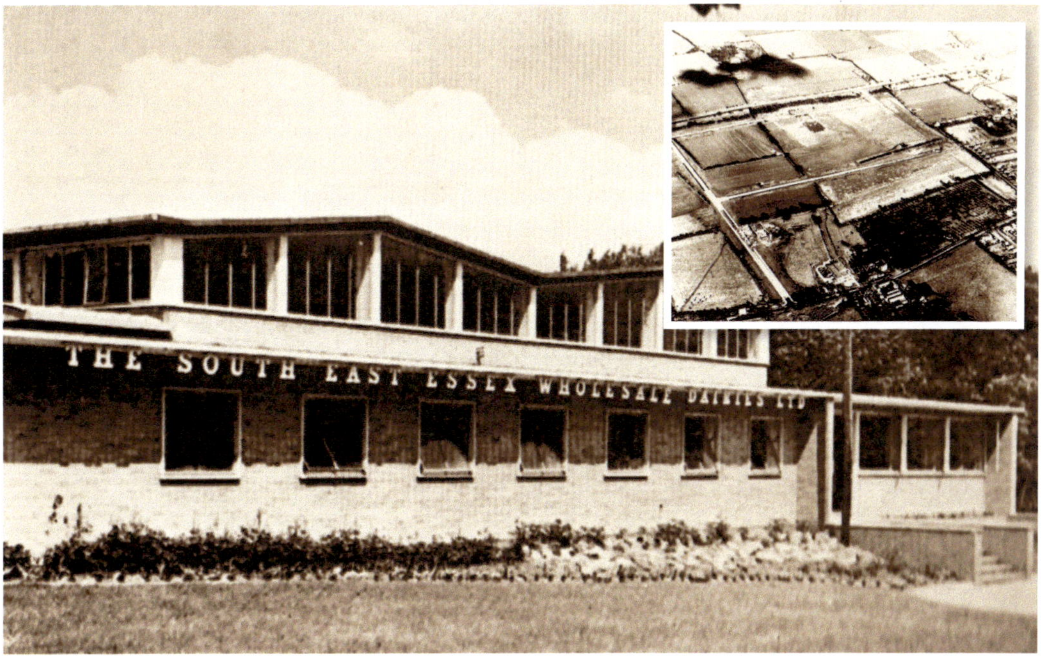

Basildon – South-East Essex Wholesale Dairies Ltd

Basildon's first new factory, South-East Essex Wholesale Dairies Ltd, opened on 10 September 1951 at No. 1 Industrial Estate, Cranes Farm Road. A foundation stone was laid by Colonel Sir Francis Whitmore, Lord Lieutenant of Essex. Charles Markham started the original business, a local dairy farmer from Laindon who ran a business in Laindon High Road. You can see an aerial view of Basildon New Towns first factory in the picture. L T Carpets, carpet factory outlet, stands on the site.

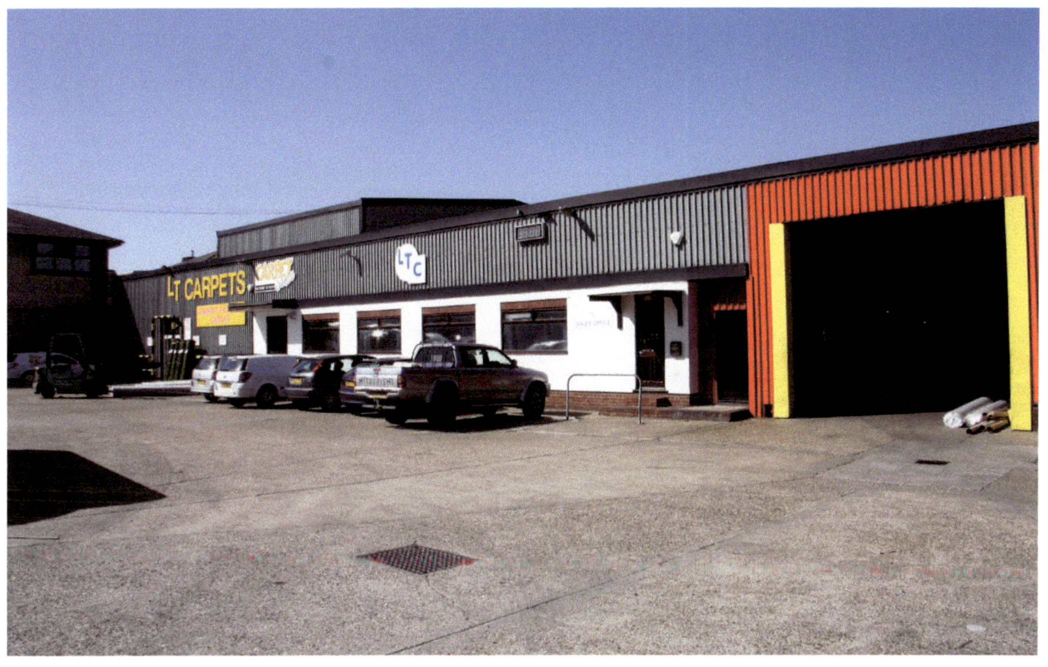

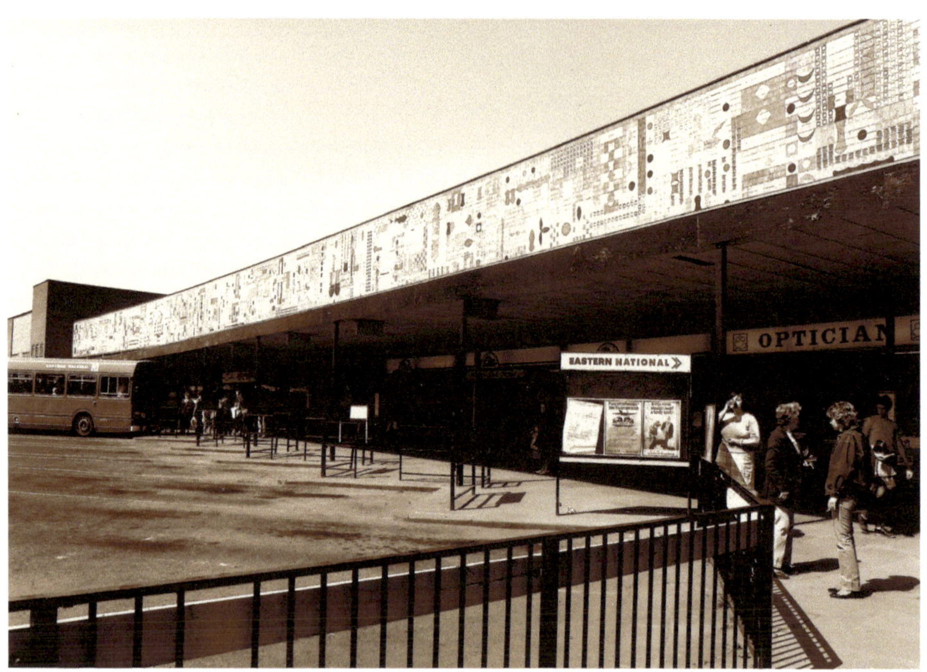

Basildon Bus Station Mosaic, Southernhay

William Gordon designed the original mosaic for Carter's of Poole. Consisting of thousands of abstract, patterned hand-printed tiles, it was said to be the largest mosaic in the country. The recent timeline of Basildon mosaic was installed after 1991 by Hollybush Construction. H & R Johnson of Stoke-on-Trent made the ceramics, and Fewster and Partners of London were the design architects. Apparently, a plaque with Mr Tony Brooks' name is installed somewhere within the mural. He was H & R Johnson's (London Office) Senior Architectural Manager and died in 1991, before it was finished.

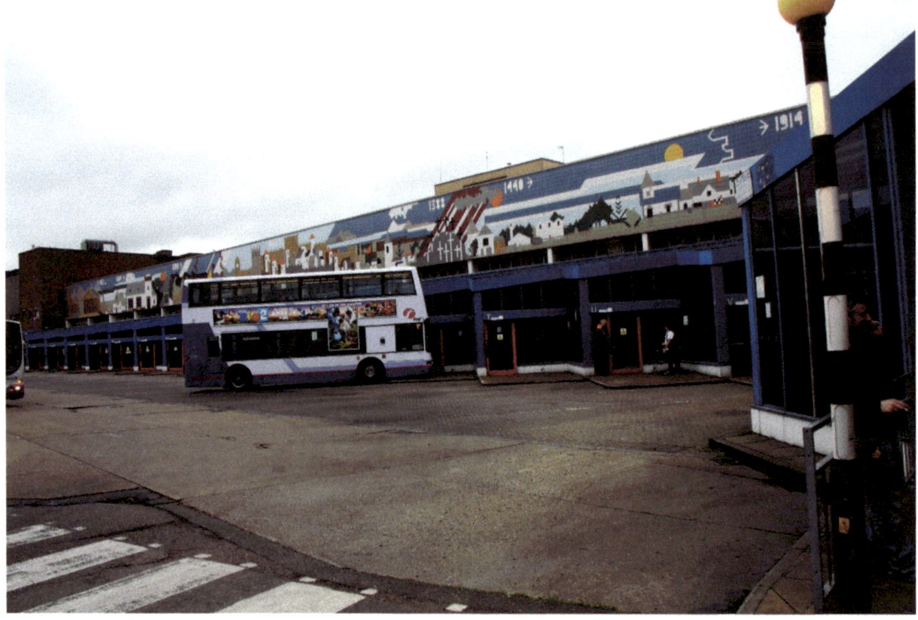

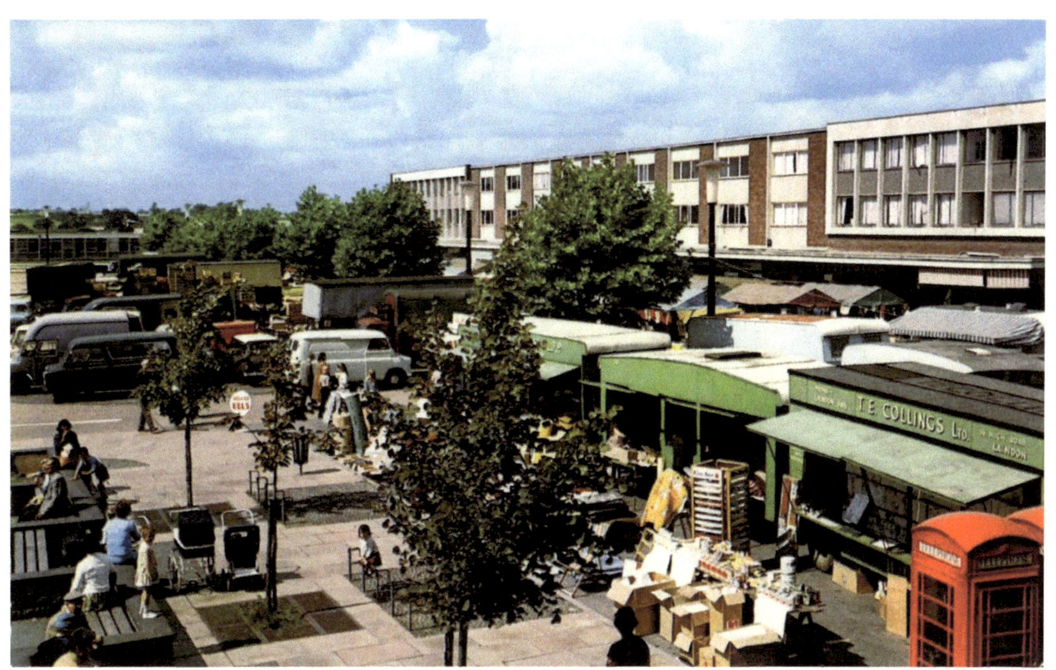

Basildon Market

On 6 September 1958, Basildon Market opened to the public; it had fifty stalls. At a time before supermarkets became quite so powerful, there were nineteen greengrocer stalls at the market. It was more of a greengrocery and produce market then, but these days it is a general market. The block of shops facing Market Square were the first to be built in the town centre. Baxter's the Butchers had sawdust on the floor, and outside the shop they would sell freshly roasted chestnuts. In 2018 the market moved from Market Square to St Martin's Square. The first day of trading in its new home was 4 October 2018..

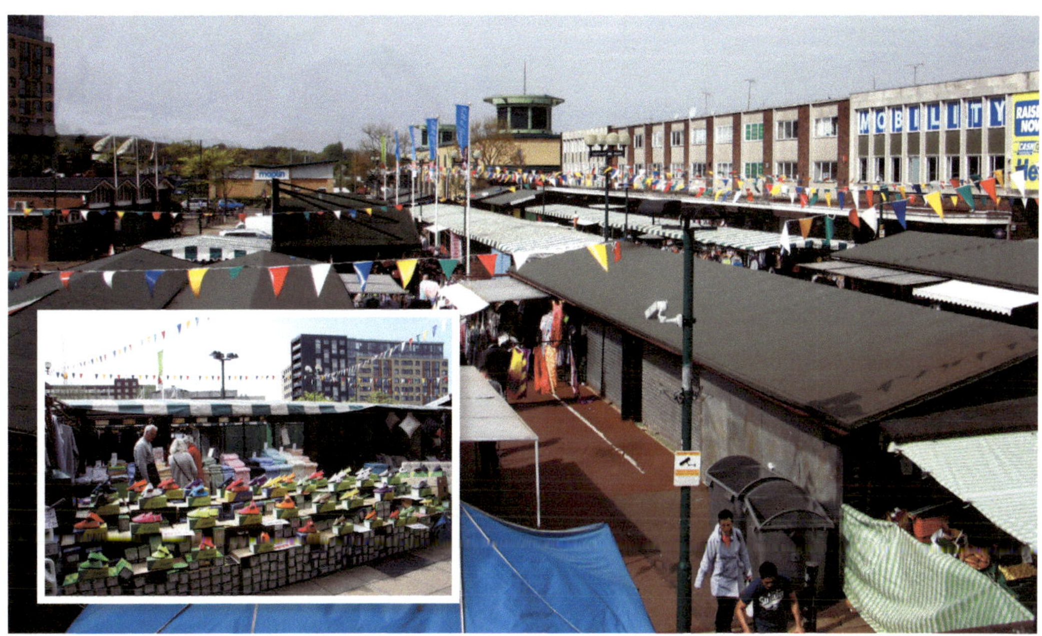

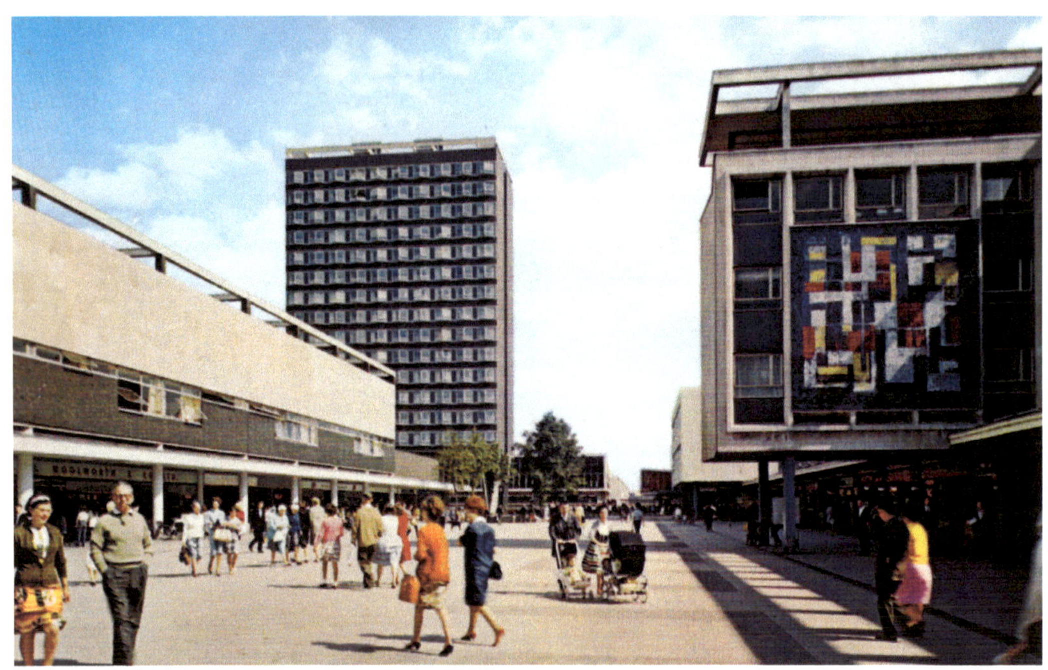

Basildon Town Square

The first phase of the Town Square was completed in 1958. Keay House, seen on the right, was named after Sir Lancelot Keay, chairman of Basildon Development Corporation. It was home to Basildon Urban District Council from 1960–65. In 1996, part of Keay House that overhung the square was demolished, including the mural by Anthony Holloway, as part of a Town Square regeneration project to create a more open plaza. The building was renamed Southgate House. Today, you can see the addition of Toni & Guy and Costa Coffee in the square.

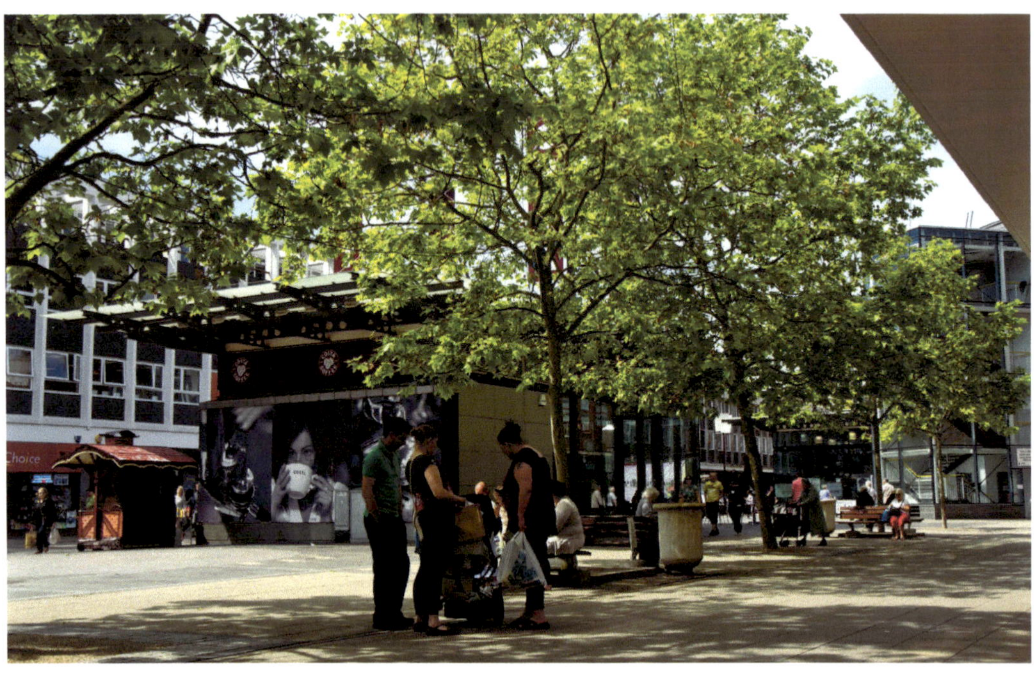

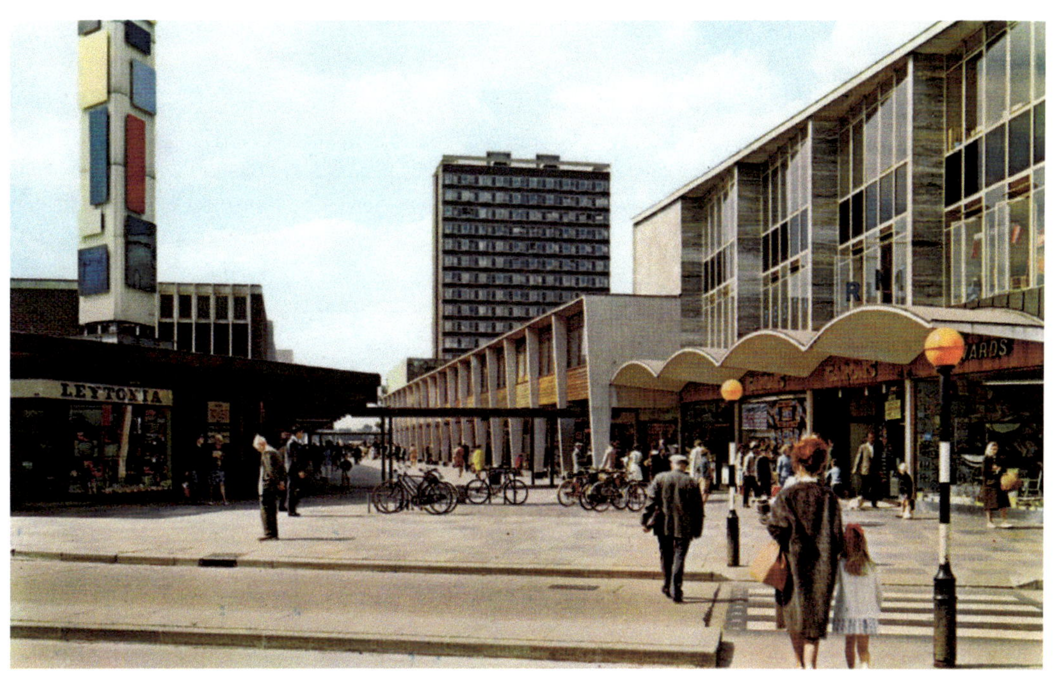

Basildon – East Walk, 1967

When you look down East Walk, you can see Brooke House, the only housing unit within the town. It is a Grade II listed building and was opened on 7 July 1962, named after the former housing minister, Henry Brooke. To the left of East Walk, before you crossed, was Barney's of Cambridge – a fashion wear shop that Wendy King's mother used to find bargains at frequently. Today, the tower on the left with the coloured rectangles is missing; this was to be used for advertising.

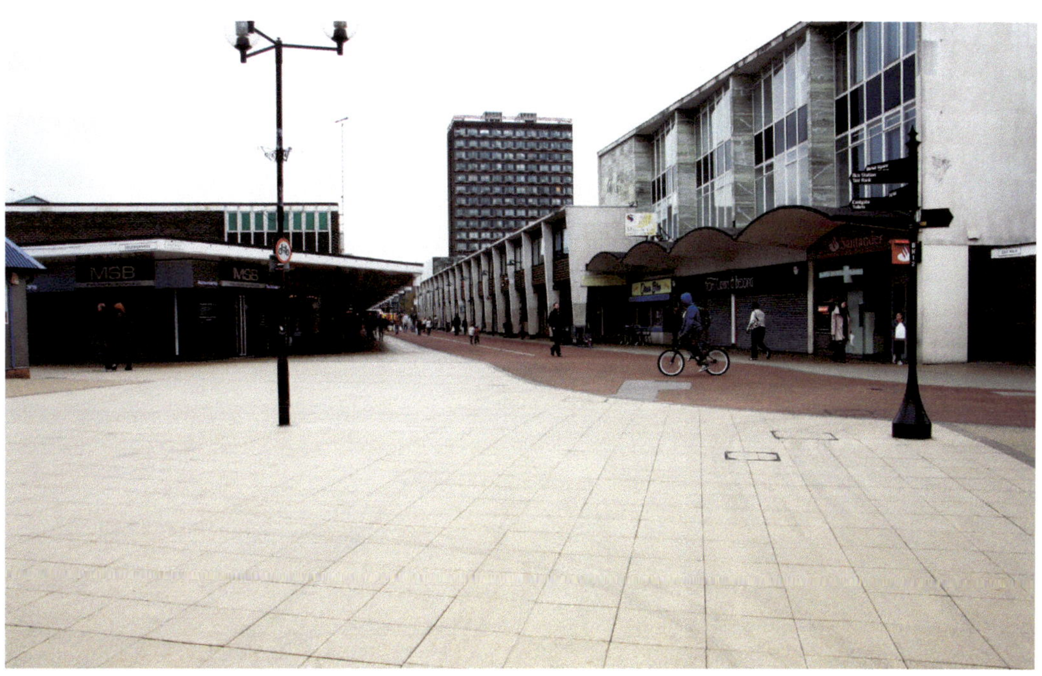

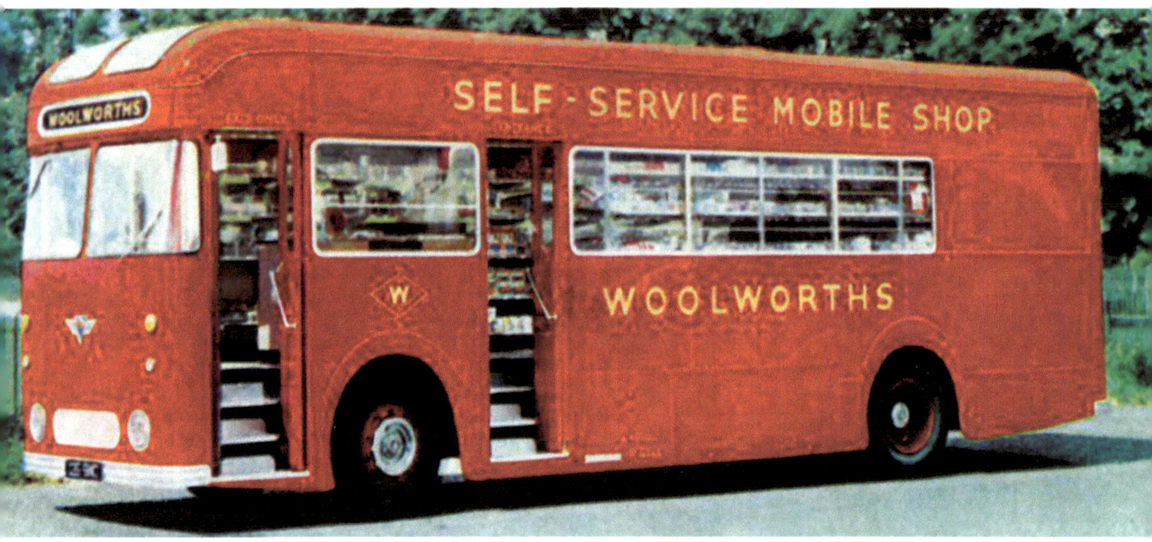

Basildon – Woolworths

Before F. W. Woolworths was established at No. 23 Town Square in February 1961, it sold its wares from a mobile van that was usually parked in Market Square. Later known as Woolworths, the store was in business for forty-seven years until Saturday 27 December 2008, when the company went into administration around the height of the recession. In 2009, the shop was divided into two units. Poundland relocated into the larger unit.

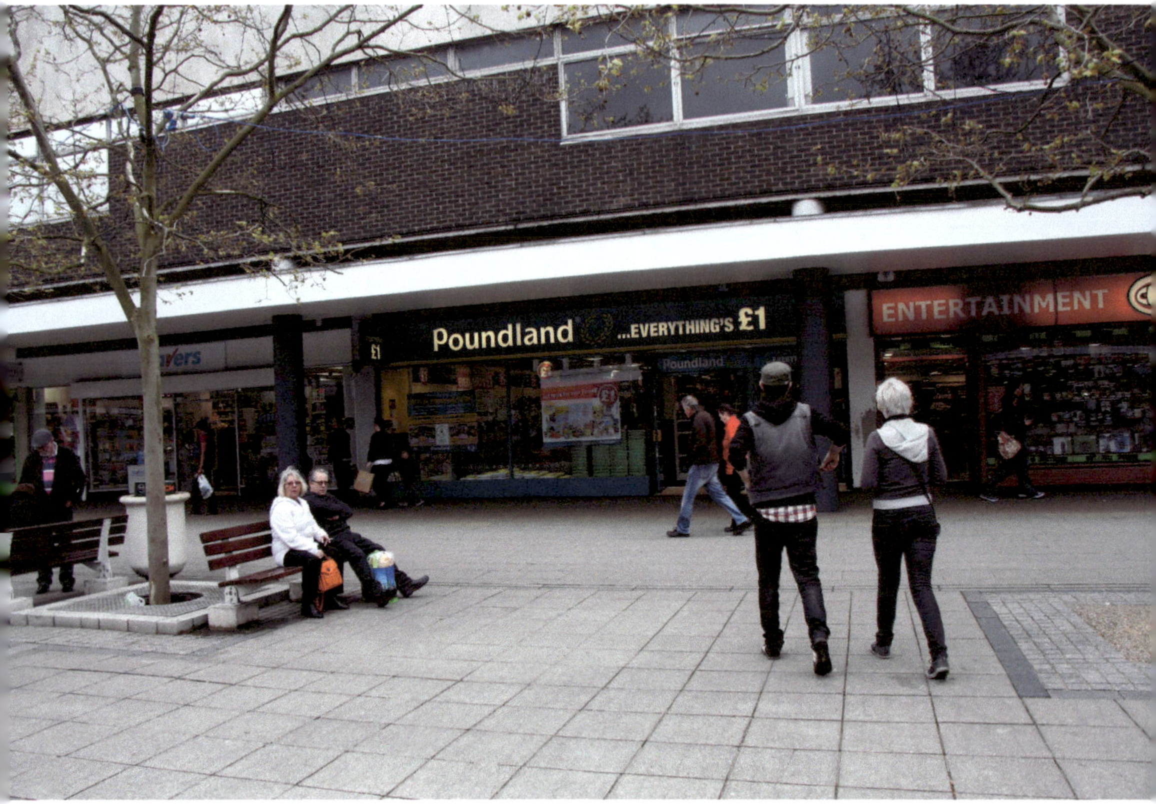

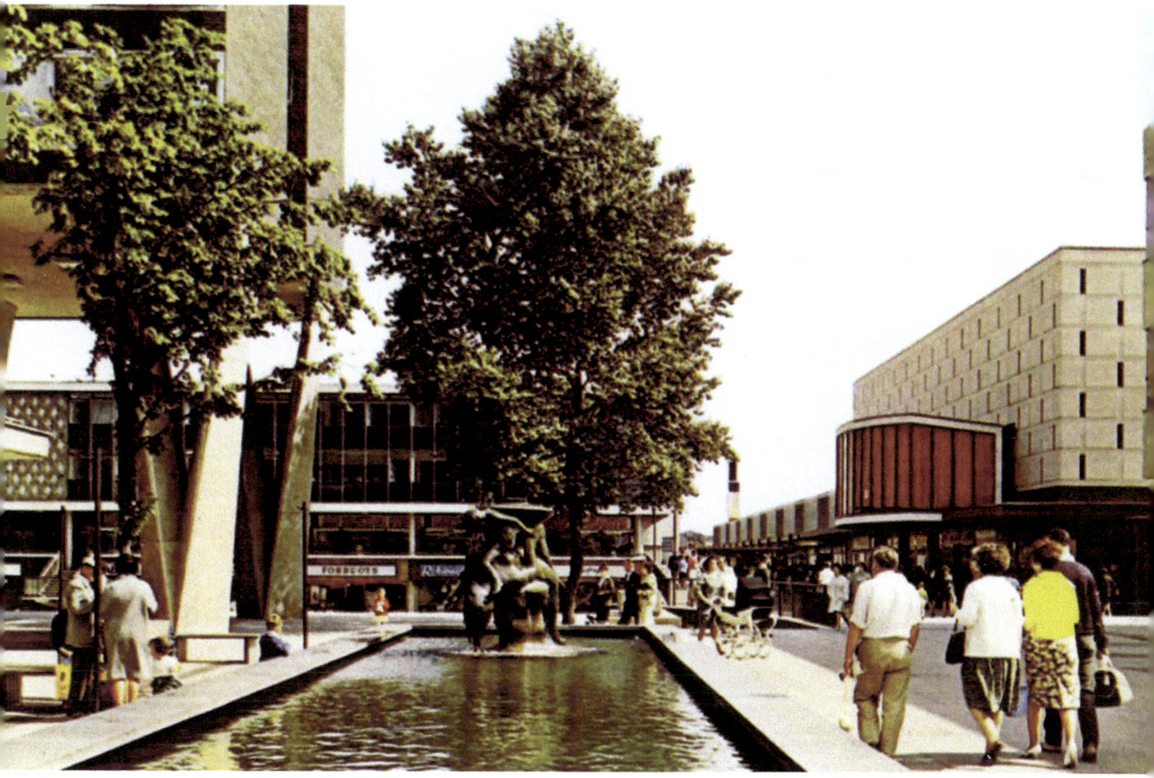

Basildon – Mother and Child Statue

The water fountain sculpture in the Town Square was commissioned in 1959 by the Development Corporation to symbolise the young and growing area of Basildon. It was designed by Paris-born sculptor Maurice Lambert R.A. (1901–64). Set in stone and finished in bronze, it cost £4,000 and was unveiled to the public on 7 July 1962. It was adopted in 1974 as the symbol to represent Basildon Council and forms the central part of the town's crest. It has Grade II listed status.

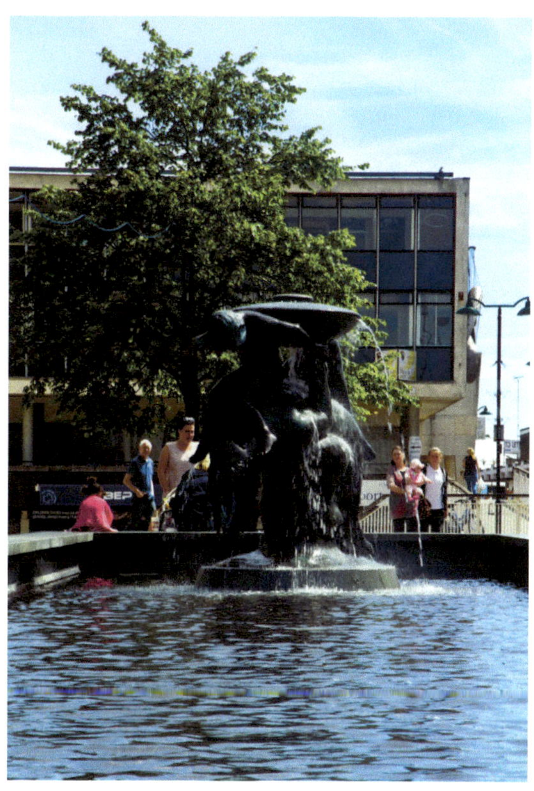

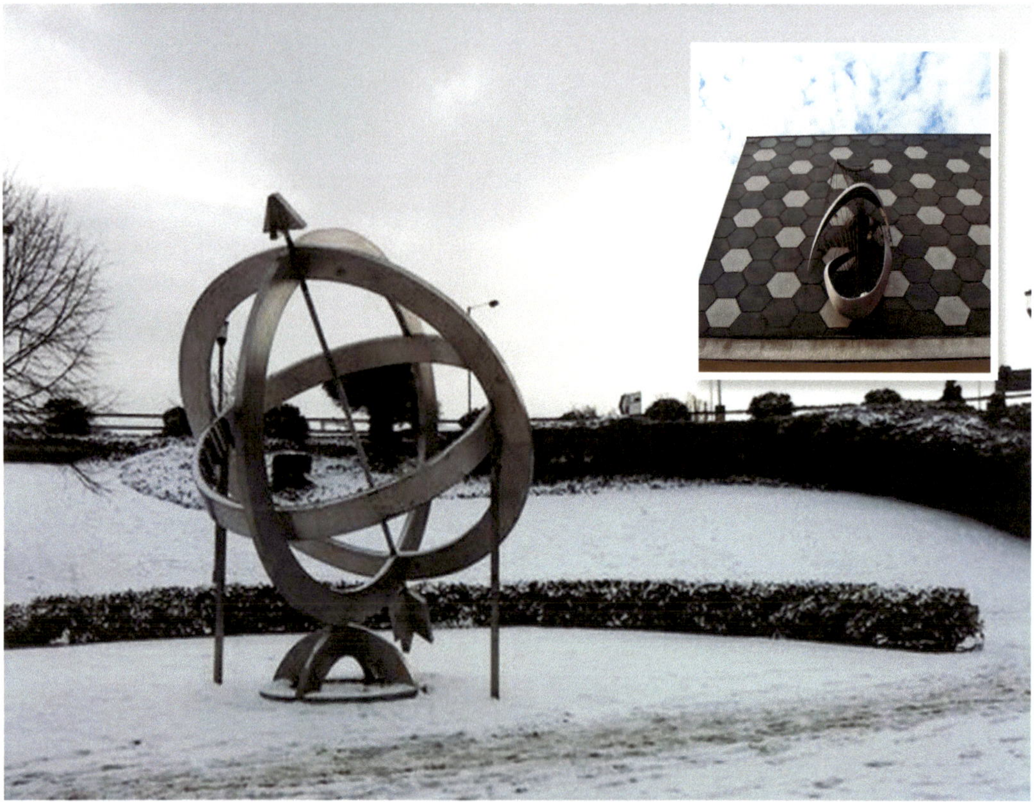

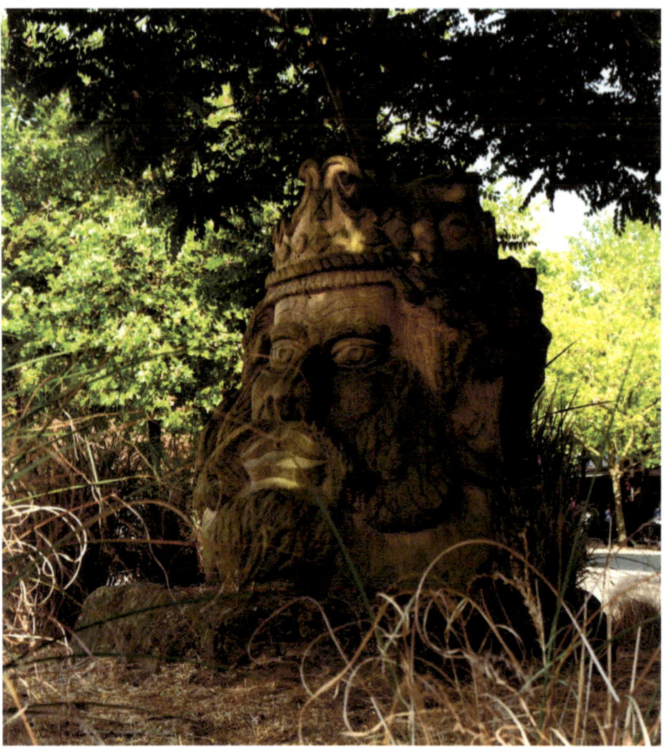

Basildon – Sculptures

Basildon has many fine pieces of twentieth-century sculpture and mosaic. These were highlighted in the Basildon Heritage Trail that was launched on 25/26 April 2009. On the wall of Freedom House is an untitled tenor clef sculpture made of aluminium and wire by A. J. Poole, erected in 1960. The Armillary Sundial by Wendy Taylor was installed in 1989 in the roundabout at Roundacre. In 2010, King Edgar's Head stone sculpture was placed in St Martin's Square. The artist, Dave Chapple, died in 2009 and was well-regarded within the region.

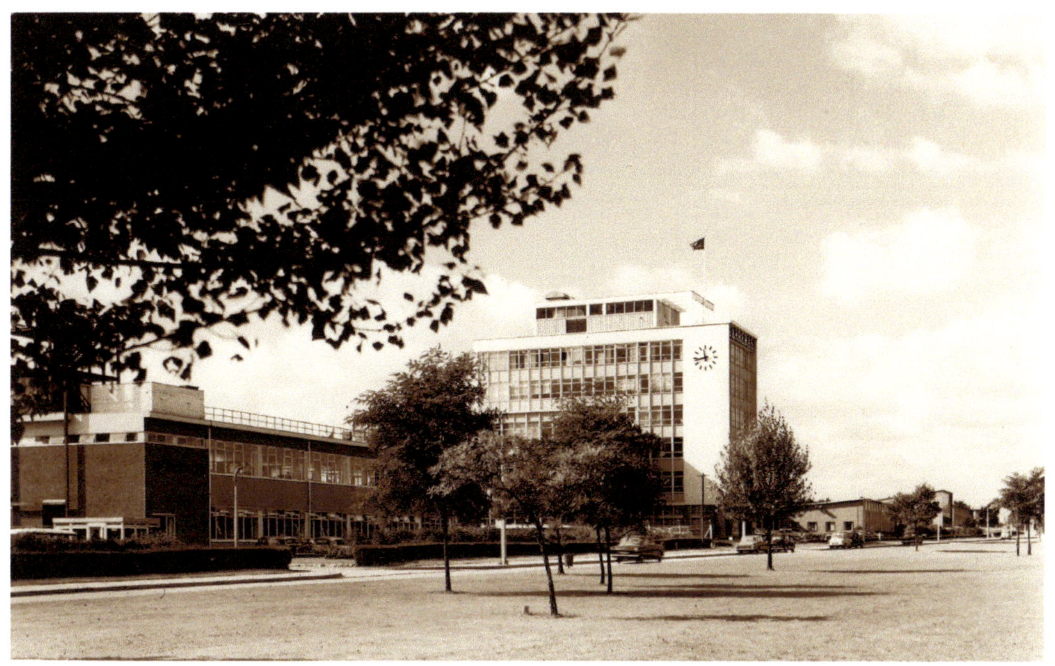

Basildon – Carreras Rothmans

In 1959, Carreras Rothmans relocated to a new factory at No. 1 Industrial Estate, Christopher Martin Road. HRH the Duke of Edinburgh officially opened the new factory in March 1960, landing in the grounds by a helicopter that he piloted. It became the world's first fully-automated cigarette manufacturing plant; at the peak of its success, it produced sixty-five per cent of all cigarettes exported from Britain. Due to competition and anti-smoking campaigns, it closed in April 1984. The building is renamed Phoenix House today, and is NHS South West Essex Community Services' head office.

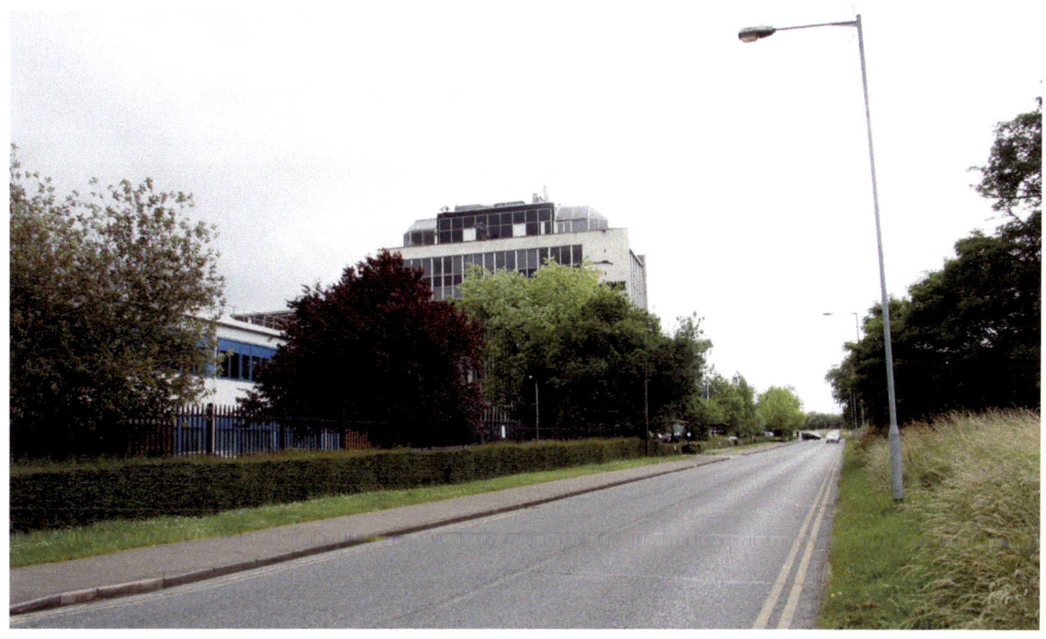

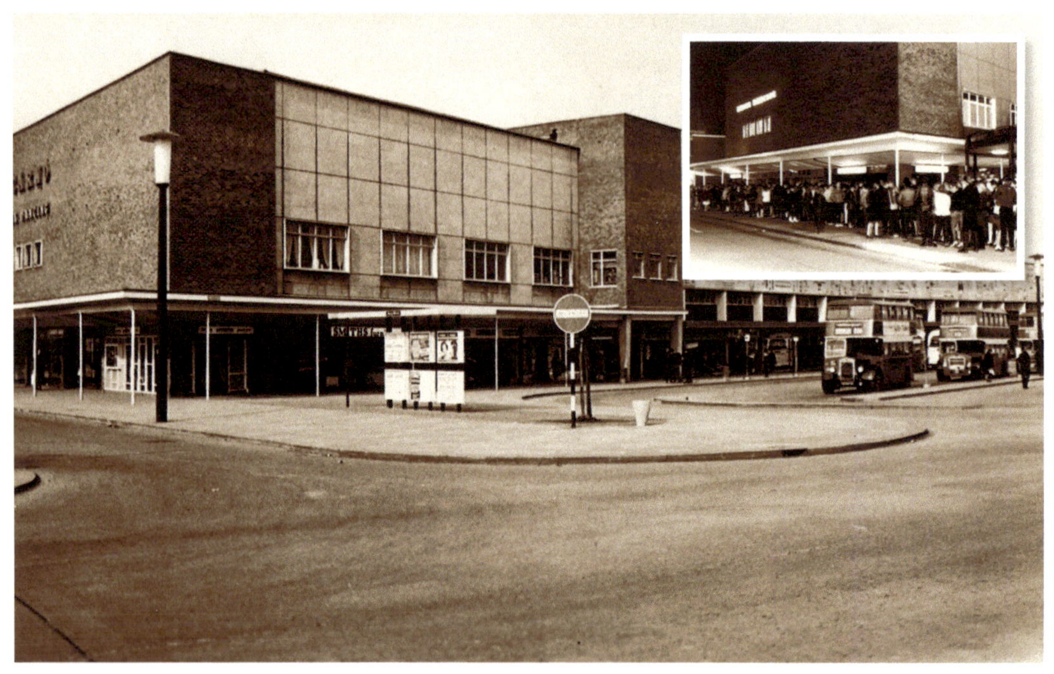

Basildon – Raquels, Formerly Locarno Ballroom

On 25 March 1961, Locarno Ballroom, Blenheim House, Market Pavement opens. Ran by The Mecca Ltd, it had a standing capacity of about 850, hosting bands like The Who, The Kinks, Herman's Hermits, Dave Clark Five and Manfred Mann. The nightclub was renamed Tiffany's from 1970–74, then Raquel's, where Depeche Mode made two appearances in 1981. Here the crowd are waiting to see them on 10 November 1981. It closed as Club Uropa in January 1998, and later opened as Riley's Sports Bar. This venue closed in 2014. (*Photograph by Robin Woosey*)

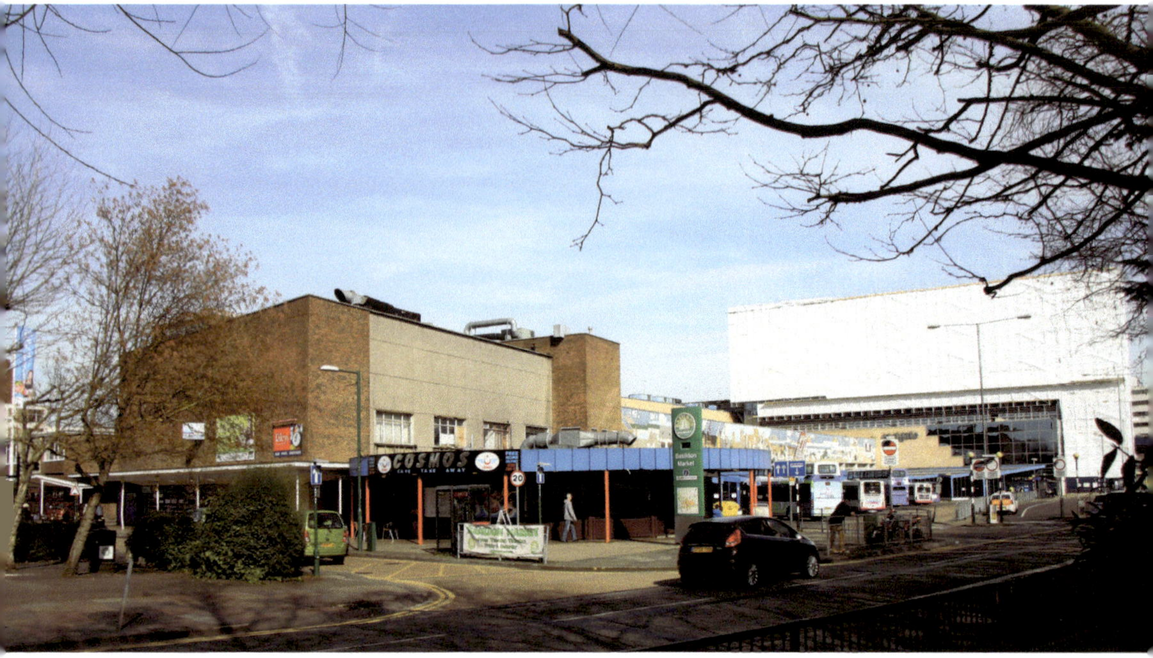

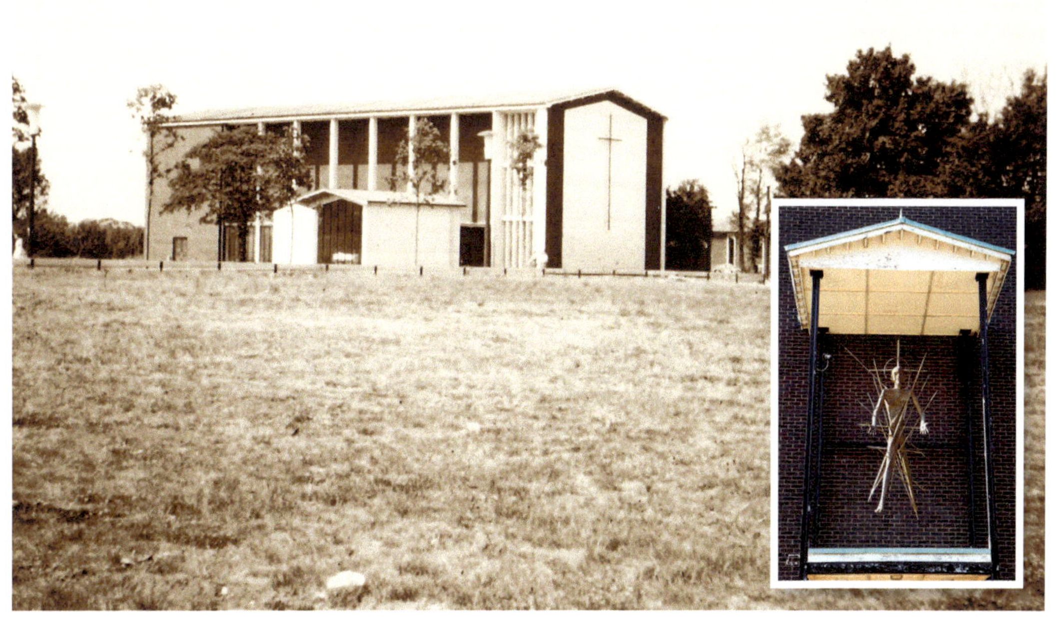

Basildon – St Martin's Le Tours Church

Designed by local architect Trena Cotton, and officially opened to the public in November 1962, the early St Martins Le Tours church was surrounded by a large expanse of grass. Part of it later became St Martin's Gardens. A fibreglass figure of Christ, designed by T. B. Huxley-Jones in 1968, is above the south door. It was the last piece of work he did before he died. In stark contrast to the above picture, the church today has buildings surrounding it and has become very pedestrian-friendly with its concrete slabbed paving.

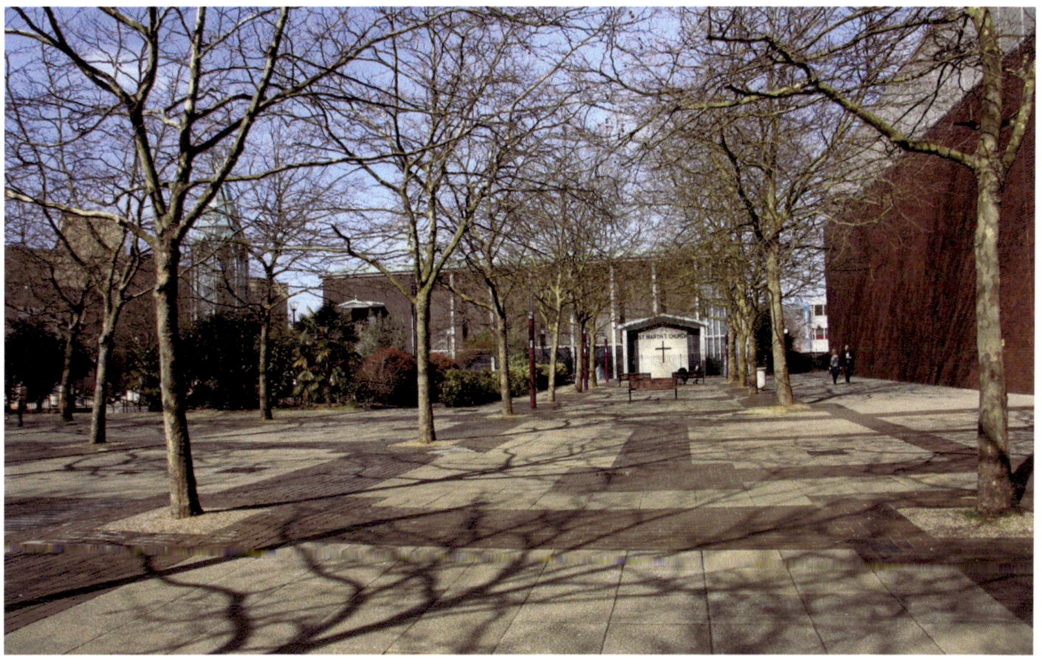

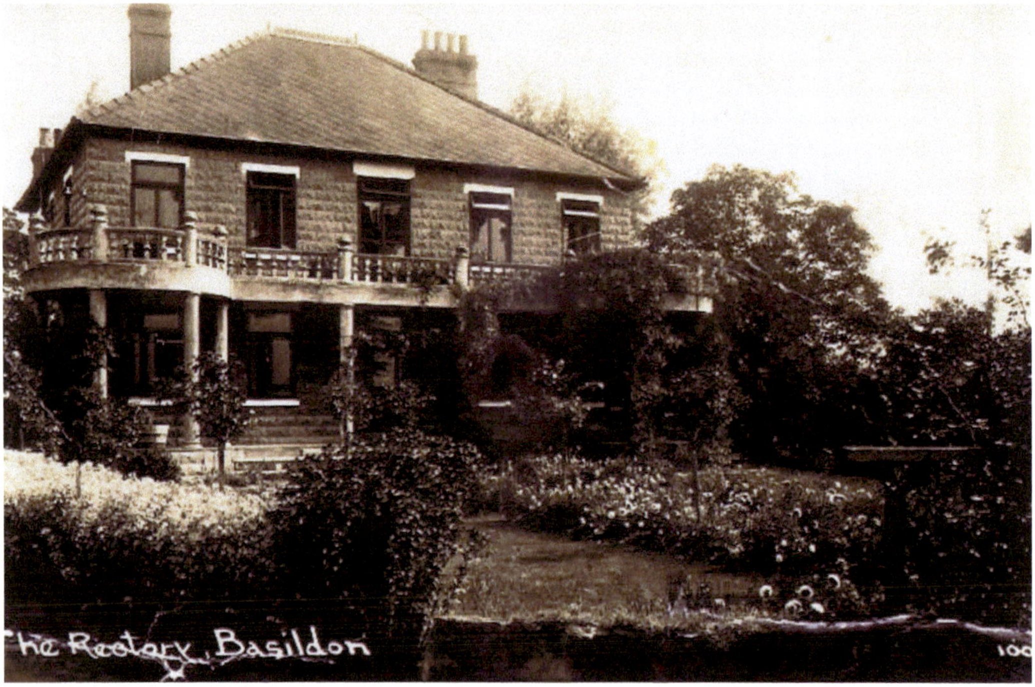

Basildon Rectory

Oliphants, a Tudor house destroyed by a fire at the start of the 1900s, was rebuilt, and in the 1930s, became Basildon's third rectory. It was demolished in 1962, and covered by the Ford Tractor Plant (now New Holland). This was part of the progressive plan for the town by Basildon Development Corporation, to try to provide work for all within the area.

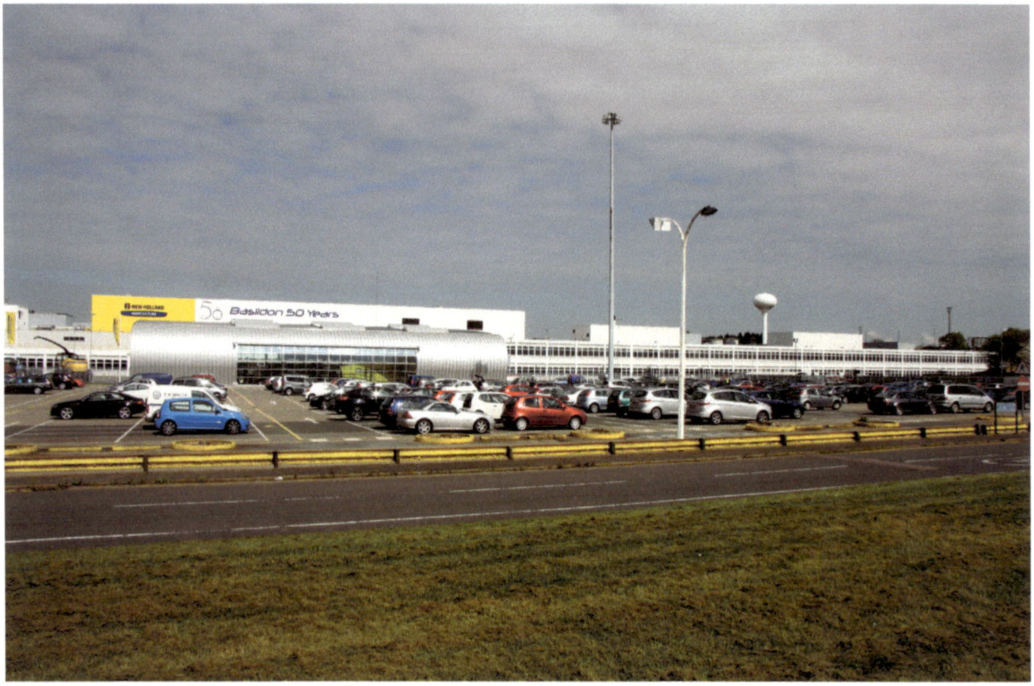

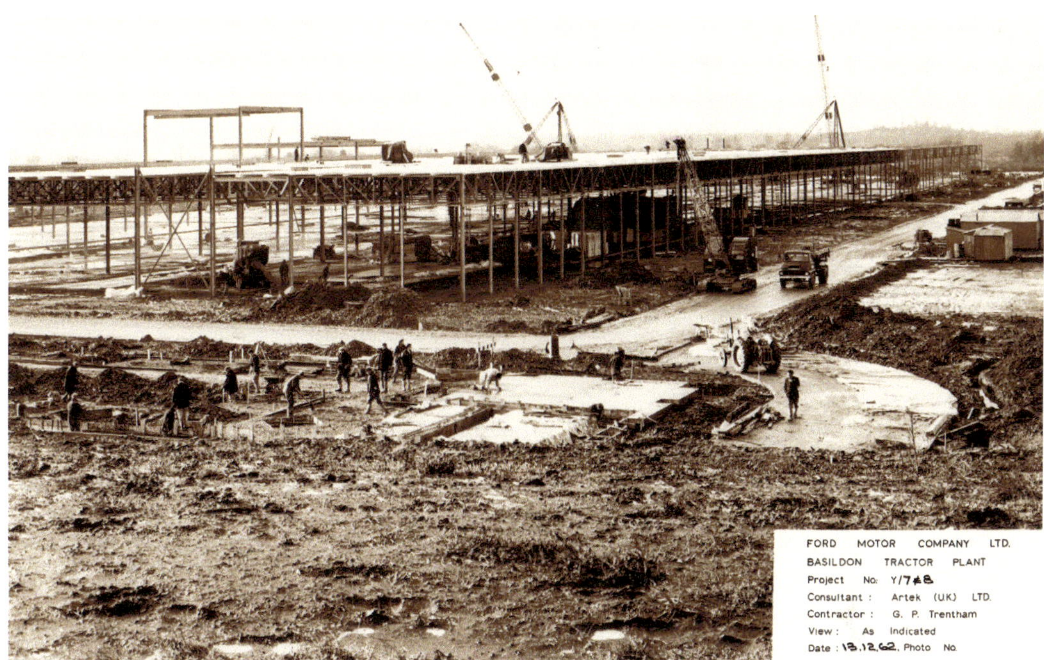

Basildon – Ford Tractor Plant, Cranes Farm Road

The Ford Tractor Plant occupied the whole of the No. 3 Industrial Estate. Built in 1964, it produced the new Ford World series tractors, Ford 6X series. The tractor production was moved from Dagenham, Essex, to allow expansion of the engine building facilities and car production lines. The Basildon Factory was transferred to New Holland when Ford sold the agricultural division to Fiat of Italy in the 1990s. New Holland celebrated the fiftieth anniversary of its flagship tractor factory this year; it employs 1,000 people and makes 23,000 tractors each year.

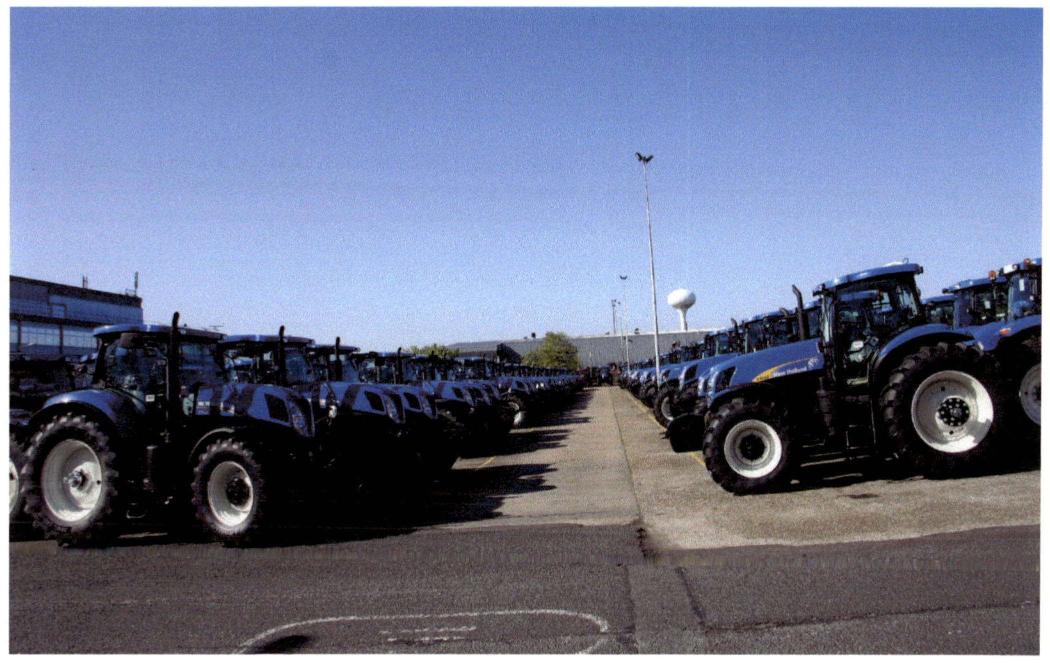

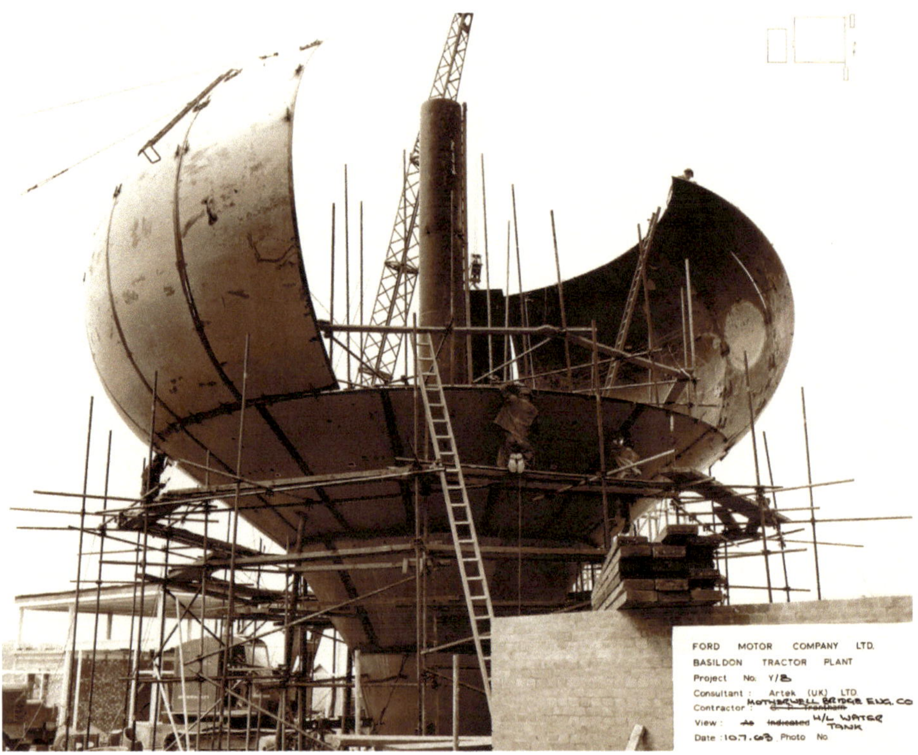

Basildon – The Water Tower, Ford Tractor Plant

The iconic 600,000 gallon water tower, known to many in the area as 'The Onion', was built at the Fords Tractor Plant in the 1960s. It can be viewed from many places and has been a landmark meaning 'near to home' for several generations living in and around Basildon. This picture of 'The Onion' in the distance is taken from the rural outskirts of Billericay.

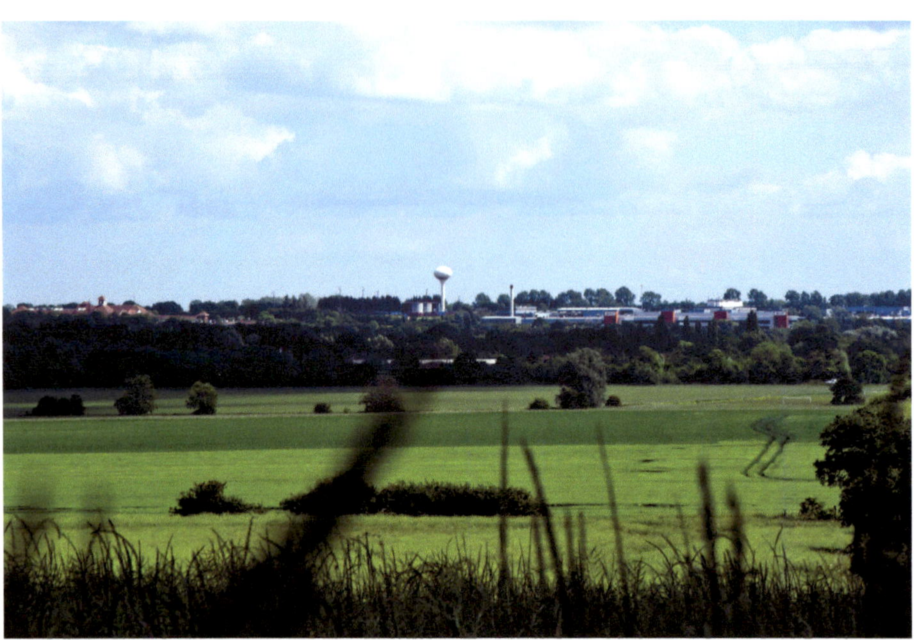

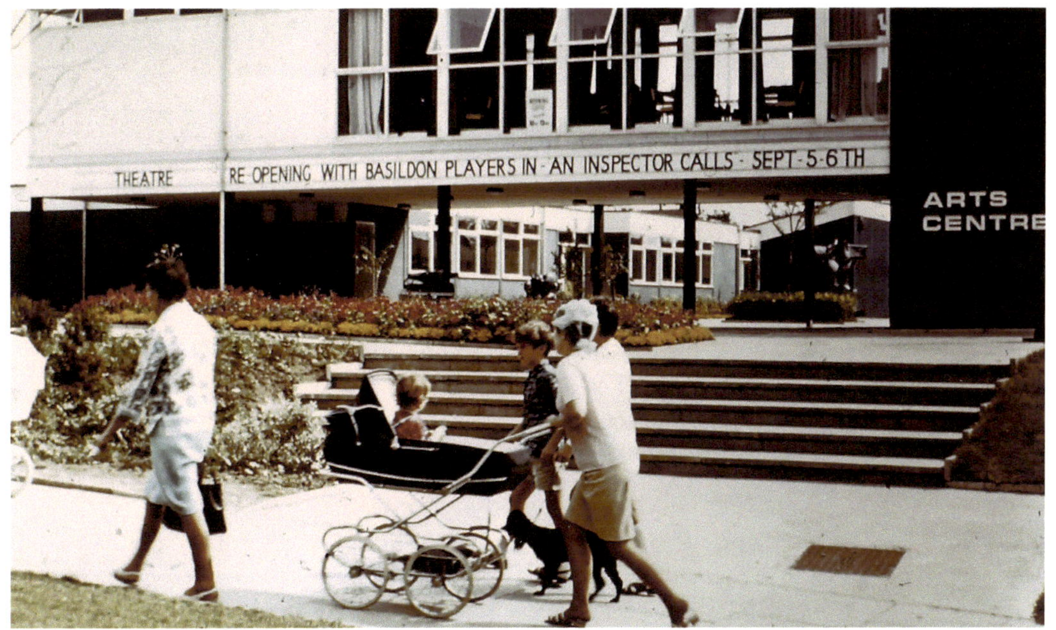

Basildon Arts Centre

This is the 500 seated Basildon Arts Centre, occupied where Westgate Shopping Centre is today. It was opened on 21 September 1968 by chairman of the Arts Council, Lord Goodman. Vin Harrop, its first Director, says, 'It was ahead of its time in the way it reached out to a very wide arts audience – it had a true following among the people of the town.' David Bowie played here in 1970 with his band The Hype, and Depeche Mode rehearsed here. It was planned to be built nearer to the Roundacre roundabout, but was built near to the temporary library. The Towngate Theatre replaced the Arts Centre in 1988.

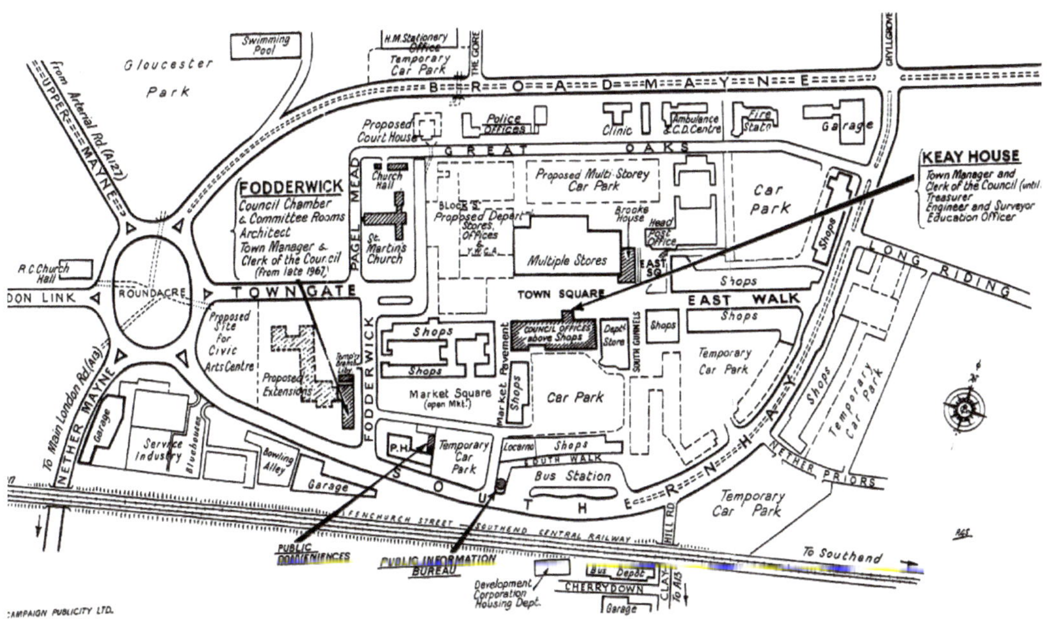

Publicity Map of Basildon - Mid 1960s

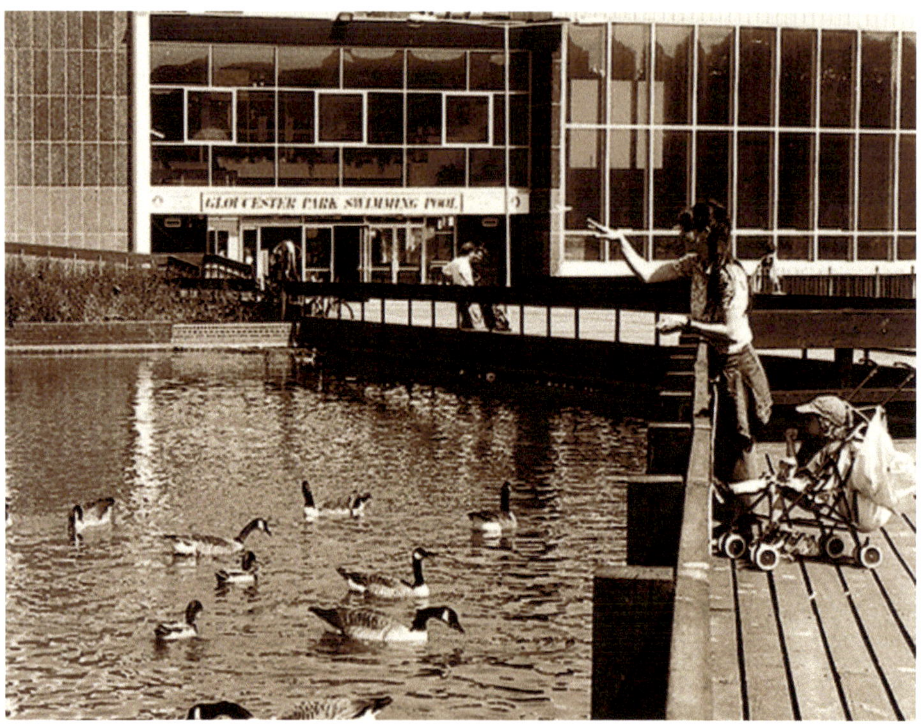

Basildon – Gloucester Park Swimming Pool

Gloucester Park Swimming Pool opened on 10 April 1968. It had a main championship-sized pool and a teaching pool housed in a postmodernist building. Despite much protest, the pool was closed on 24 April 2011, replaced by the Sporting Village, which opened later in April with its Olympic-sized swimming pool. Acacia Park, a development by Barratt Homes, is being built where the iconic swimming pool used to be.

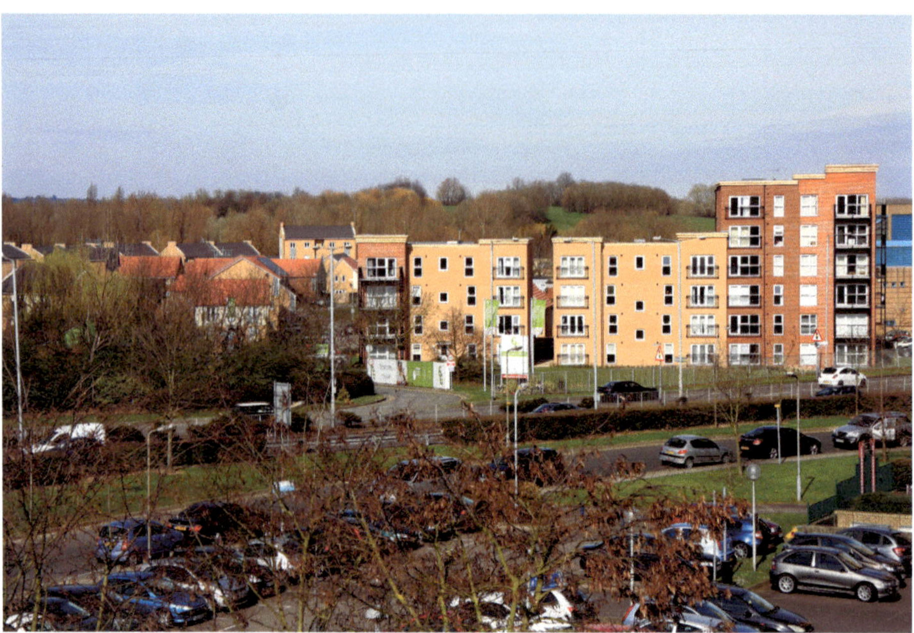

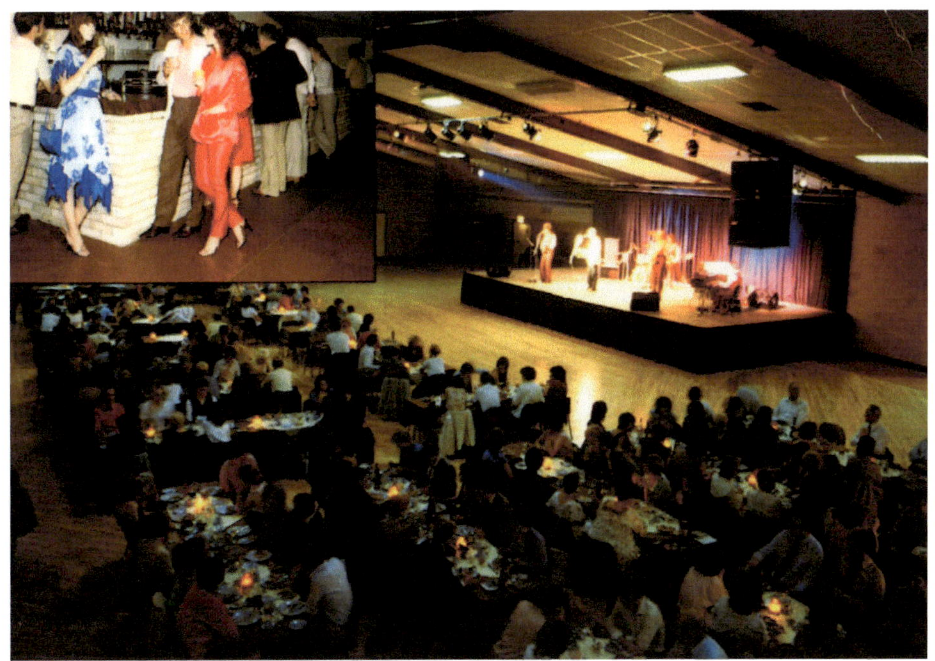

Basildon – Festival Hall

In 1982, Festival Hall opened on the site of Aquatels Zoo and Ecology Centre. It seated 1,500 and held pop concerts with names such as David Essex and Bucks Fizz. It also hosted boxing contests featuring the likes of Big Daddy and Giant Haystacks. Gary Clark remembers that Terry Marsh fought his title fight in the Super Tent on 3 April 1987. The hall was demolished in 1996, and The Festival Leisure Park opened in 1997. At present, the Toby Carvery, TGI Fridays and Harvester restaurant are on the site where the hall stood.

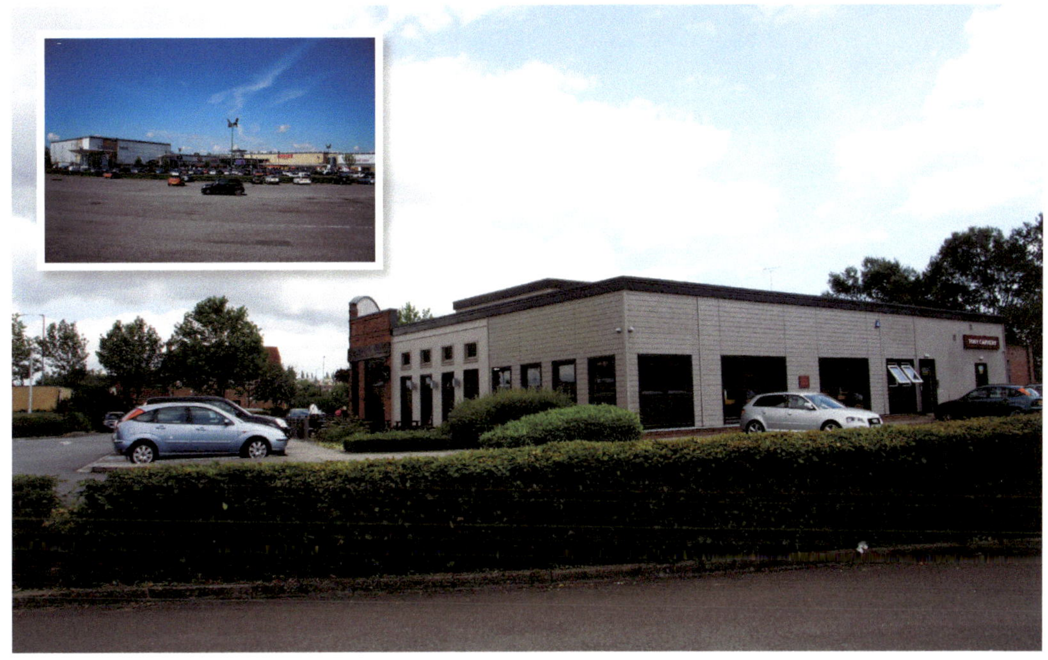

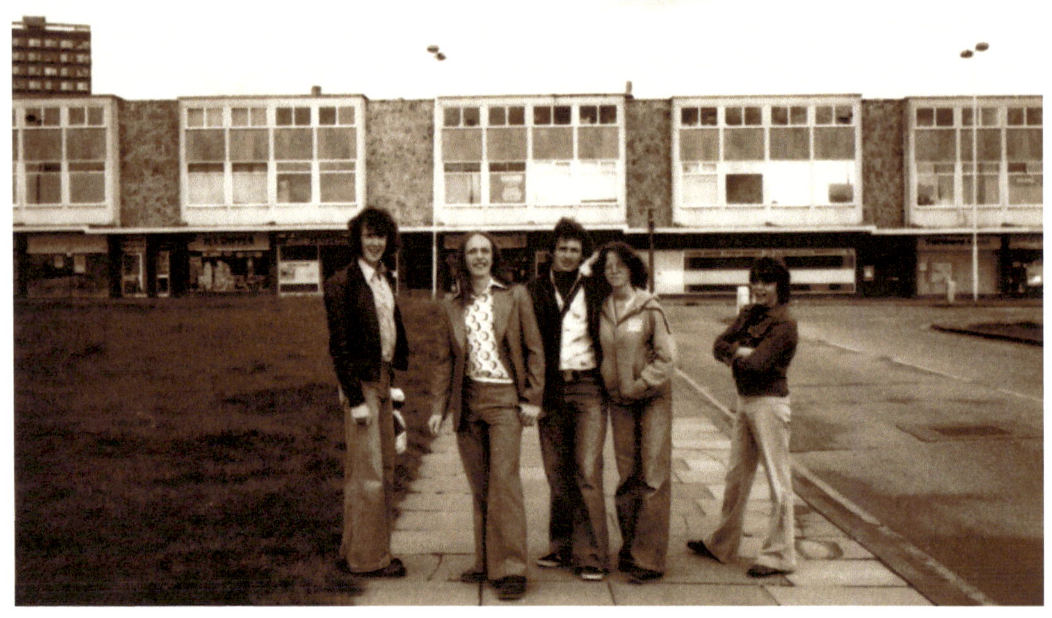

Basildon – Toys R Us

In the 1970s, some young men and a young lady stand where Toys R Us was then built in 1985 (opposite the shops at Southernhay). It was one of the first five Toys R Us superstores to open in Britain. You can also see H. T. Dwyer Newsagents. Wendy King and her brother Adrian were taken there by their mother for sweeties every Sunday in the 1960s; it was one of the rare shops open on a Sunday then.Toys R Us closed in 2018 after thirty-three years as the global firm had gone into administration. There was a total of 105 stores in the UK.

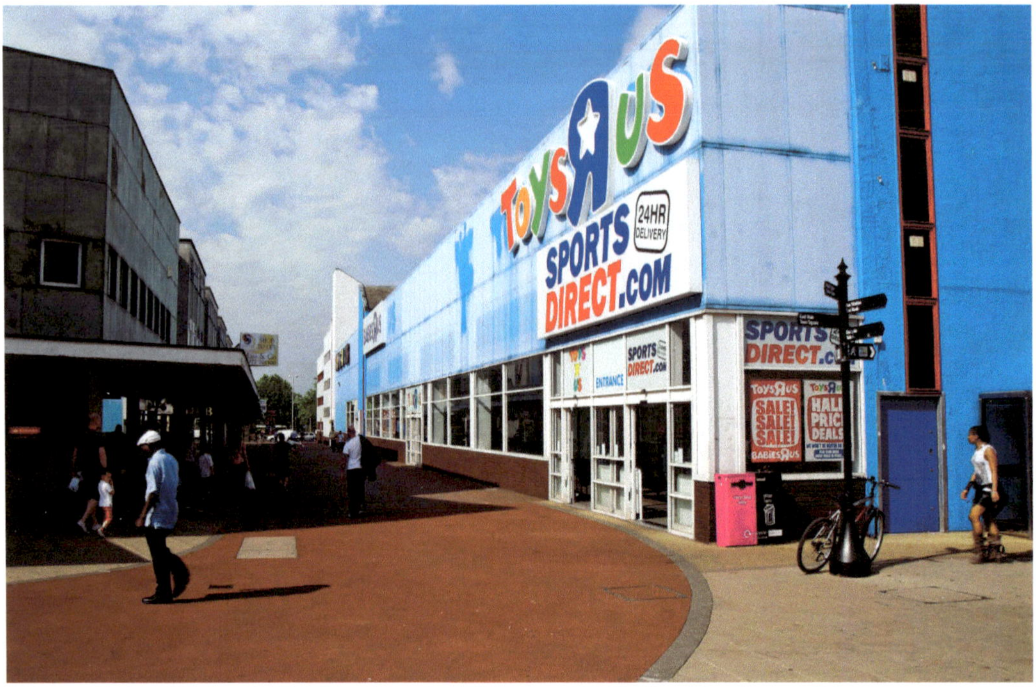

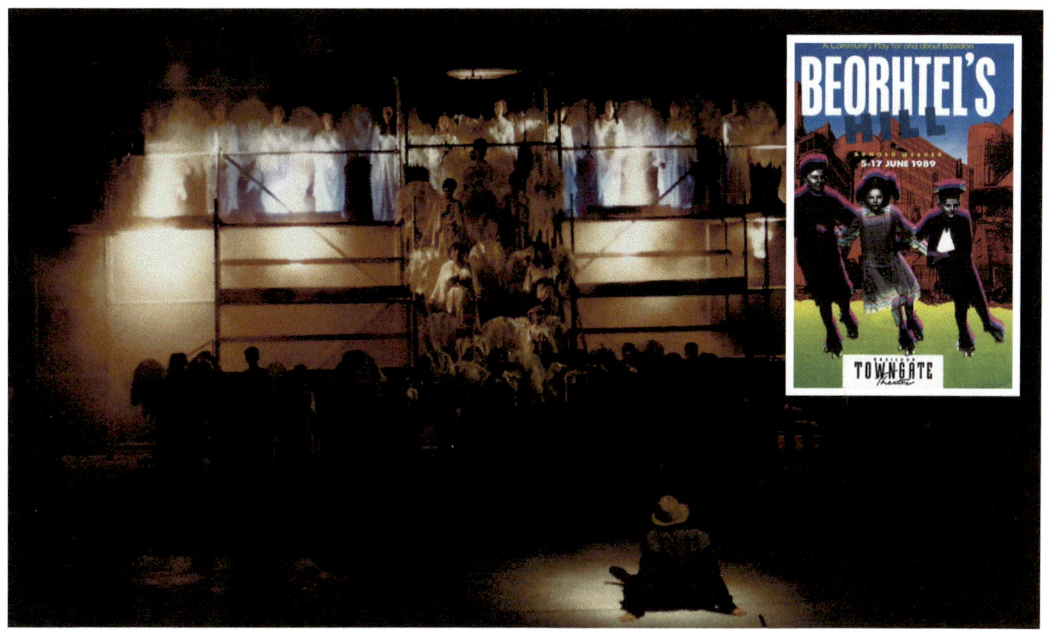

Basildon – Beorhtel's Hill

For the fortieth anniversary of Basildon New Town, *Beorhtel's Hill*, a play written by international playwright Arnold Wesker, was shown at the new Towngate Theatre in 1989. A community play was produced by Colway Theatre Trust and directed by Jon Oram and Steve Woodward. The theatre's outreach team, headed by Richard Lee, had a large involvement. It was written for and about the people of Basildon, covering three eras of time from the 1900s – the plotlanders, the New Town's new residents, and the people of Basildon in the 1980s. It was researched for two years and involved over 1,000 people (*see page 8*).

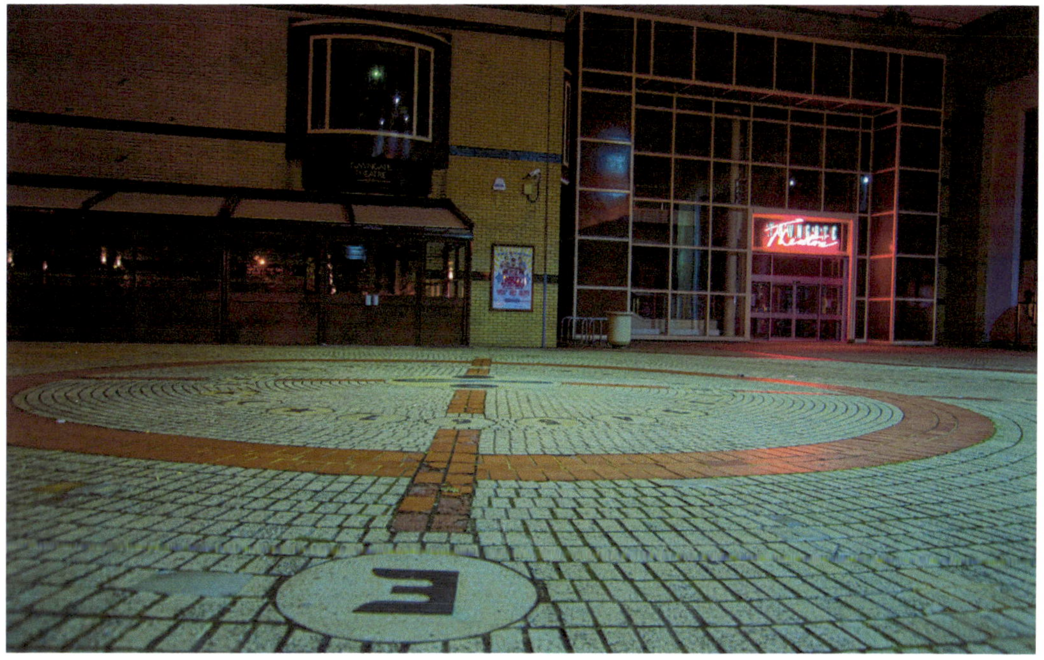

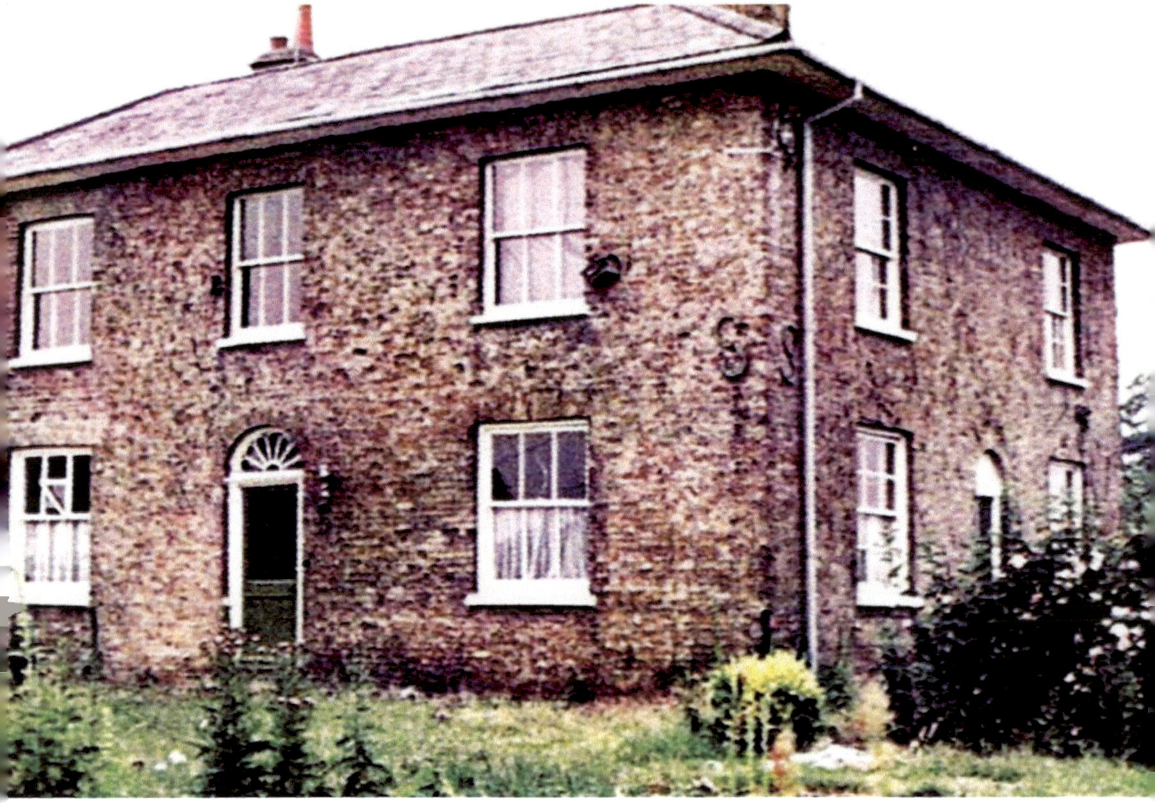

Basildon – St Lukes Hospice

Fobbing Farmhouse is a Grade II listed building that is over 200 years old. It was a corn farm owned by the Osborne family. Community nurse, Trudy Westmore-Cox, realised there was a desperate need for a hospice in Basildon. Supported by her husband Les, friends, family and the local community of Basildon and Thurrock, they started fundraising towards this vision. They became a registered charity and formed a management committee, approaching the Basildon Development Corporation, who offered them Fobbing Farm. Trudy and Les became the co-founders of St Luke's Hospice, which officially opened on 26 September 1990. Since then, hospice care and the building itself have developed, extending to serve the growing needs of the population, now housing an eight bed inpatient unit, day hospice, counselling and therapy areas, in addition to hospice at home and outpatient facilities, as well as many other end of-life-care services.

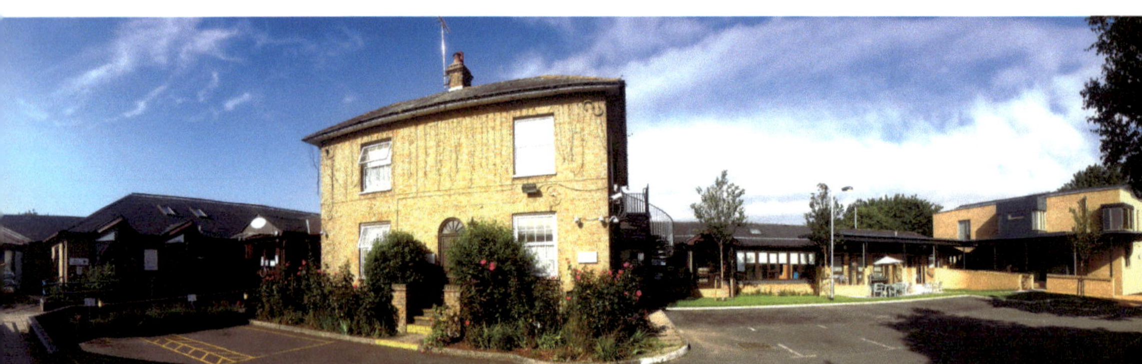

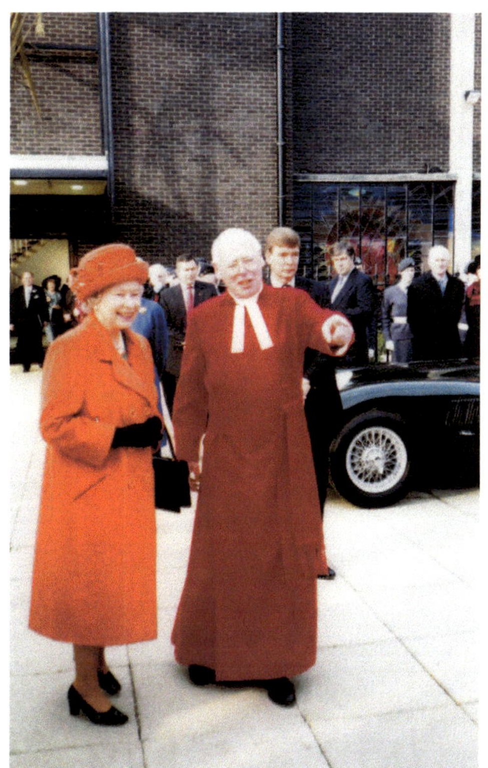

Basildon – St Martins Bell Tower

The Queen officially opened St Martin's Bell Tower on 12 March 1999 to celebrate Basildon's fiftieth birthday and mark the Millennium. She is seen talking to Cannon Lionel Webber, Rector of St Martin's church. It's an 85 foot, unique, freestanding, faceted glass and steel tower of neo-Gothic design, created by Douglas Galloway. The bell tower has eight bells; six are from the redundant St Nicholas church, Colchester. The eighth bell, the Tenor Bell, weighs 565 kg. It was made by Joanna Hille in 1441, the first recorded bell cast by a woman.

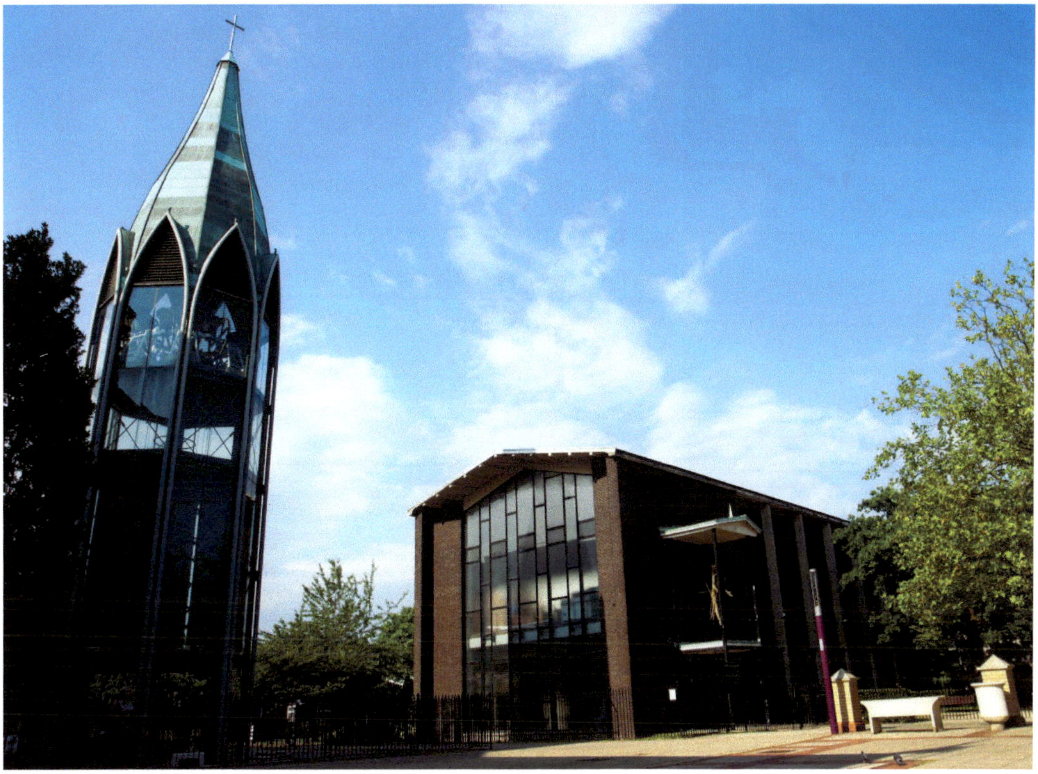

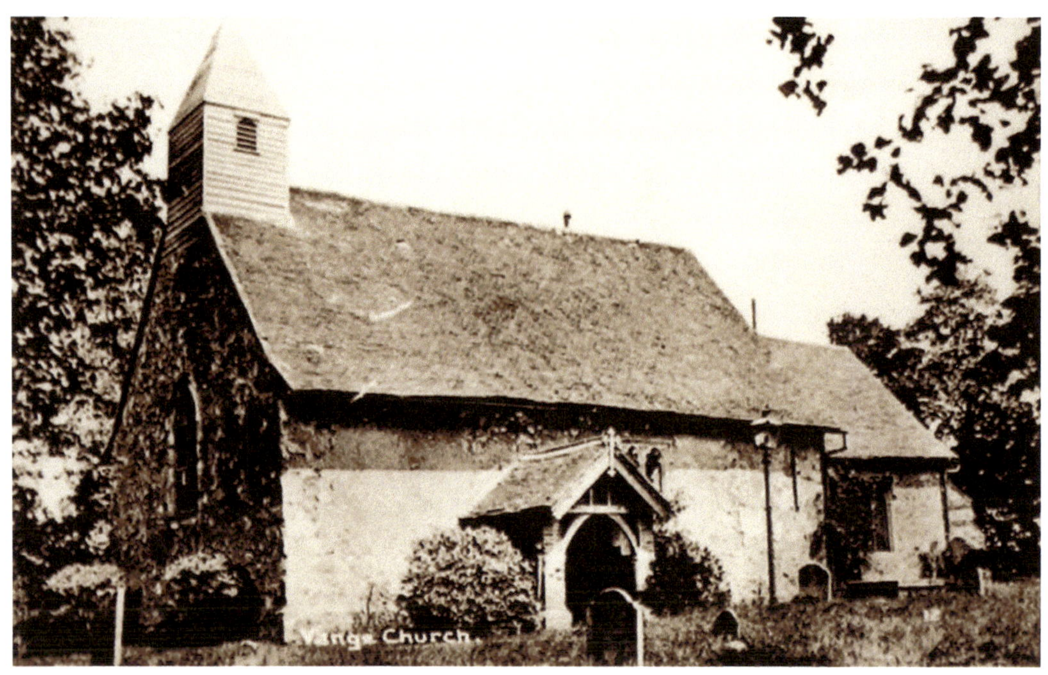

Vange – All Saints' Church

All Saints' church, London Road, is believed to be the oldest surviving church in Basildon. The nave dates back to the late eleventh century, other parts the twelfth century. Due to its size and location it was deemed inadequate for the population of Vange in the late 1950s, so St Chads was built in Clay Hill Road. The church was made redundant in 1996. It is now a Grade II listed building, and in 2003, the Churches Conservation Trust took over the care of the building.

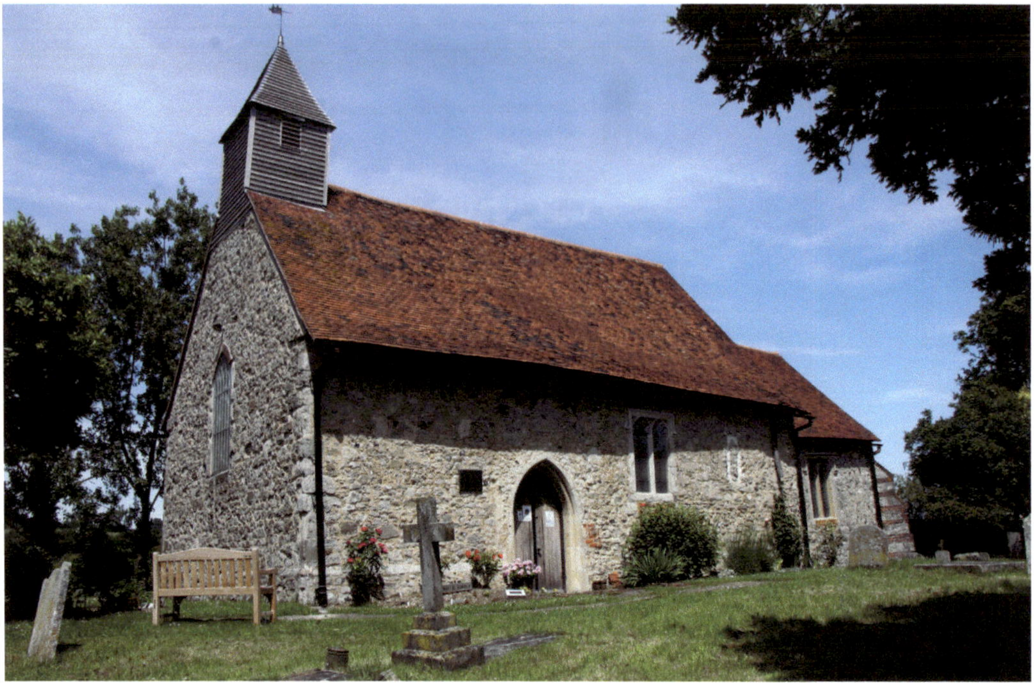

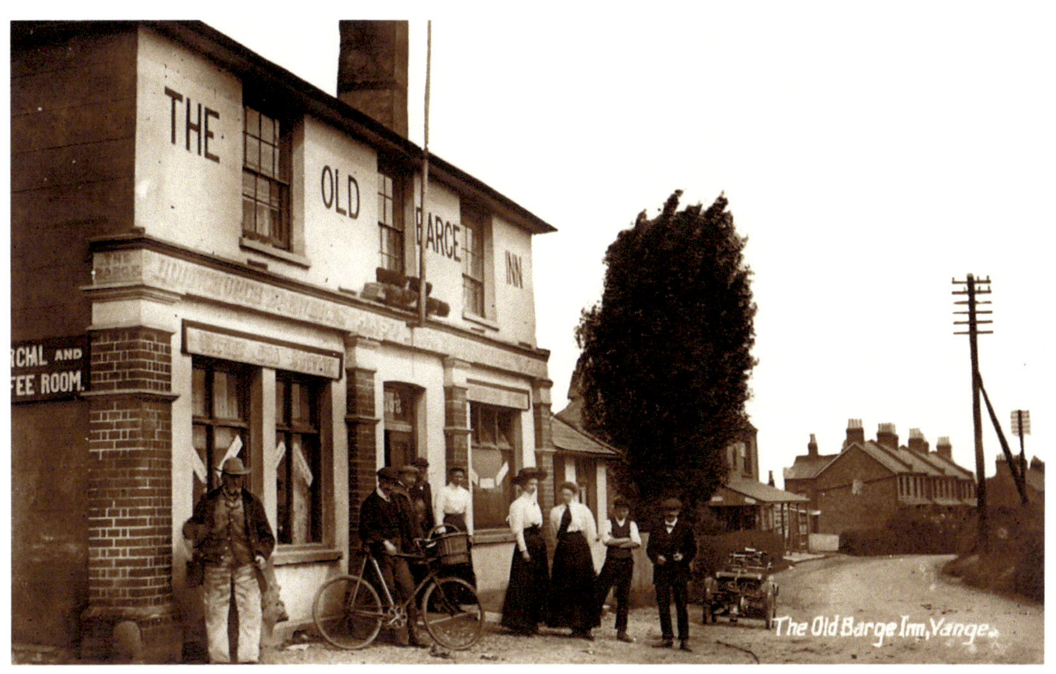

Vange – The Old Barge Inn, 1910

It is said that many a skipper drank at the Old Barge Inn after mooring near Vange Wharf. At one time a private house, one of its first names was Man with Seven Wives. The innkeeper was called Mr Wife, so presumably his family numbered seven. Records date it back to 1840, but it is said that it has been the site of a pub for 400 years. Notably, the Evans family ran the pub for seven decades from 1937–2007. Recently, publican Mark Bassett has managed it.

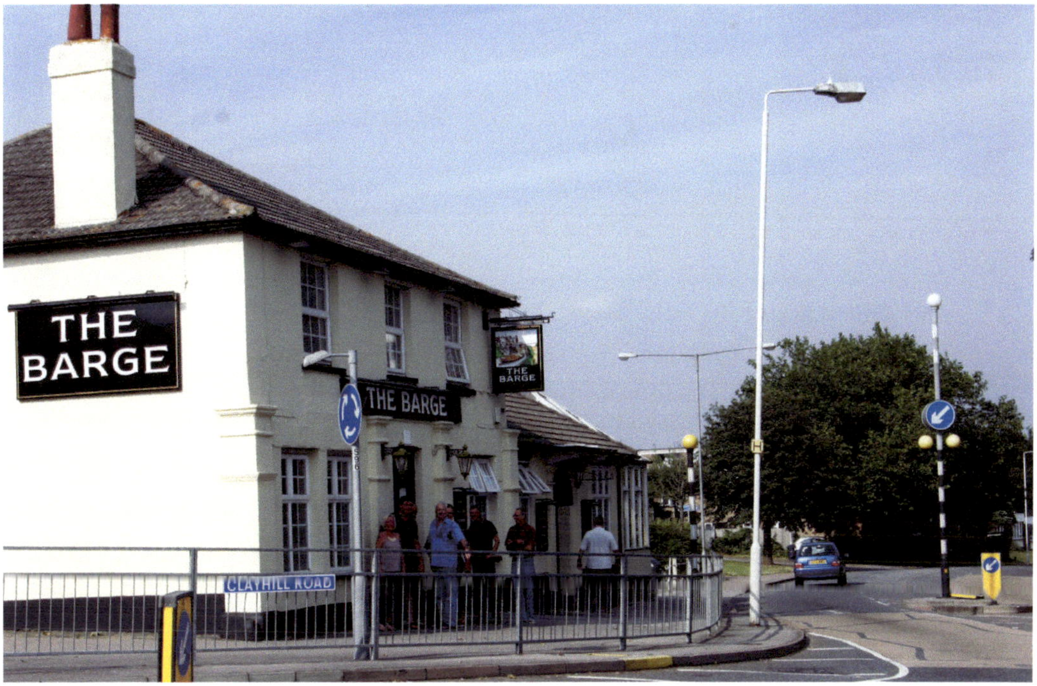

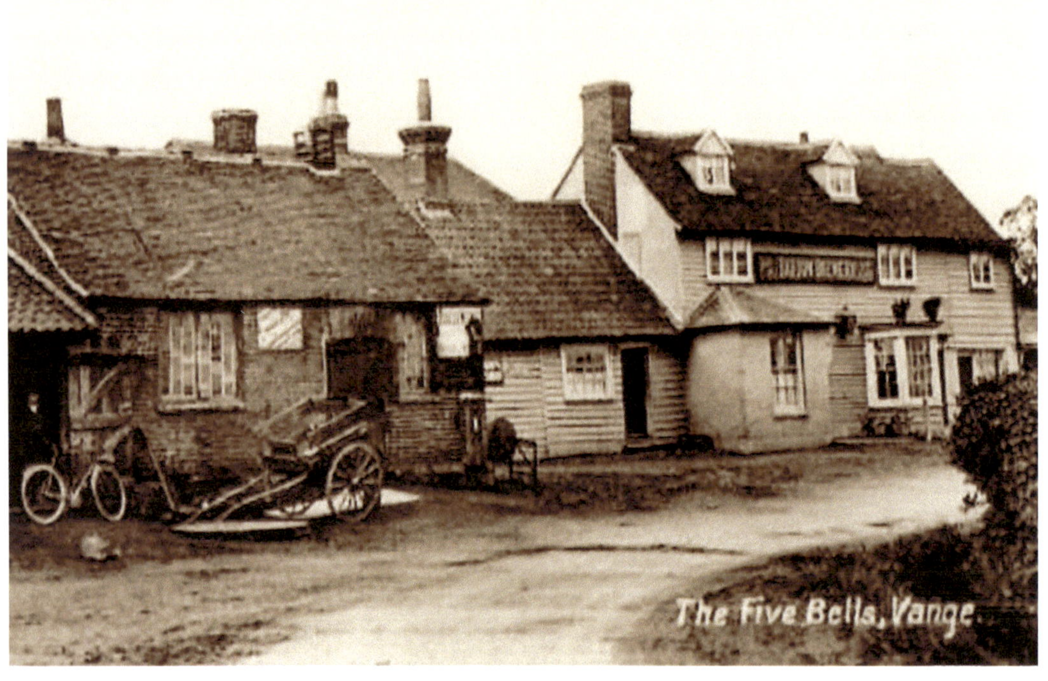

Vange – The Five Bells

This is the Five Bells and adjoining Old Forge in the 1910s, but there has been a public house situated on the corner of London Road and Five Bells Hill for centuries. The first recorded occupant was Henry Brown in 1841. The Old Forge went in the 1950s, but The Five Bells public house is now a Harvester restaurant serving walkers, locals and passing travellers from the busy A13.

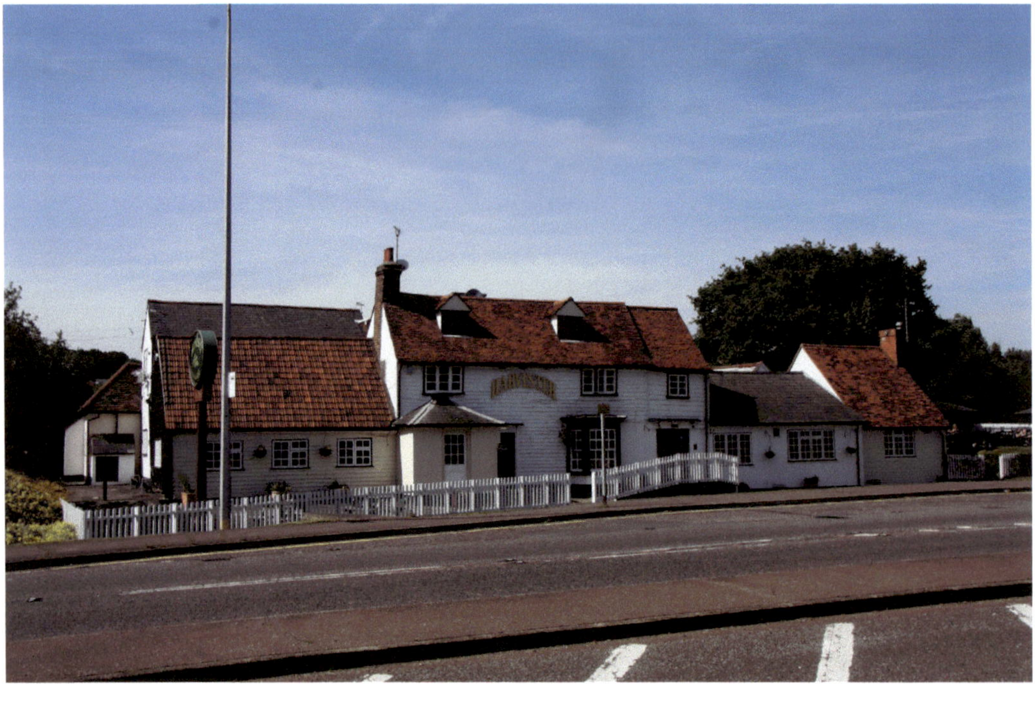

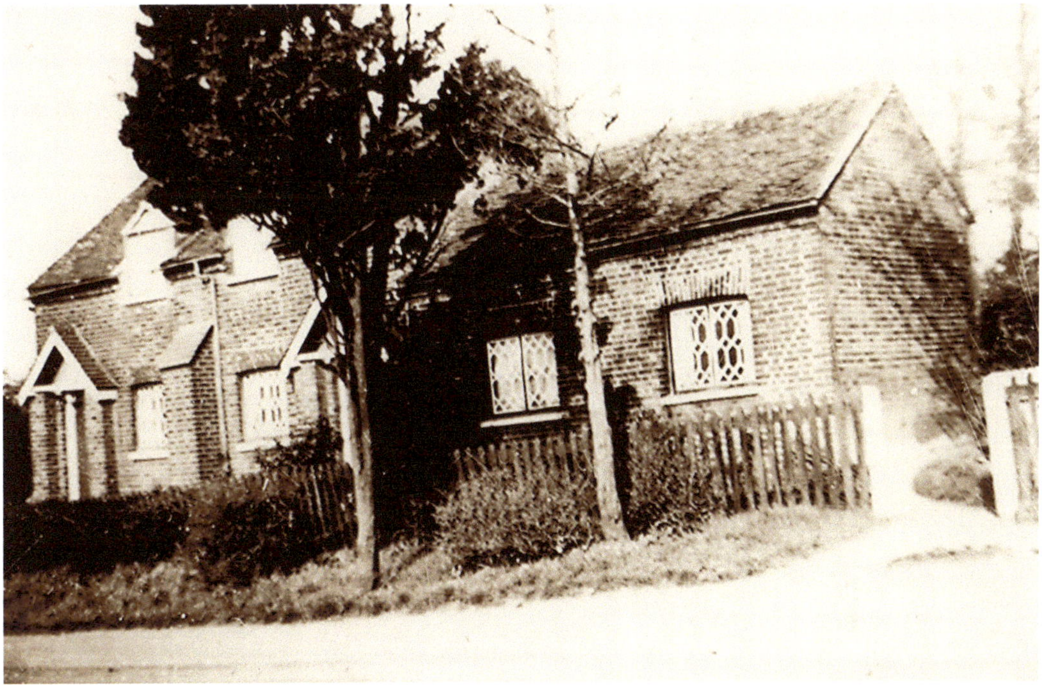

Vange Old School, 1950s
Rectory Cottages was the first school in Vange. The small one-storey building to the right was the schoolroom, and the cottage next to it was inhabited by the headmistress. This was the first school in Vange and was built around 1858. The school that is now Vange Primary School was built in 1876. Today, it is a residential building.

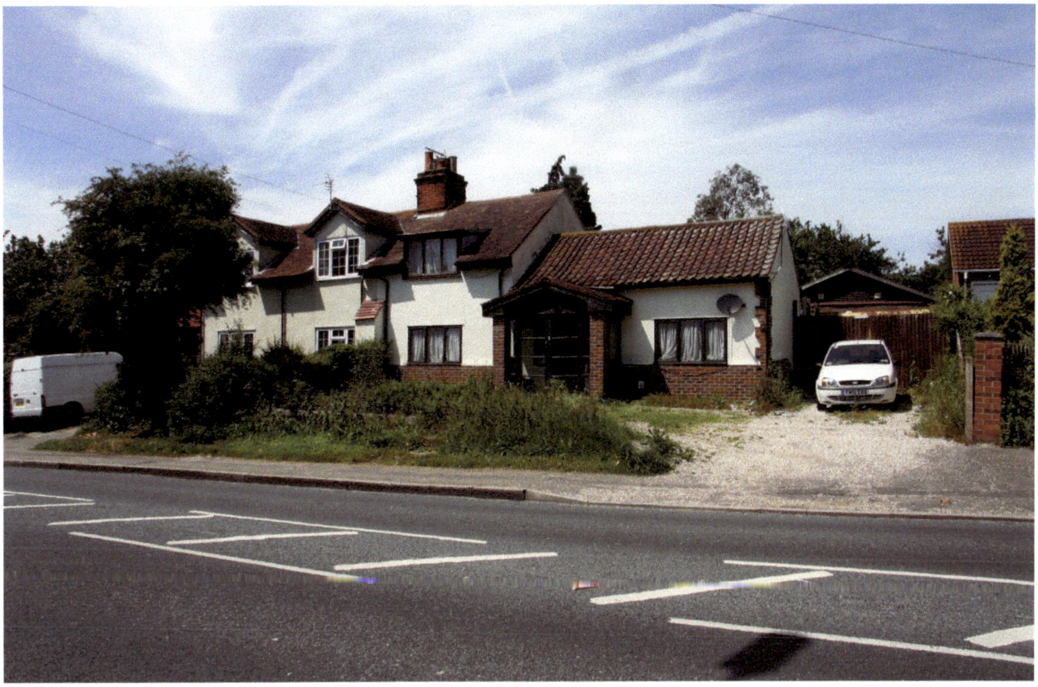

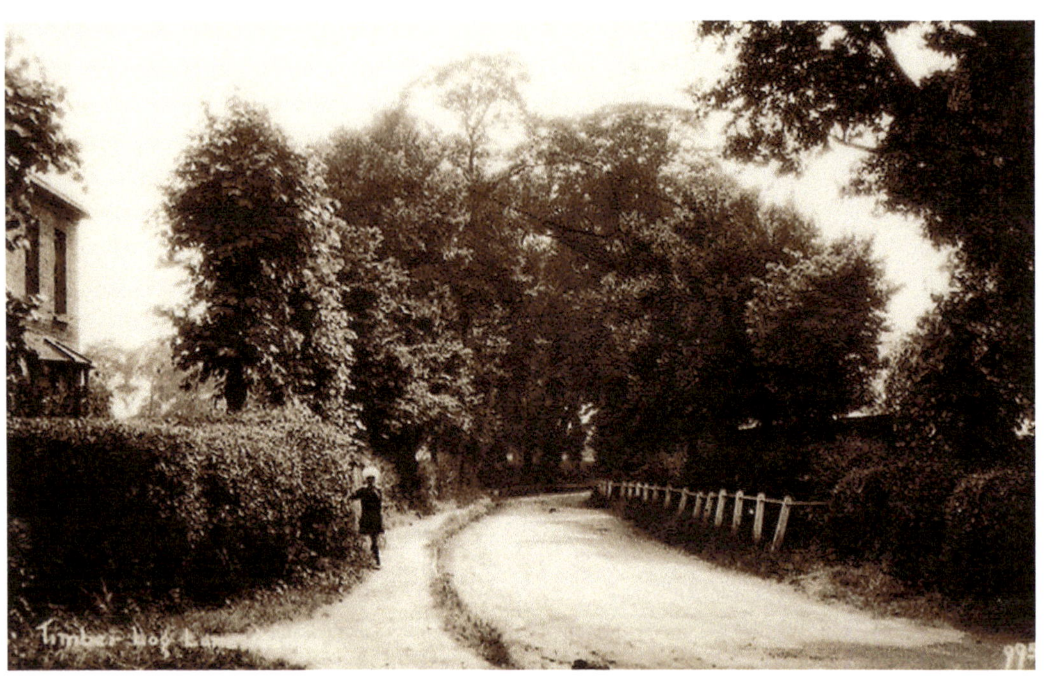

Vange – Timberlog Lane

The name of this lane derives from the time when the old timber carts used to come round from the river at Vange Wharf, winding around the newly enclosed fields. These logs and timber were probably shipped down to shipyards, notably Brightlingsea. It is said that the Romans dragged timber down this lane too. This picture was taken *c.* 1930s. Today, Timberlog Lane is a built up area with residential developments, quite a stark contrast to the country lane it once was.

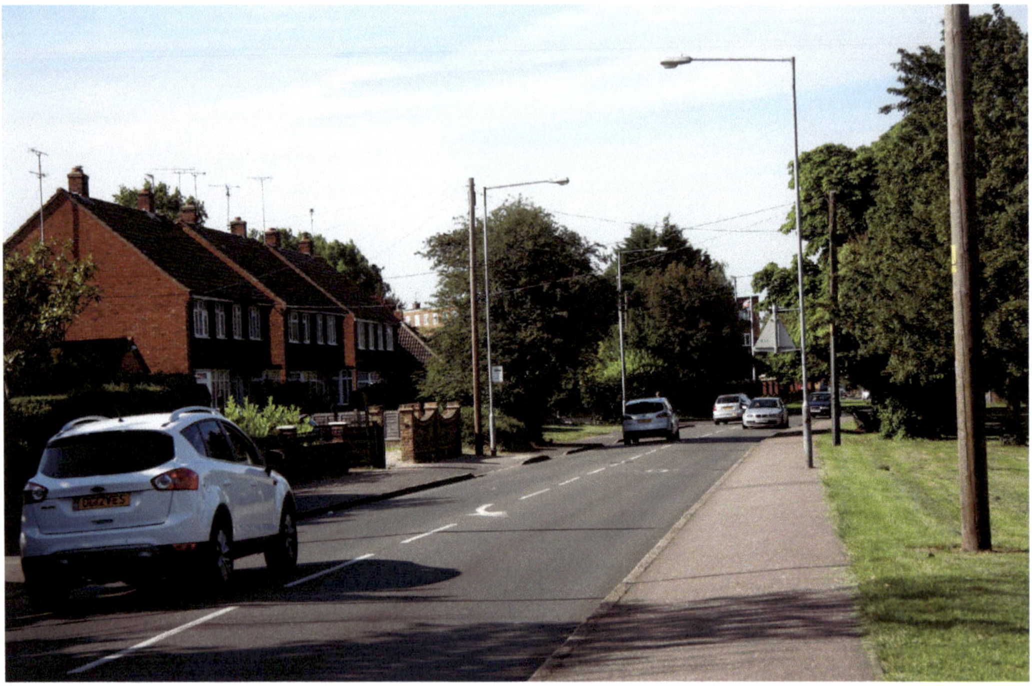

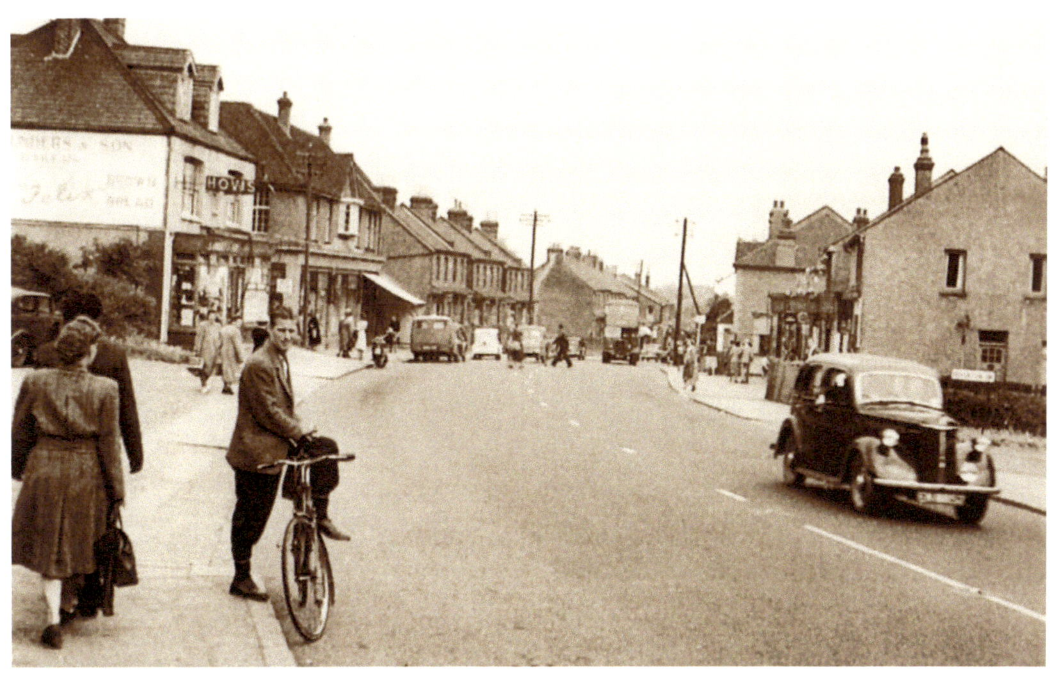

Vange – High Road

The High Road, Vange looking east from the barge in the 1950s. You can just make out 'Saunders & Son Bakers' on the wall of the shop on the left, with its Hovis sign protruding from the front of the building. Today's Vange is unrecognisable compared to how it looked when almost the entire length had some form of development providing a public service. Instead, the road is lined with modern residential estates.

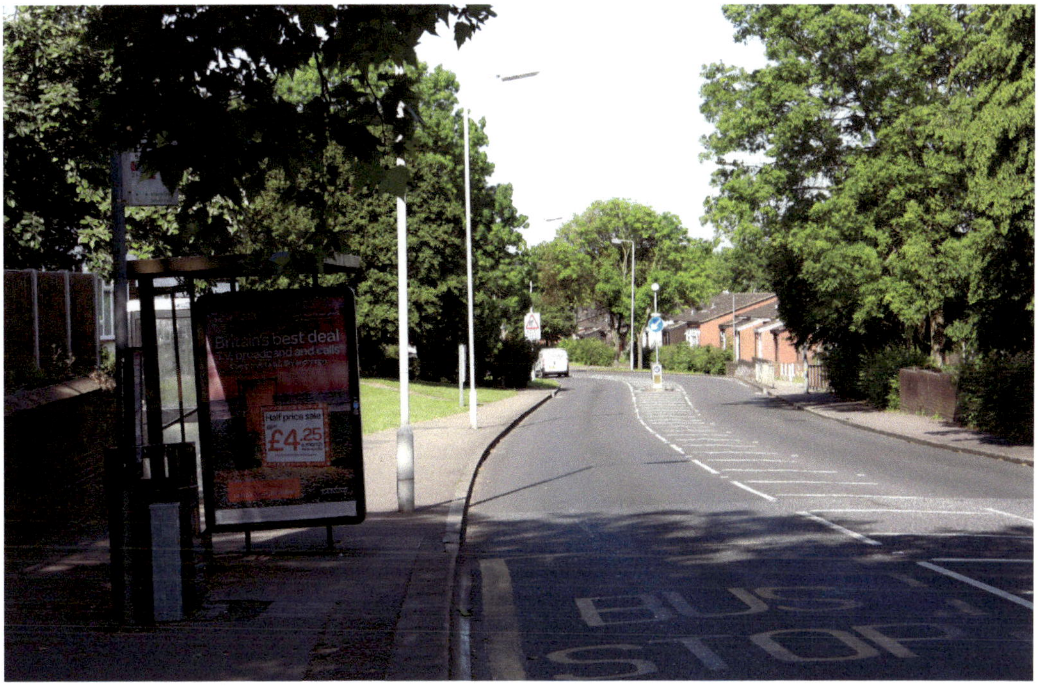

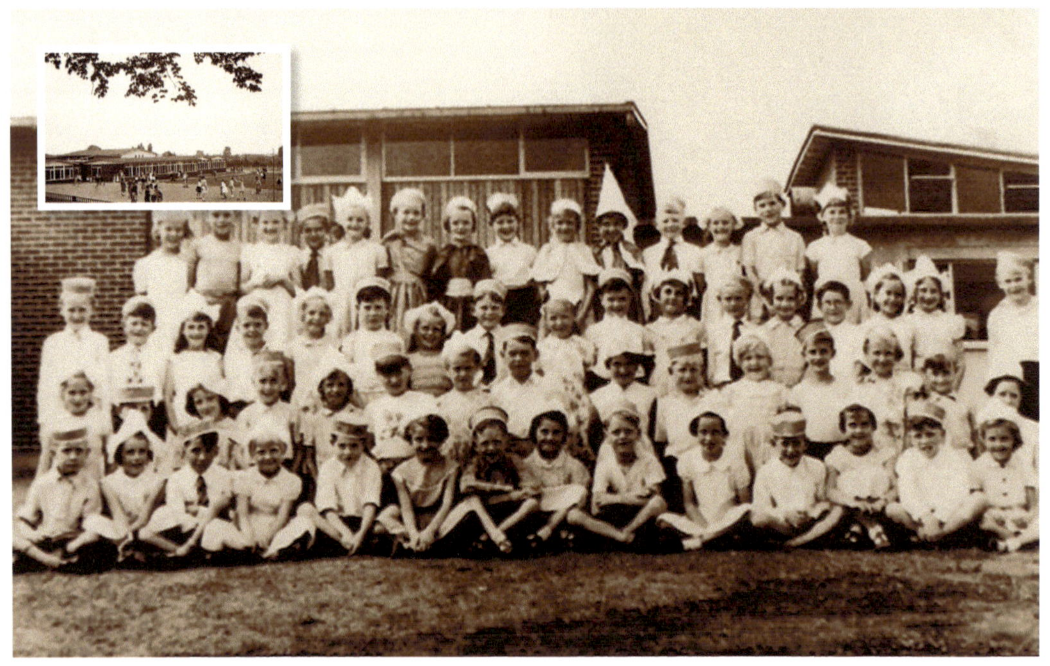

Vange – Swan Mead School, Church Road

During the building of Swan Mead County Junior and Infant School in 1953, a quantity of Bronze Age metalwork, including partly finished axes, were found in what has become known as the Vange Hoard. It was the first school to open in Basildon New Town in 1954. Mr Bernard Goodfellow was head of the junior school and Mrs. Davis was head of the infant school. Here, the schoolchildren are seen sitting down in 1957. It became Cherry Tree Primary School in 2001, and today it still functions as a primary school and nursery.

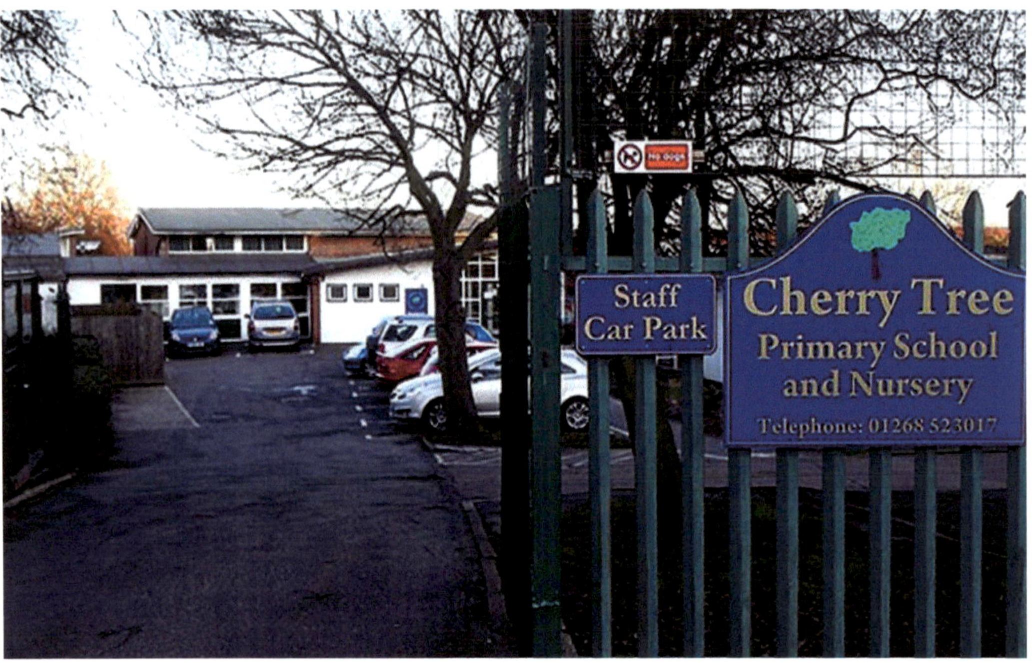

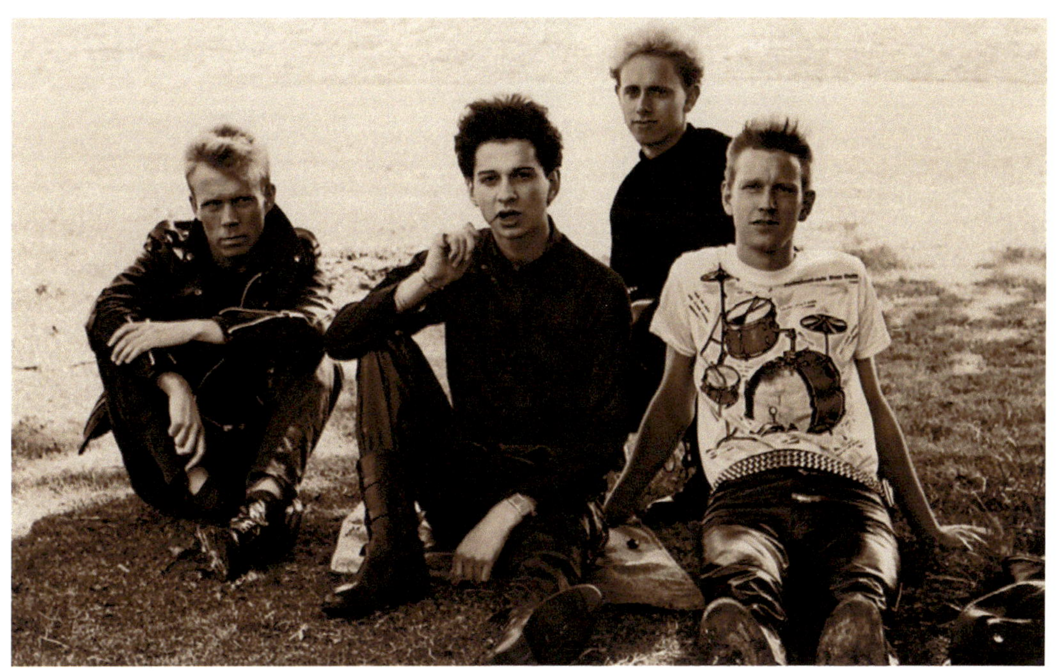

Vange – Depeche Mode

Depeche Mode, sitting below the embankment on Vange Hill Drive on 21 June 1981. Tim Williams, a photographer, said, 'I took this photo from over the road to Vince Clarke's flat, it was their first official photoshoot.' The annual Bas Depeche Mode Bus Tour visits the spot outside Vince's flat, and visitors from around the globe listen to anecdotes and hear private Vince Clarke/Yazoo demos. This is the same spot today, a few yards from where the community centre has since been built.

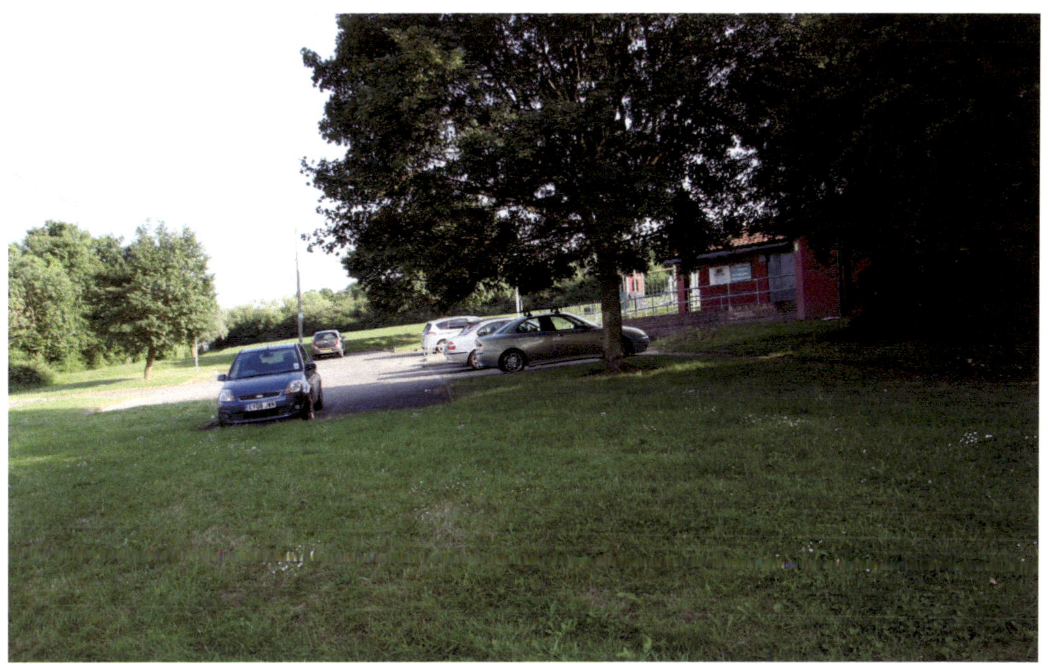

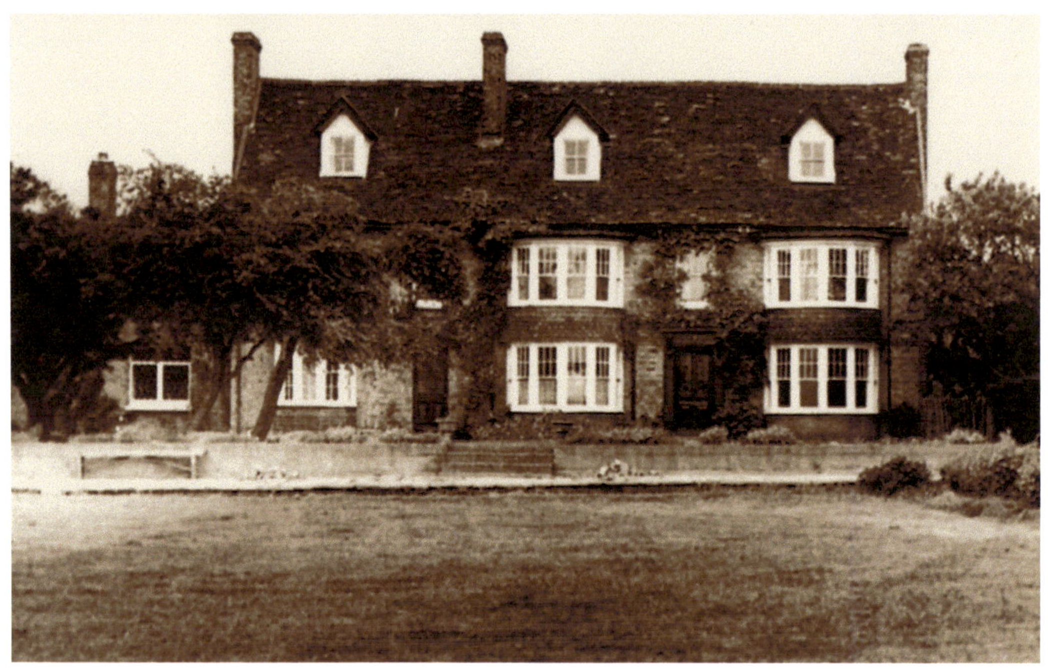

Pitsea Hall/Cromwell Manor 1960s

Pitsea Hall was built *c.* 1500 on the site of a Norman manor house. Pitsea Hall Farm can be traced back to *Domesday* records when it had 1,720 acres. Over the years, land has been sold to enable the railway to pass through Pitsea, and later, to Wat Tyler Country Park. It is said that illicit goods were smuggled here and kept in a pit in a yard protected by a fierce dog. It has been given Grade II listed status and is now a licensed venue for weddings and other functions.

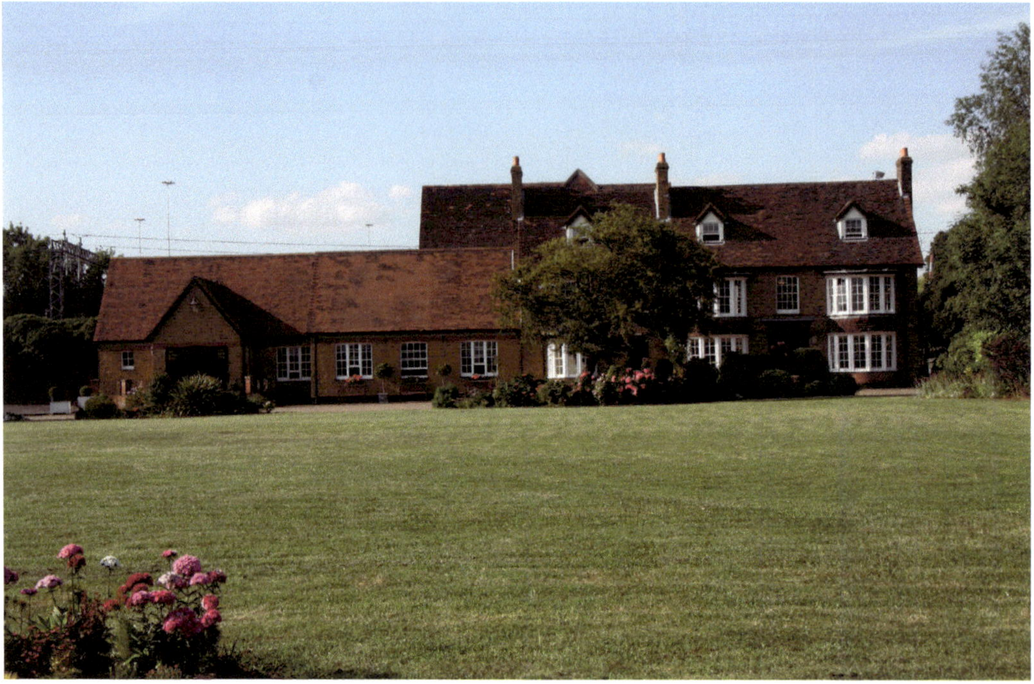

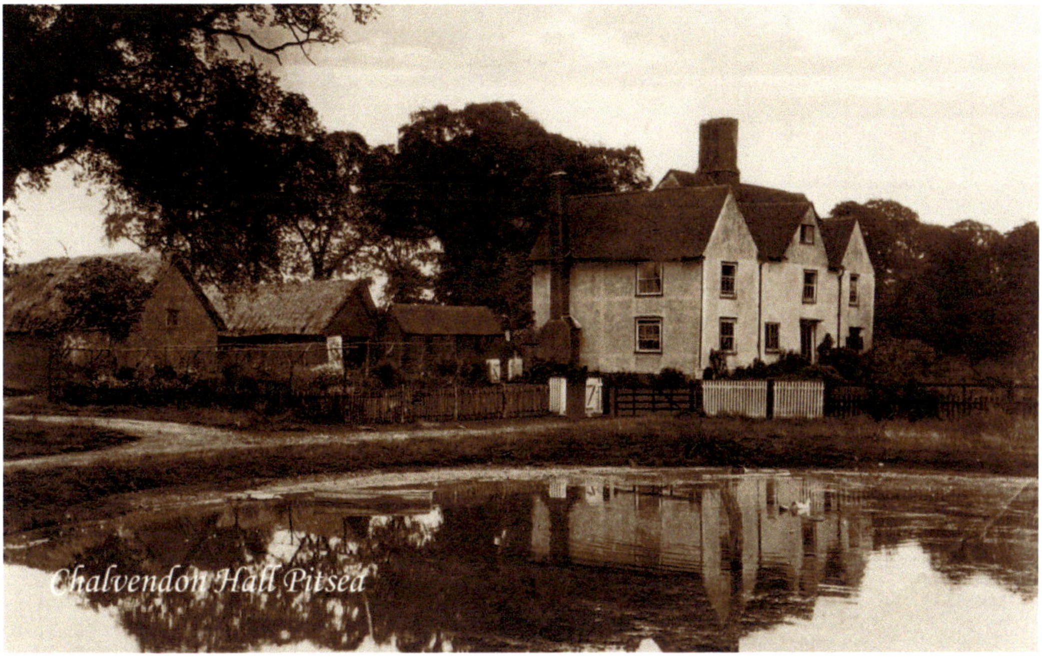

Pitsea – Great Chalvedon Hall

Great Chalvedon Hall, built *c.* 1500, was a private residence until 1977. The hall had a secret underground passage heading towards Pitsea Marshes; the entrance to the tunnel was boarded up for two centuries after part of the tunnel collapsed in the 1700s. There was also a small secret room next to the attic called a 'priest's hole', built in the reign of Queen Elizabeth I when Catholics were being persecuted. This historic building has Grade II listed status and is a public house today; it has a smaller pond within its grounds and is surrounded by a housing estate.

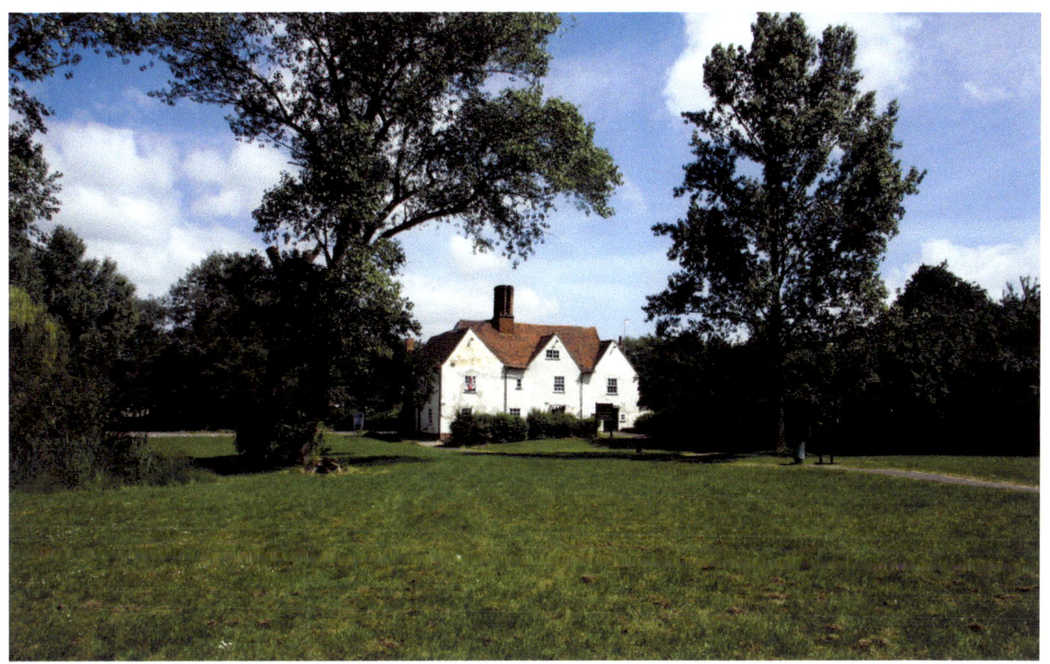

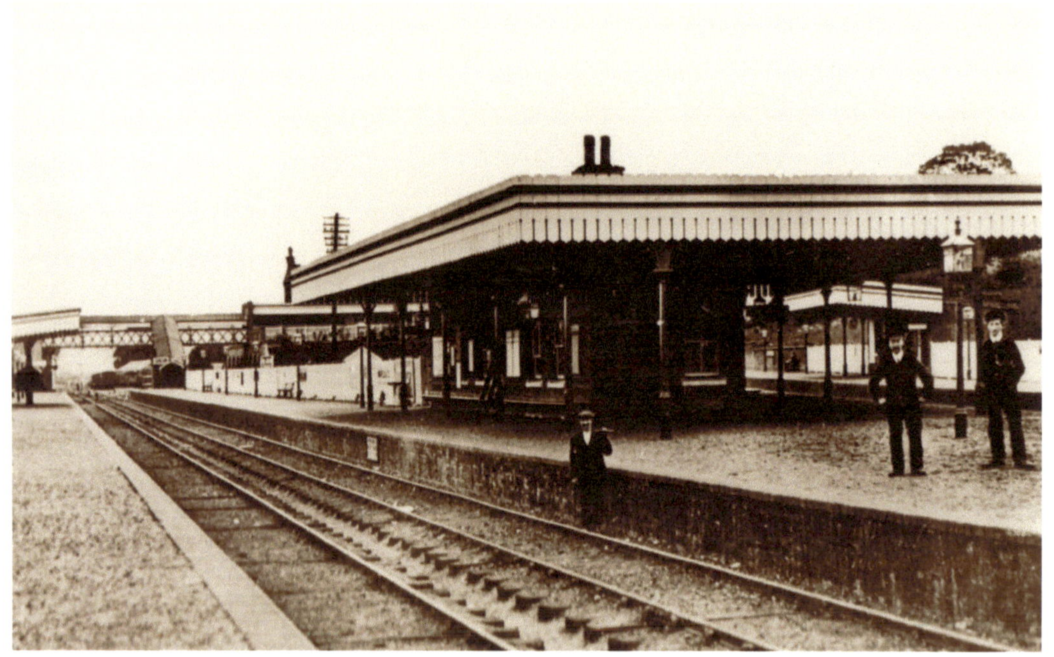

Pitsea Station

Here we are looking east to Tilbury around 1935. Following an Act of Parliament in 1852, the new railway line linking Southend with London was constructed in various stages, and Pitsea Railway Station opened on 1 July 1855. In June 1888, the railway was slightly relocated to accommodate the extra platforms when the new direct route to London opened. At this time, land was being sold to developers as farming had hit a depression, unable to compete with the cheap imported grain from America and Canada. The modernised Pitsea Station is seen here also.

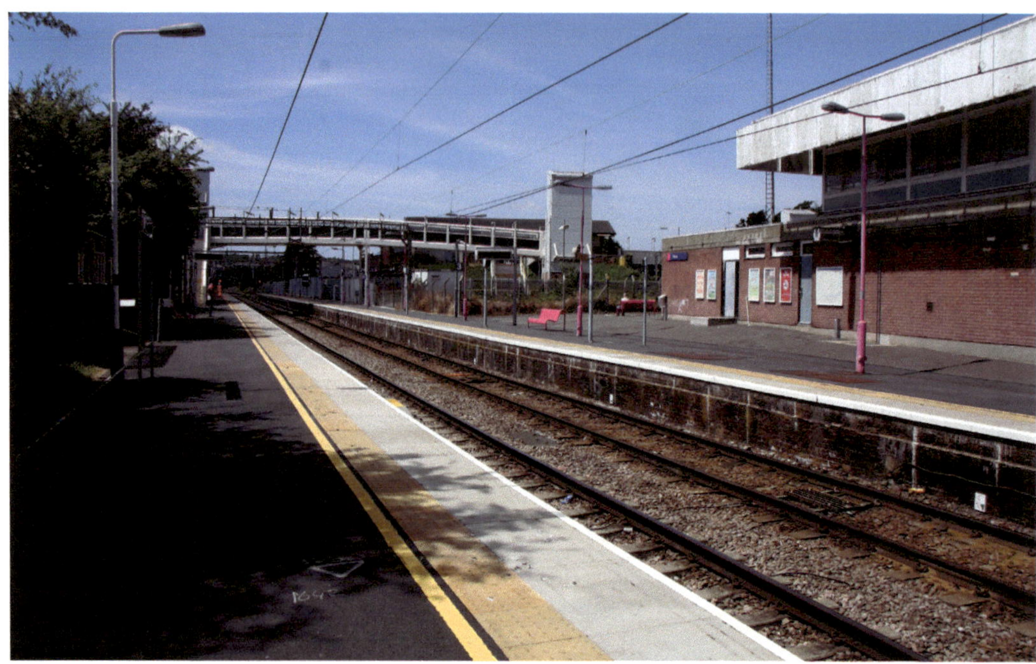

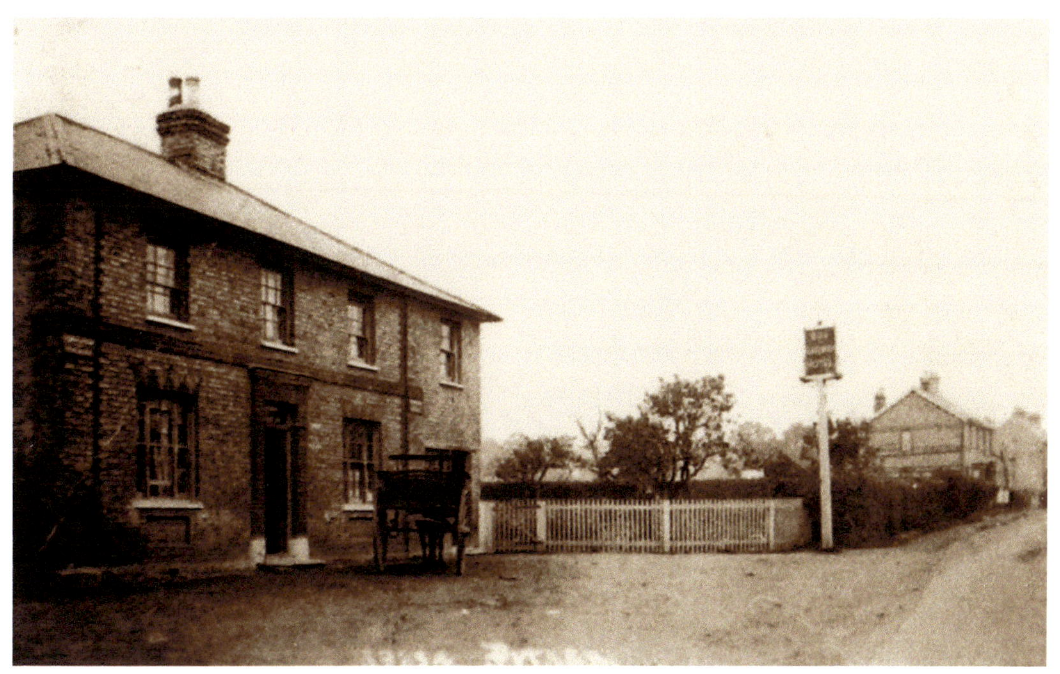

Pitsea – Railway Tavern

After the Pitsea Railway was built in 1855, the Railway Company stated that there should be a public house, and The Railway Tavern was built around 1859. It closed when The Railway Hotel opened, part of Harold George Howard's vision for Pitsea. The old Railway Tavern became a post office and a second shop. It was later demolished, and residential buildings are now on the site near to Rectory Road on the north side.

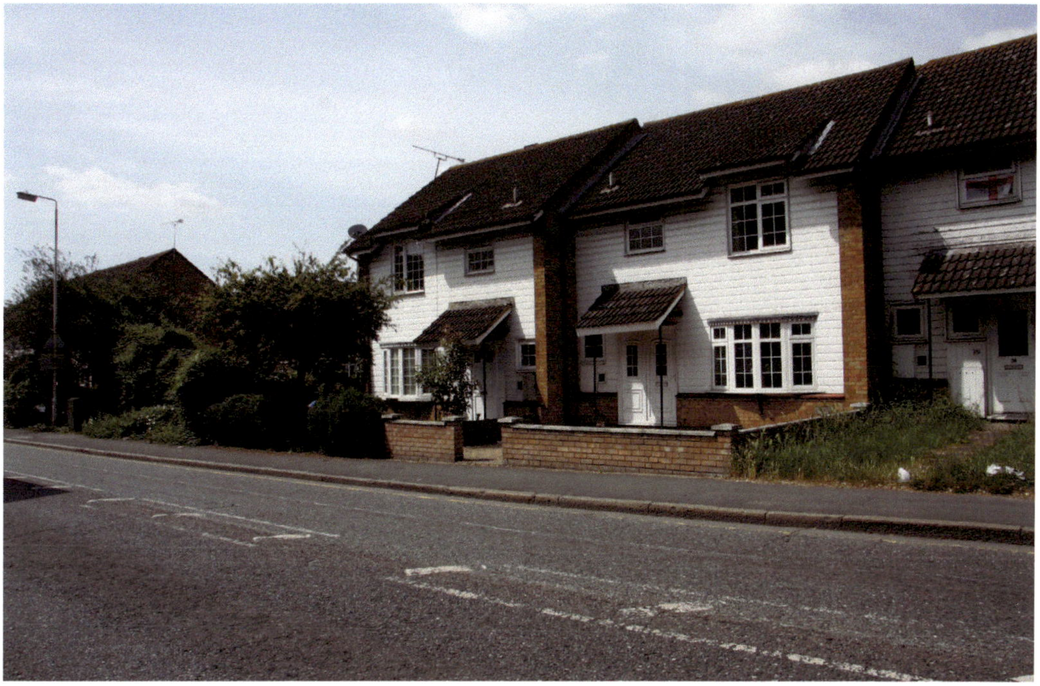

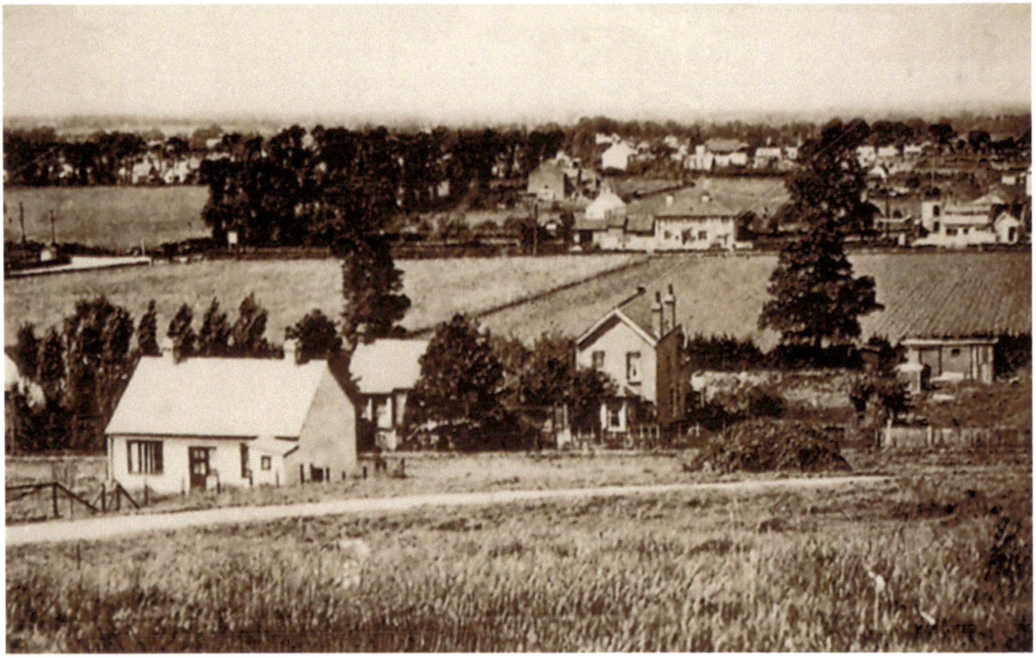

This view is of the Northlands Estate from St Michael's Church Hill in the 1910s. After the second expanse of field you can see a building with four windows on the first floor close to the centre of the picture. This was the Railway Tavern, which was located on the High Road just before Rectory Road. Today, much of the view is blocked by trees, but you can see how the area has built up – gone is that sleepy village of yesteryear.

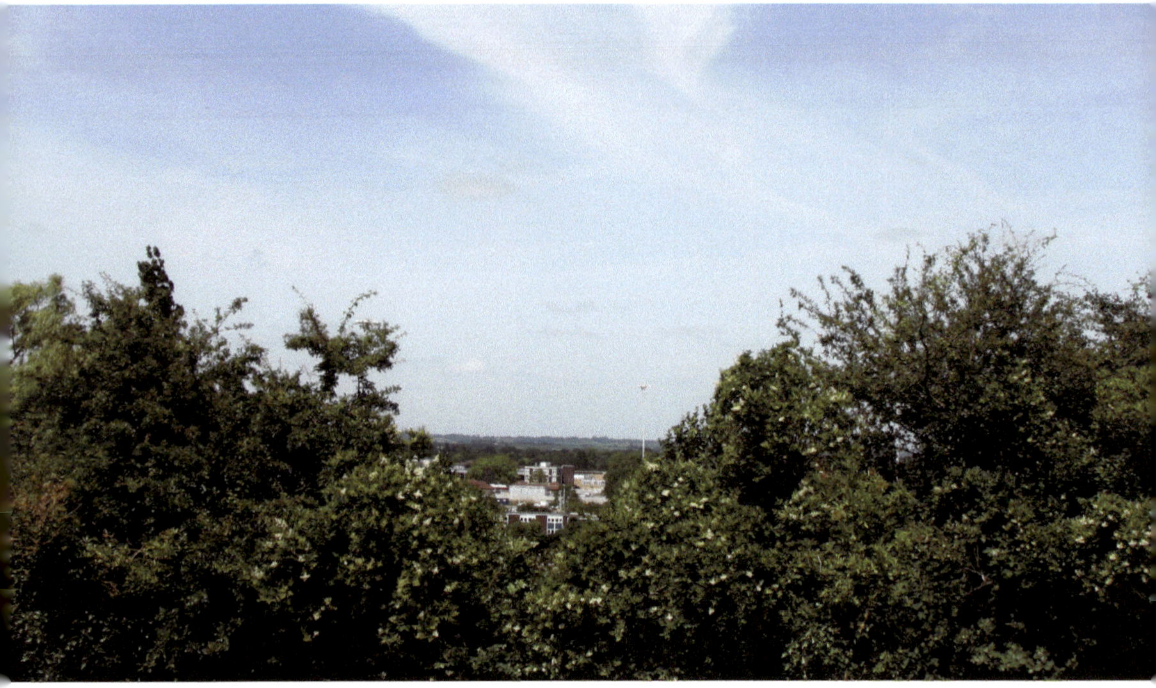

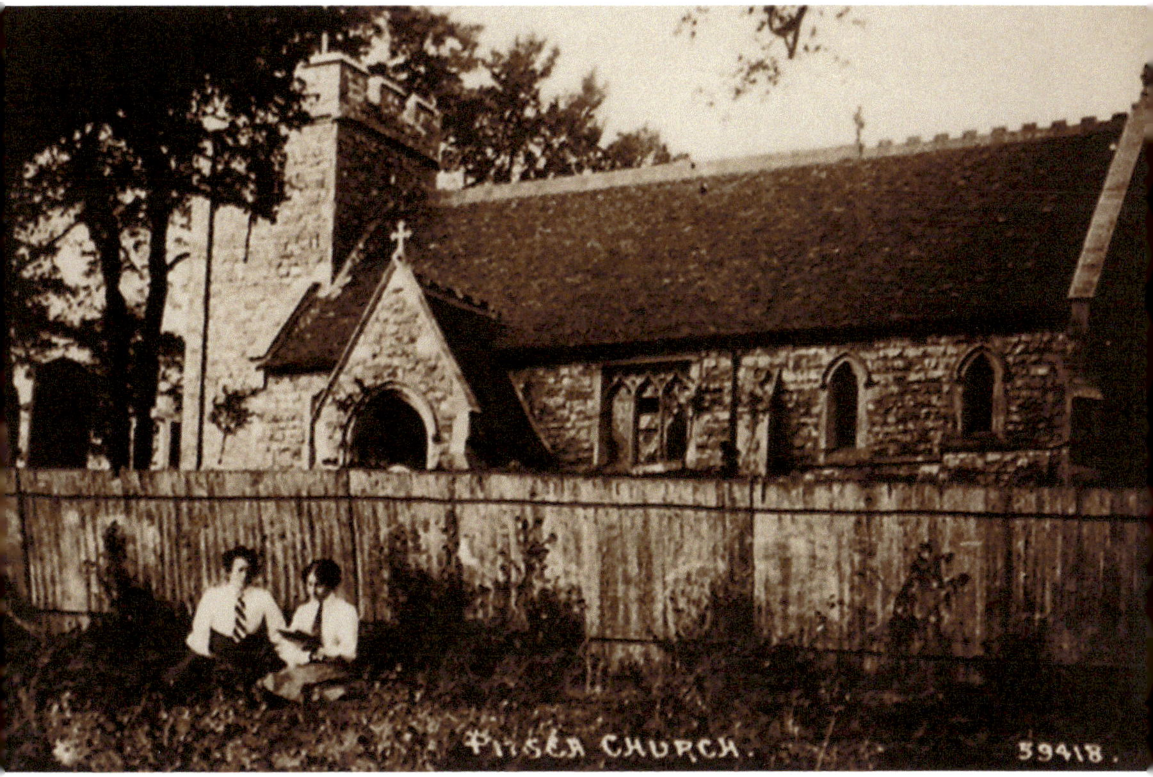

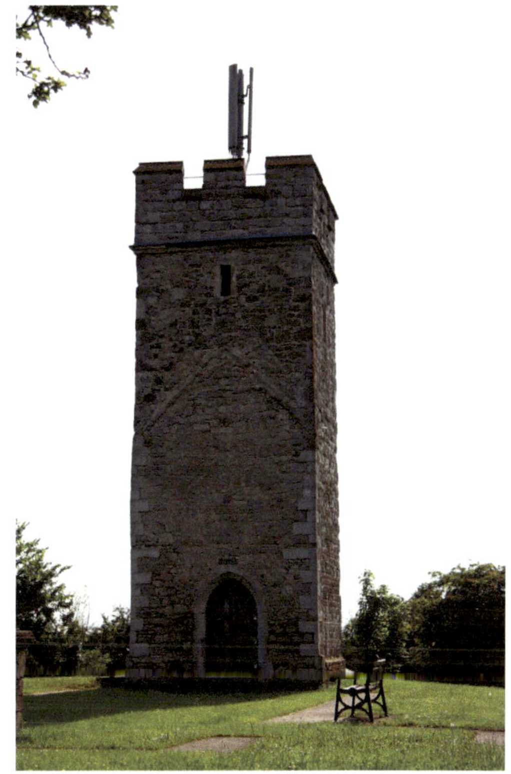

Pitsea – St Michael's Church

A church has stood on this site for over 700 years on a small hill overlooking the parish of Pitsea and creeks leading to the River Thames. It was last rebuilt in the 1870s. It was in use until the 1970s, but later abandoned and, consequently, it became vandalised. For a while it was considered for use as a museum, but this never materialised. In 1998, the nave and chancel were demolished, leaving the sixteenth-century tower remaining. This Grade II listed building now supports a mobile phone mast for Orange (telecommunications).

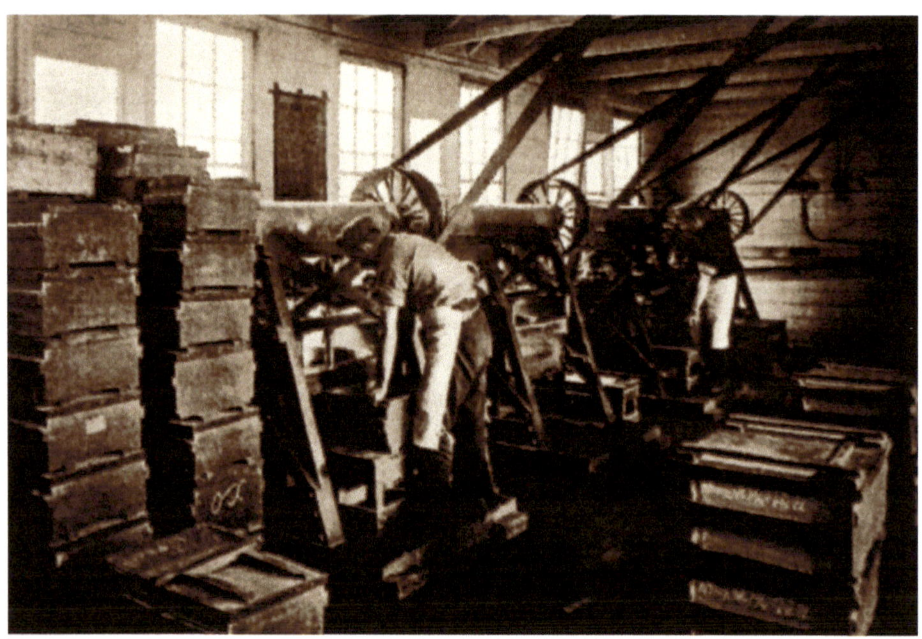

Pitsea – The British Explosives Syndicate

In 1891, the British Explosives Syndicate built a factory in Pitsea. The explosives were mainly used for mining, but later they were used in the First World War. Although the factory operated a stringent safety practice, in May 1916 a chemist and his assistant were killed when the chemist dropped a small bottle of Nitroglycerine, the main ingredient in explosives. You can see by the different coloured bricks where the laboratory has been rebuilt. The factory closed in peacetime, 1929. Allsorts Professional Dog Grooming and The Laboratory Art Studio are based in the old laboratory today, in Wat Tyler Country Park.

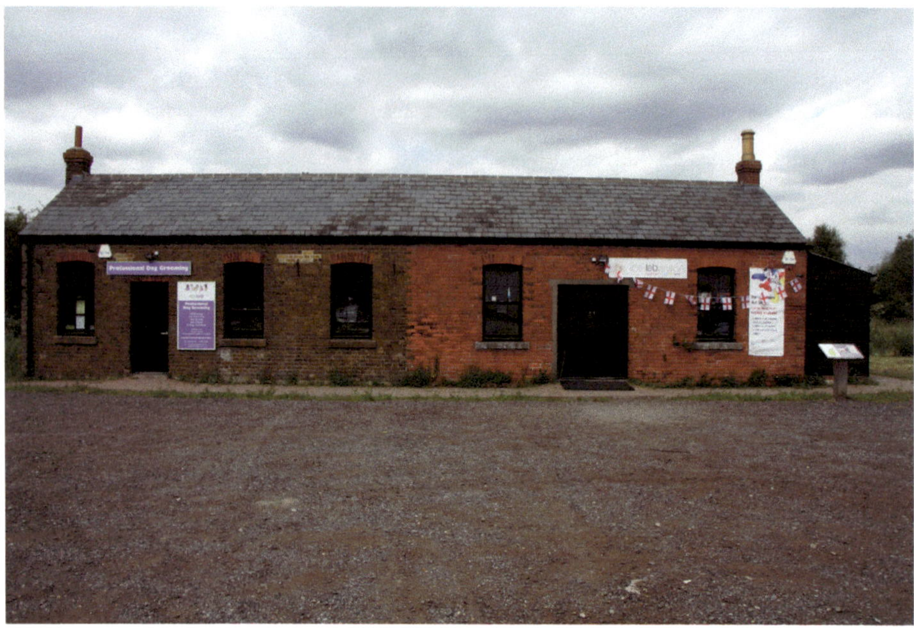

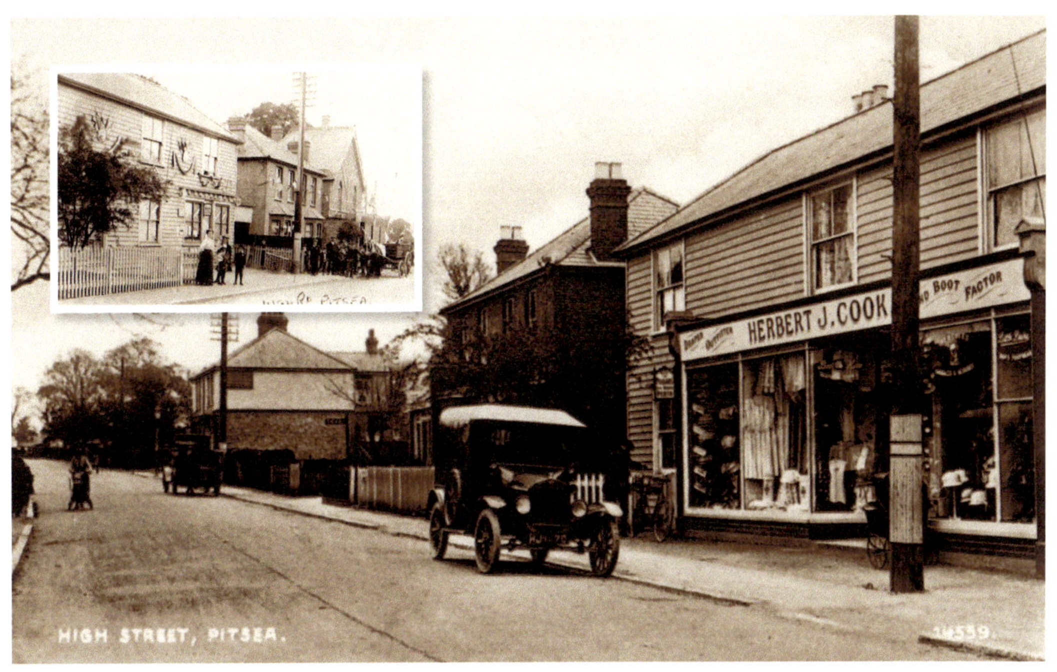

Pitsea – Herbert J Cook's Drapery Store

Standing on the south side of the High Road, east of the market car park, stood Herbert J Cook's business from 1897 to 1964. Here we see Cook's Drapery decorated for Edward VII's coronation in 1901. Mr Cook opened the first post and telegraph office here in 1897, the nearest for Vange and Bowers Gifford. By the 1920s, the shop had been extended. It stood close to where the A13 was built opposite Howard Diamond Jubilee Park.

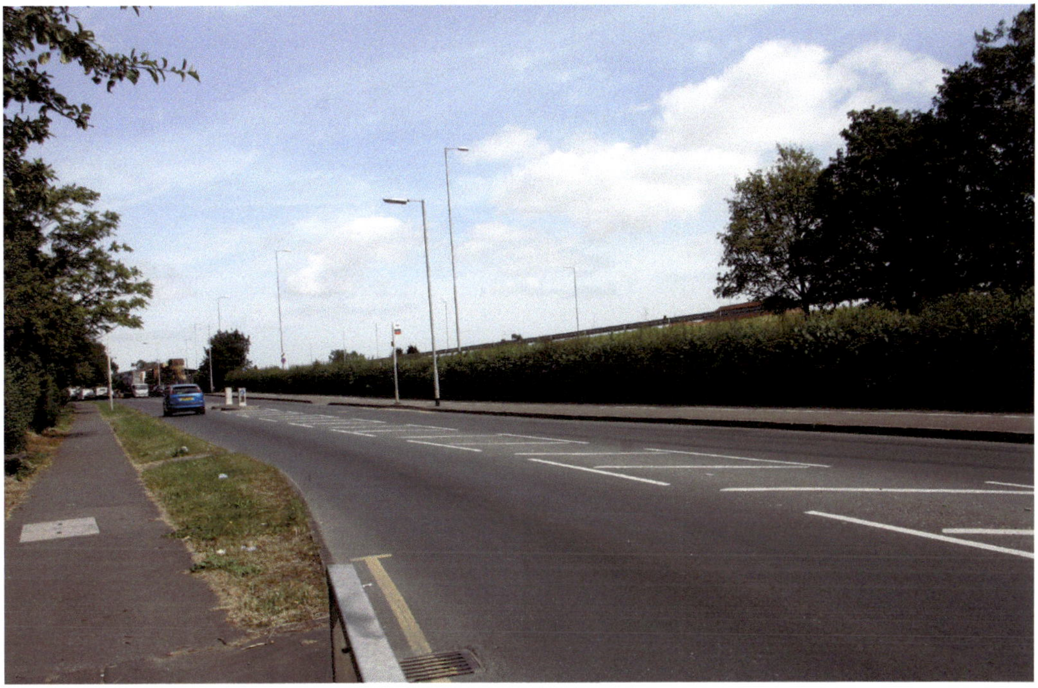

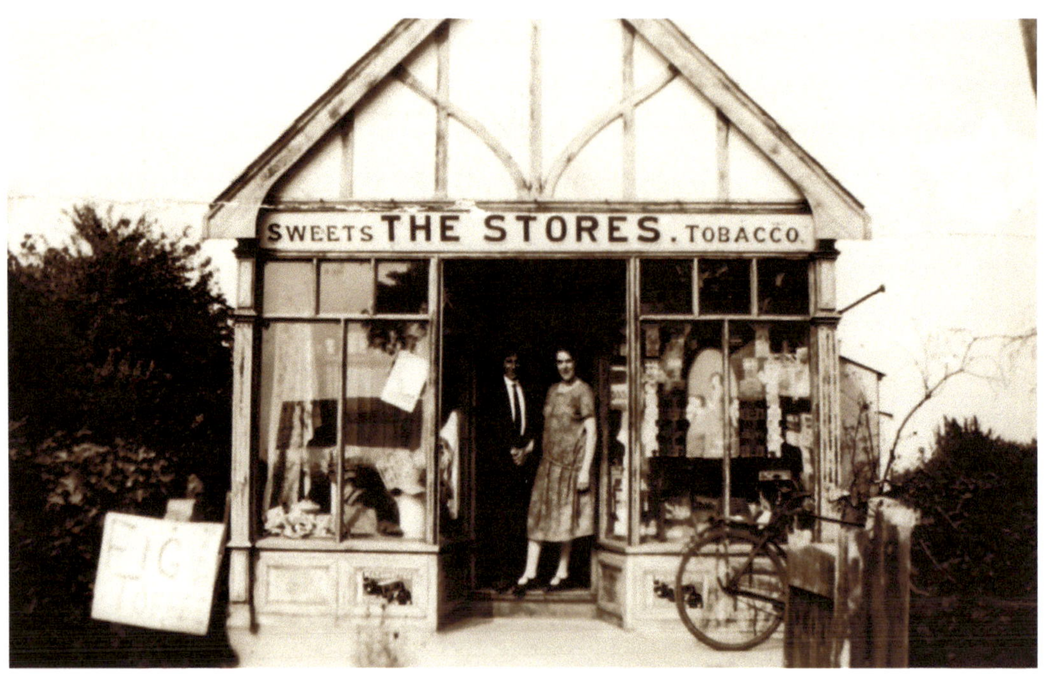

Pitsea – The Stores, Burnt Mills Road

The Stores was located at Burnt Mills Road, at the end of Rectory Road. Victor Beauchamp Guy and Mary Elizabeth Jane Guy are the couple seen here. Underneath the windows of the shop there are two identical adverts either side of the door for the Mazawattee Tea Company. In later years, the shop was replaced by the couple's home in 1929, which they called Marie. Today, Burnt Mills Florist stands near the site. Bradley Green at the end of Tenterfields has replaced where Rectory Road met Burnt Mills Road.

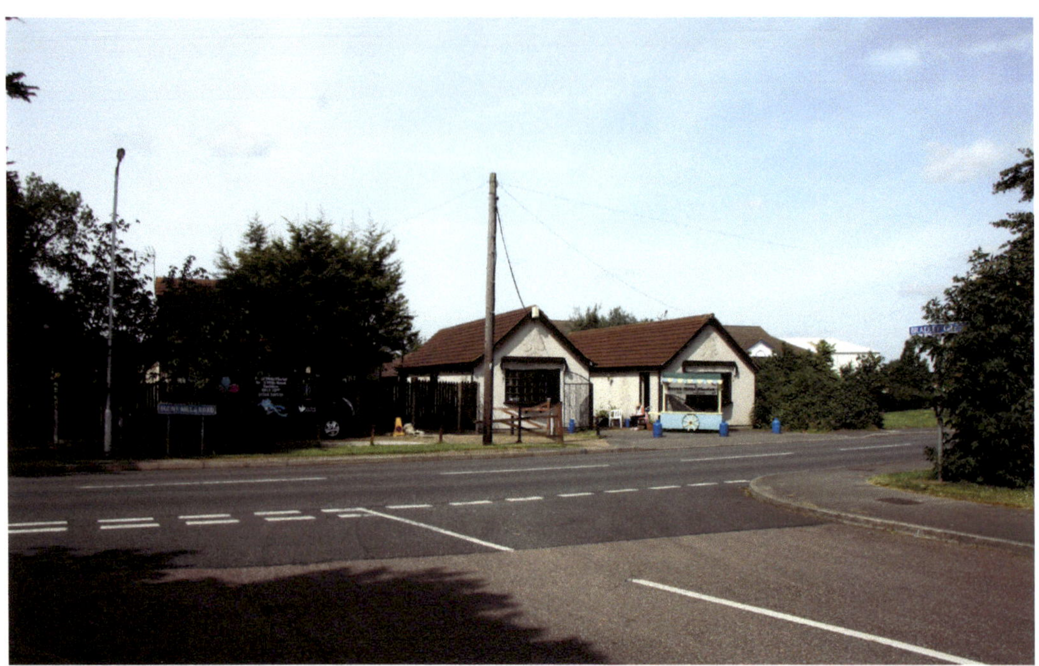

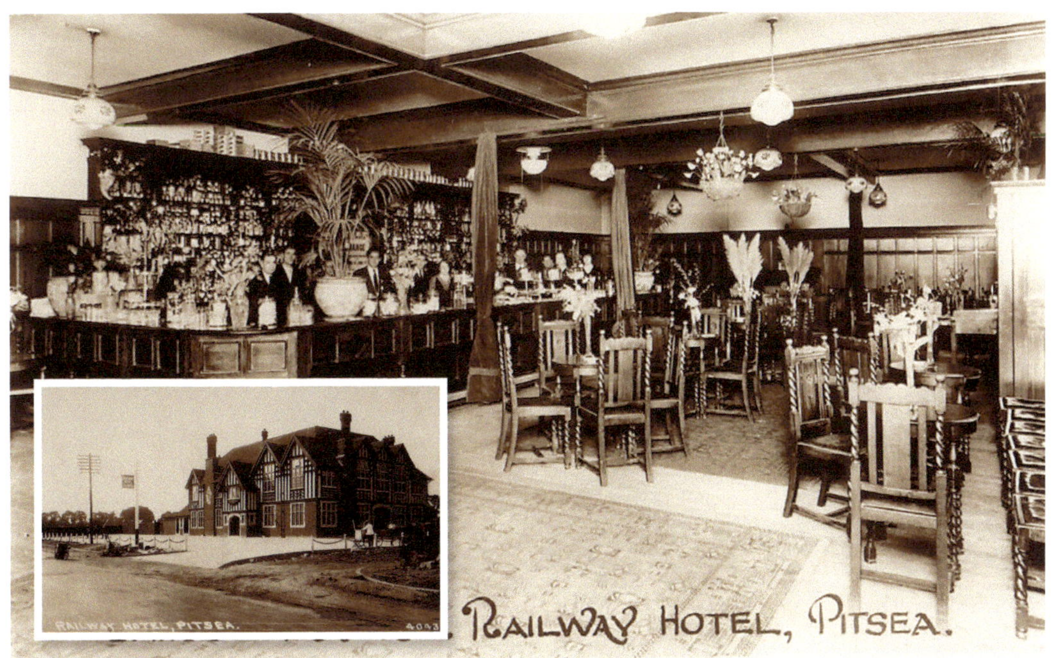

Pitsea – Railway Hotel, 1930s

The Railway Hotel, designed by Harold George Howard, opened in 1927 in order to cope with the increasing amount of visitors due to car ownership and replace The Railway Tavern. Its facilities included a banquet hall and a bowls green. Near the end of its life it got a bad name, some called it the Flying Bottle. It was demolished in May 2013 to make way for a new site for the market and an Aldi in a Pitsea regeneration project.

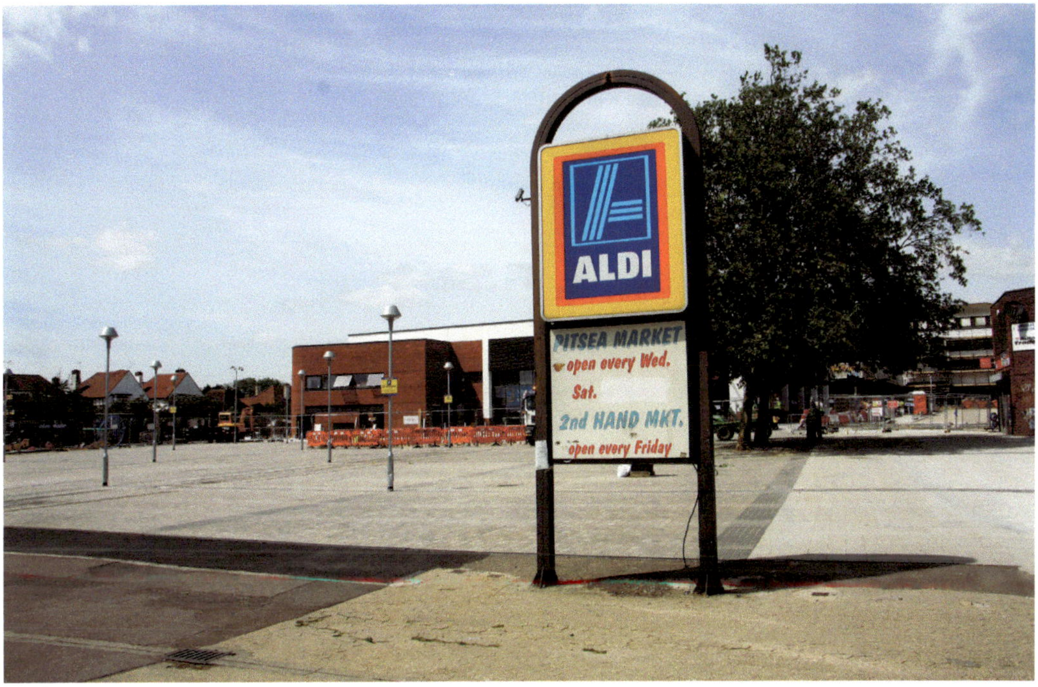

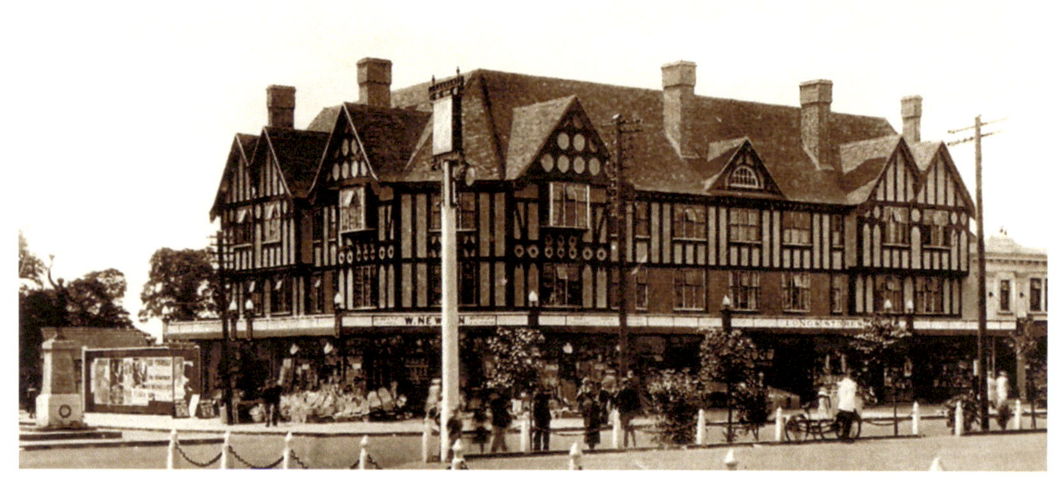

Pitsea – The Broadway

Harold George Howard, a farmer and landowner, drew up plans to turn Pitsea into a thriving Tudor-style town in the late 1920s. The Railway Hotel was the first building, then two blocks of shops, Tudor mansions and the Broadway cinema were built in 1929. The collection of shops became known as The Broadway. The Second World War put his plans on hold, followed by plans for the New Town, which led to his planning permission being refused. He sadly compared it to an unfinished symphony. The Broadway shops are altered, but still standing, and the cinema has gone.

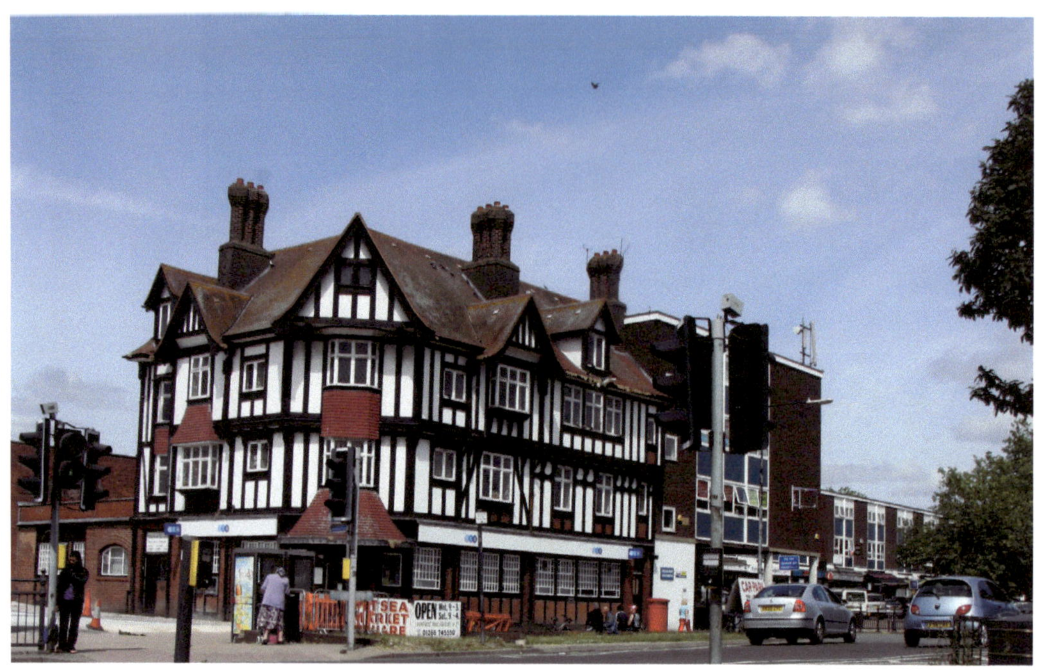

BROADWAY CINEMA
✦ and New Shopping Centre ✦

OFFICIAL OPENING
MARCH 28th, at 8 p.m.   Admission 1/-
:: *Proceeds to Local British Legion and Nursing Association.* ::

For the convenience of patrons from Southend, additional buses will run on Friday & Saturday Evenings from Victoria Circus, stopping at usual places en route.

White Shadows in the South Seas

Monday, March 31st, for three days *(Wednesday at 2.30).*

MARION DAVIES & WILLIAM HAINES	KARL DANE & GEORGE K. ARTHUR
in	in
# SHOW PEOPLE	# BROTHERLY LOVE

POPULAR PRICES—6d., 9d., 1/- & 1/6 (Including tax).

Daily 5.15-10.30   Wed. & Sat. 2.30-10.30   Free Car Park

Pitsea – Broadway Cinema

Broadway Cinema officially opened on 28 March 1930. It also hosted variety shows and later, professional wrestling. After renovations in 1955, it was renamed The Century. Bingo was introduced when cinema viewing dwindled due to television ownership, leading to the cinema closing in 1970 when it was turned into a bingo hall. An article in a local newspaper shows children protesting at its last Saturday morning cinema showing. The Gala Bingo hall finally closed its doors on 27 July 2009. Today, the part of the building that housed the cinema has gone, and a betting shop stands at the corner of The Broadway.

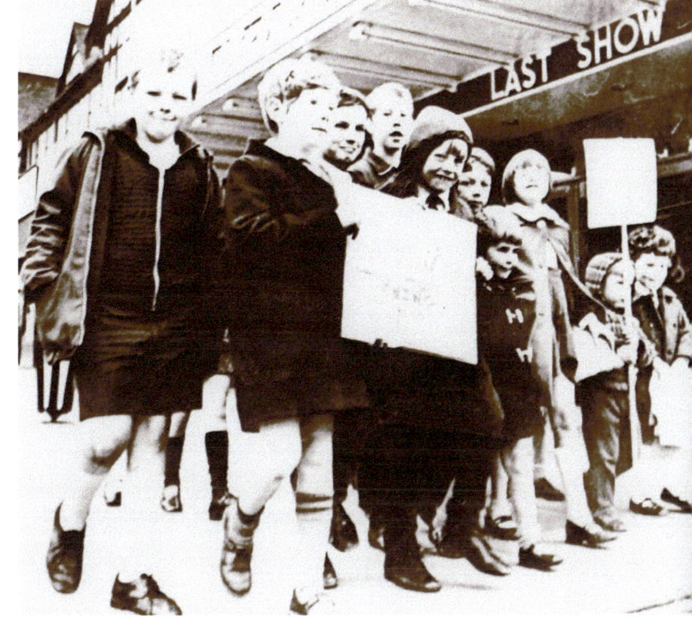

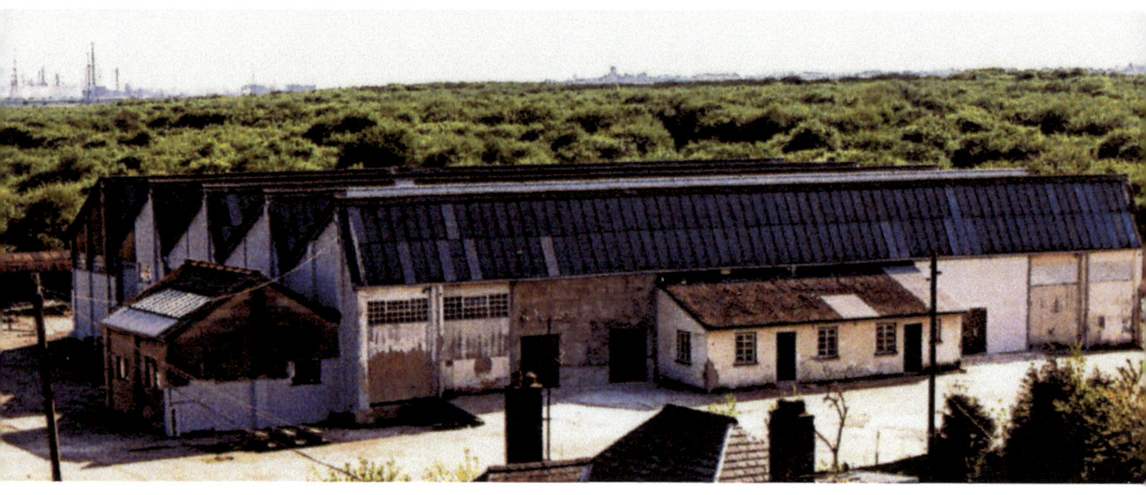

Pitsea – Sea Transport Stores

In 1929, the Ministry of War bought the site when the explosives factory closed. It set up the Sea Transport Stores to store equipment for hospital and troop ships. It is rumoured that in The Second World War, it equipped landing craft and troop ships for D-Day. For many years this building was a motor boat museum within Wat Tyler Country Park, and later, in 2011, it opened as the Green Centre, specialising in educating visitors about the environmental challenges facing the modern world. It is home to the Basildon Borough Heritage & Museum Group and the Essex Field Club.

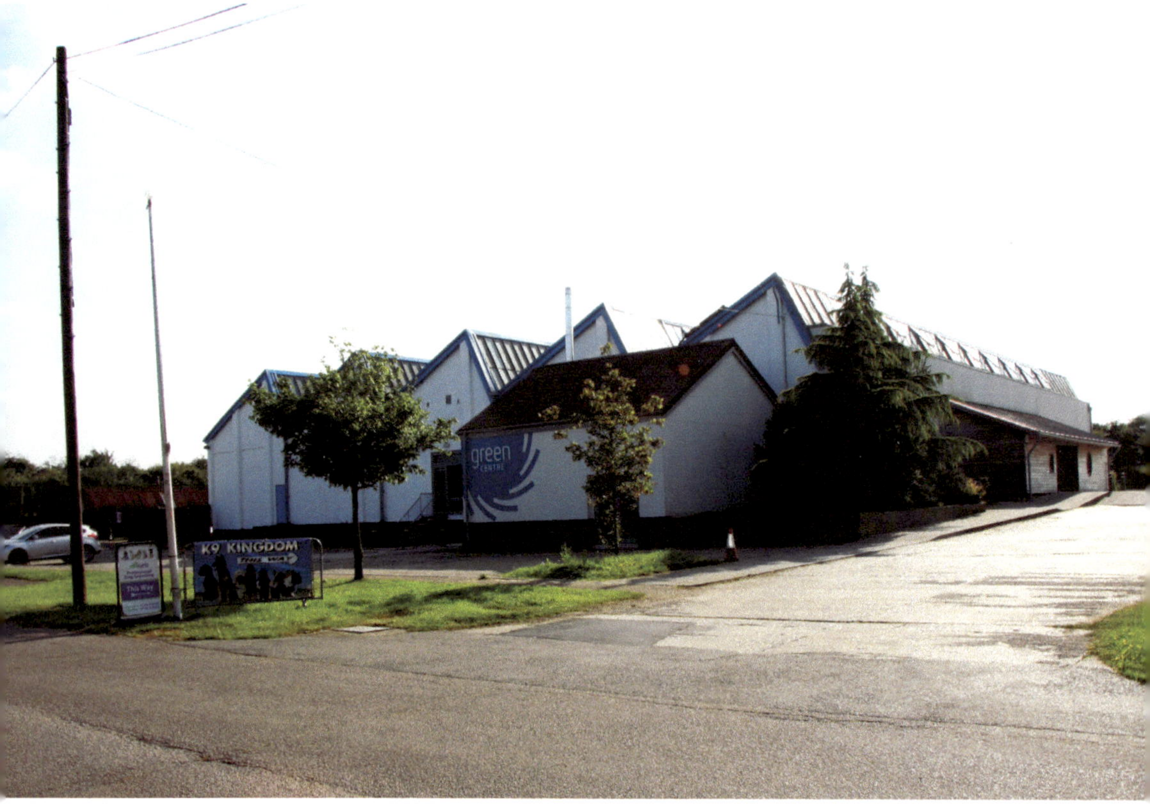

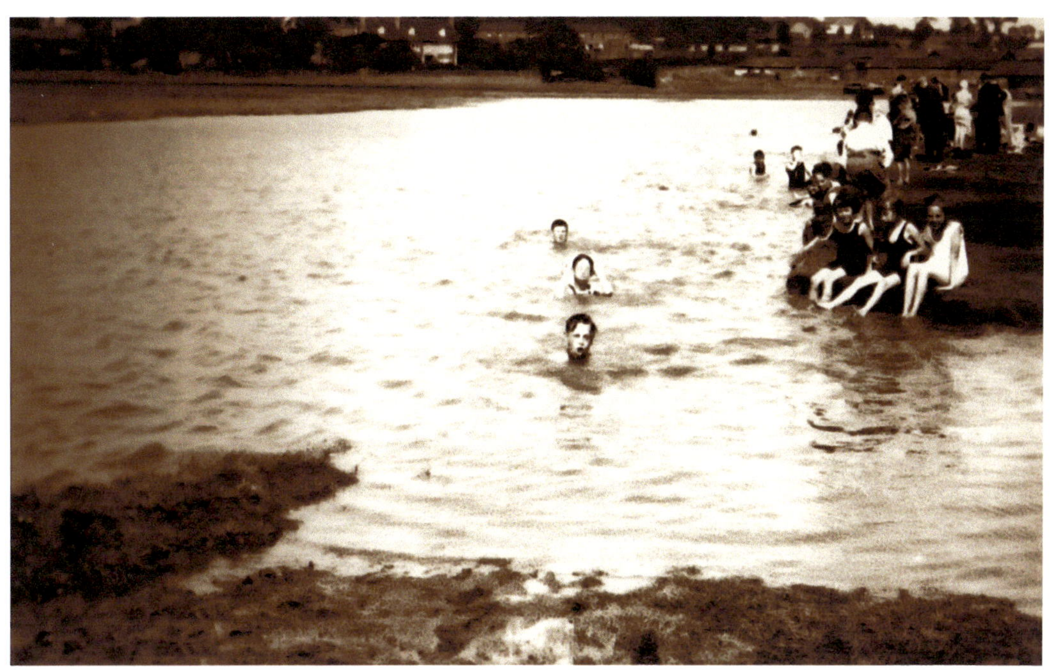

Pitsea Creek

In the 1930s when this picture was taken, swimming in Pitsea Creek was a natural event and very popular amongst pre-war children. This was before there was a council rubbish tip. You can see Pitsea Hall in the background. Note its position: a lot of land has been reclaimed from the creek, and some of it has been used to create Wat Tyler Country Park. Today, the country parks marina is located at the end of a much narrower Pitsea Creek.

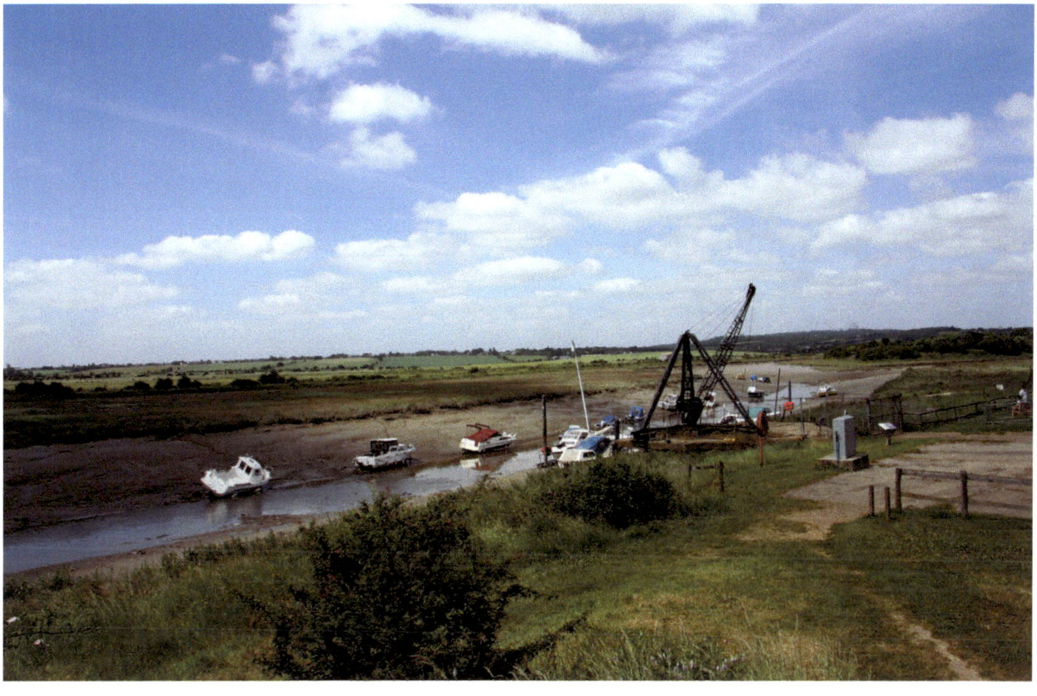

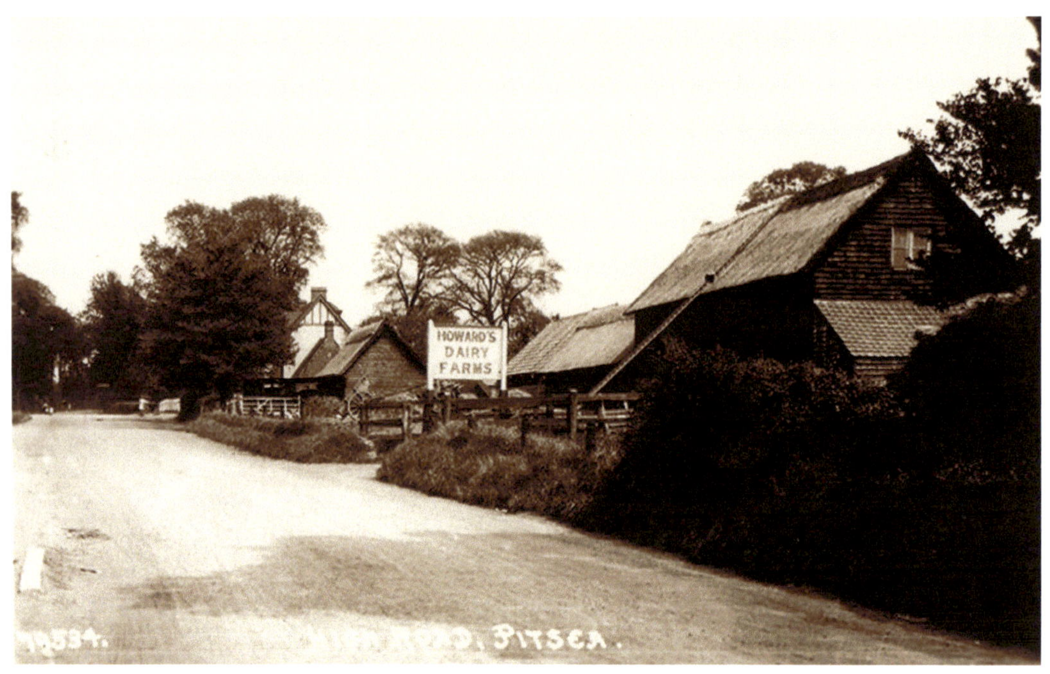

Pitsea – Howard's Dairy Farm

One of Harold George Howard's dairy farms was on High Road/London Road, where the A13 is now. The prosperous farmer and landowner built up his business from a humble dairy round. Mr Howard contributed the war memorial that originally stood at Station Lane, then got moved to Howards Park, which he gifted the town. It was renamed Howard Diamond Jubilee Park in 2012 in honour of the sixty-year reign of Queen Elizabeth II.

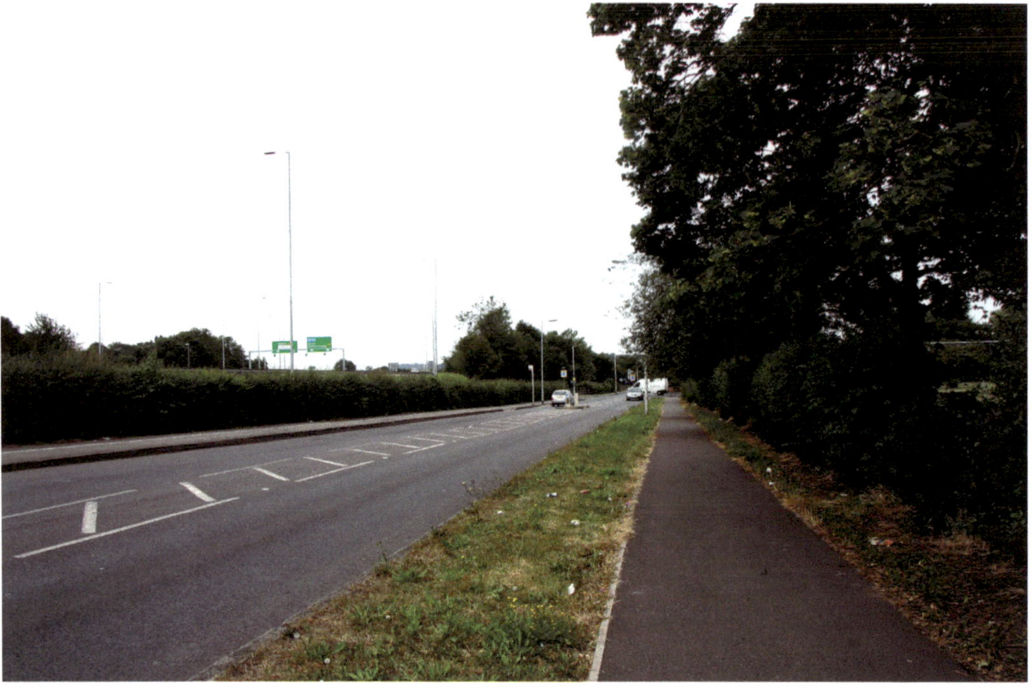

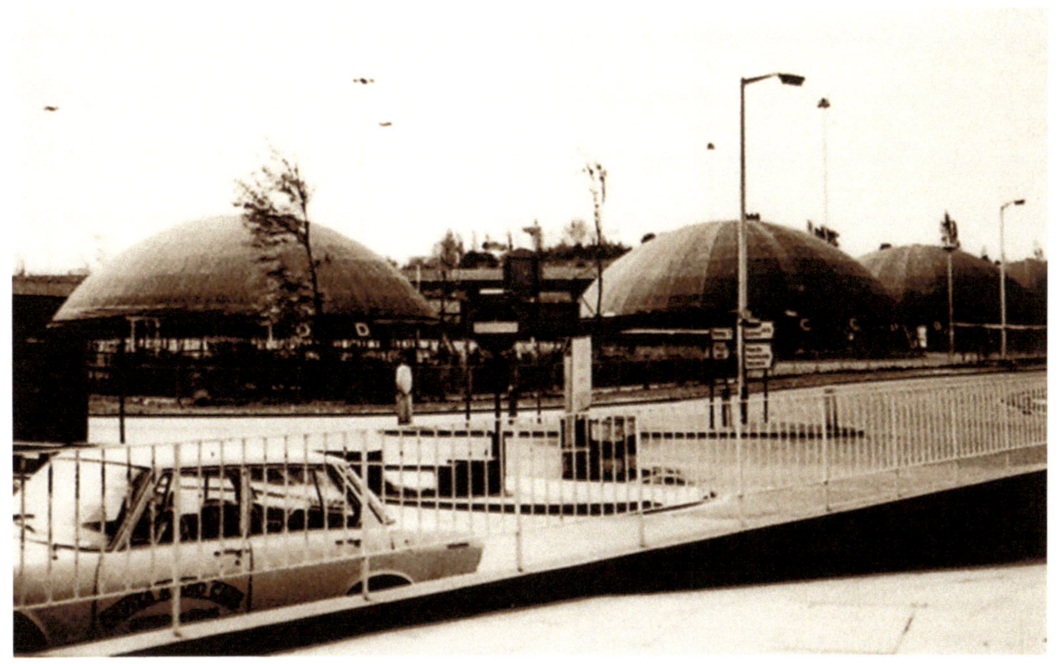

Pitsea Market

In 1969, the market that had thrived in Pitsea from 1925 had to be moved from where Tesco Extra is now in order to make way for major road improvements. It was moved to a former field on the south side of the high street, and for the customers' comfort, they erected four 30 foot domes with an 80 foot diameter; each dome could hold forty-three stalls. The Great Storm of 1987 ripped the domes apart, sealing their fate as a temporary solution. The site is now partly covered by Pitsea Retail Park and the new road structure. Pitsea market is still active within the town.

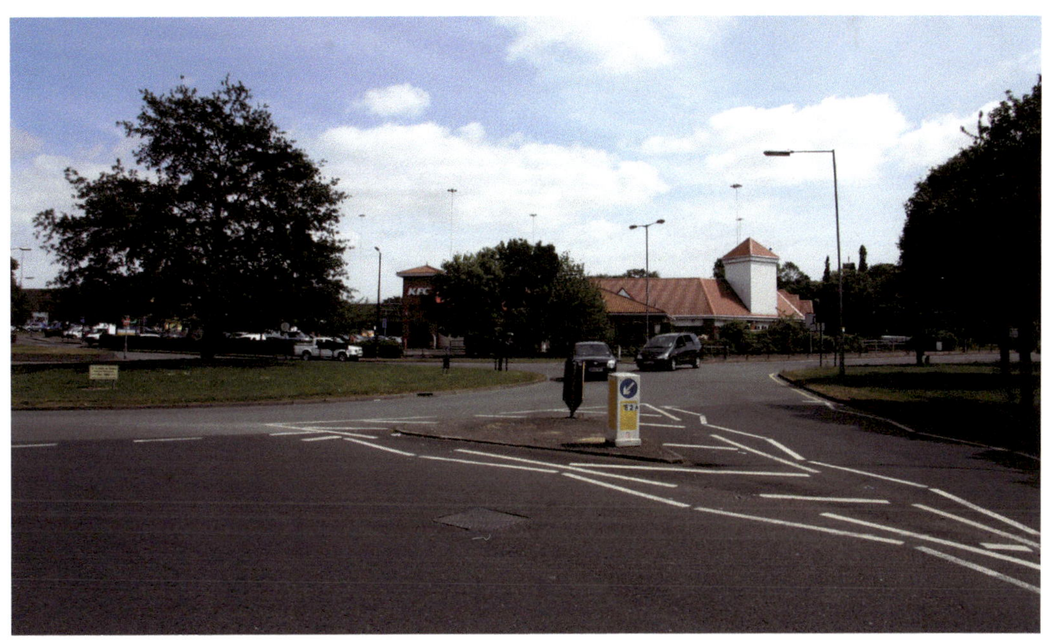

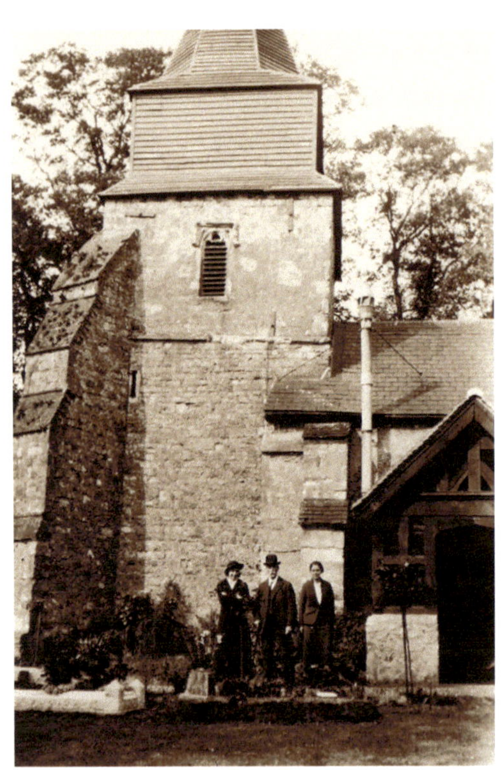

Bowers Gifford – St Margaret of Antioch

St Margaret of Antioch was built by Sir John Giffard *c.* 1400. Its tower and wooden spire were added in Tudor times. It was a gift from the Giffards, Lords of the manor, who gave their name to Bowers Gifford. Sir John fought in the battle of Crecy in 1346 with Edward III, and there is part of a brass depicting him in his armour in the Sanctuary. It is believed that a church has stood here from Saxon times, and that the first building was made from wood. Today, it is only used on a Sunday; it is a very remote building.

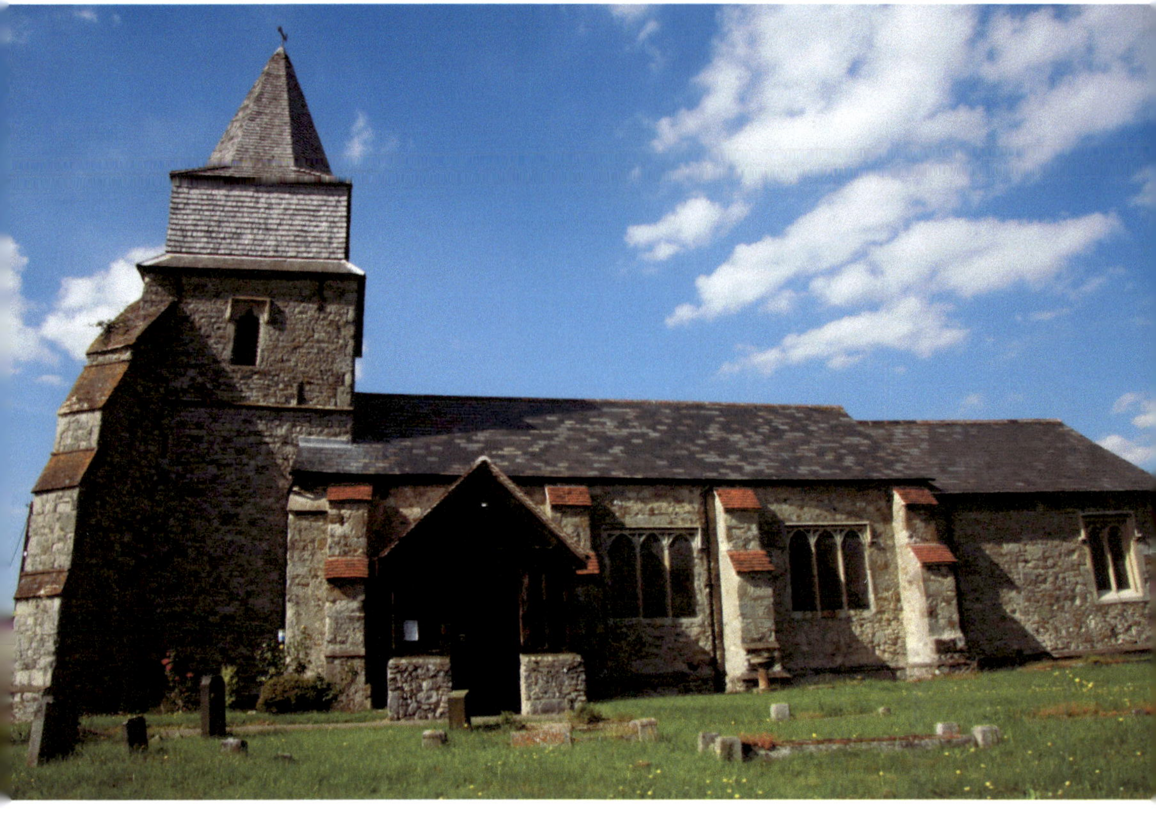

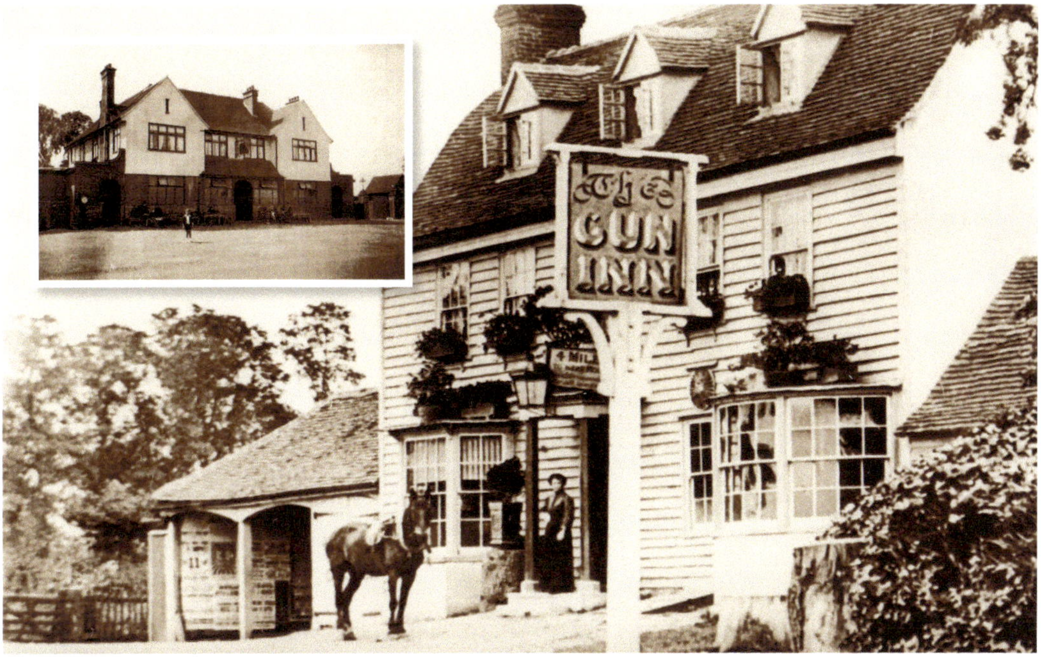

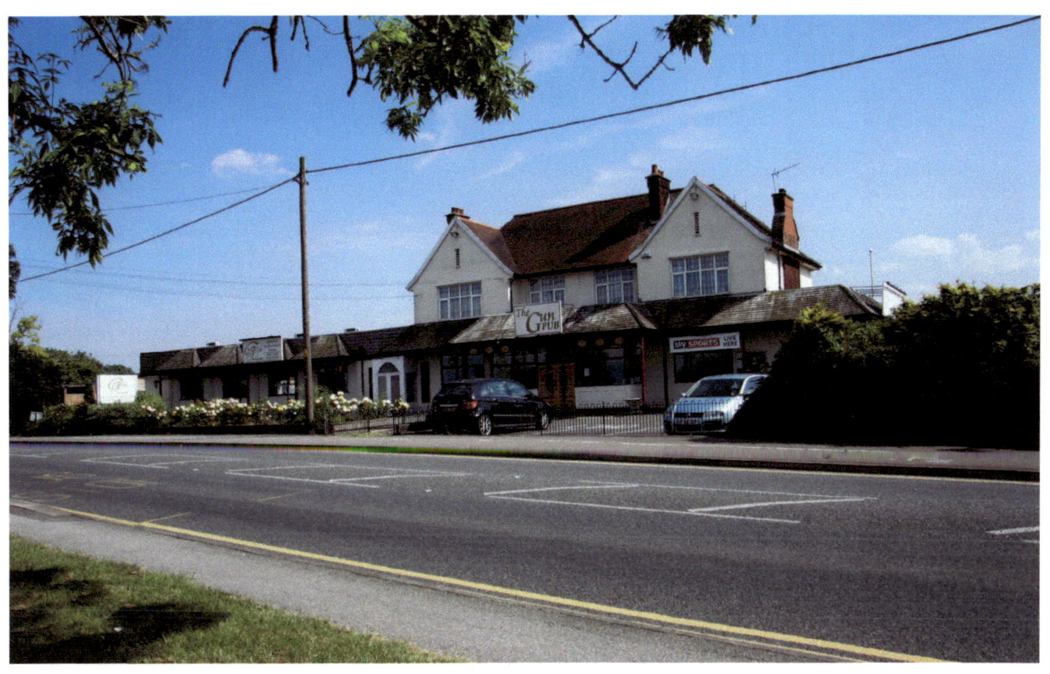

Bowers Gifford – The Gun Inn, London Road

The Gun Inn of the 1900s dates back to at least 1769, when the first recorded landlord owned it. A huge iron cage stood outside – drunks were put in here to cool off! It was rebuilt after the First World War and was popular for dances and singsongs around the piano. After recent years, having acquired a reputation as a rough pub, it was put up for sale. The new owners have turned the reputation around, and it is now known as the Gun & Golzar, serving English pub food and Persian food within its restaurant.

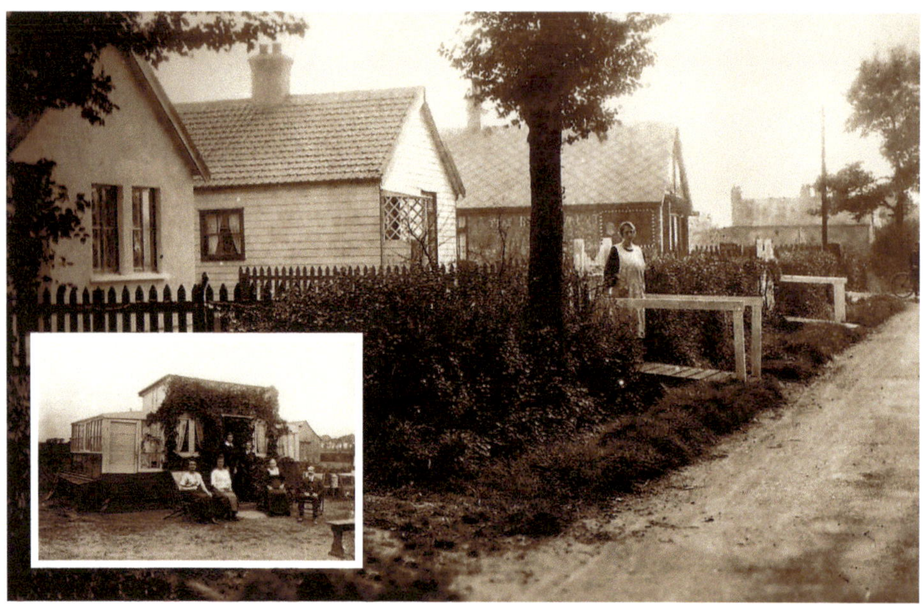

Above is a family outside its plotland home in 1910. The lady in the next picture is crossing a footbridge from her plotland home in Pound Lane in the 1920s. She is wearing an apron that was commonly worn for domestic activities around that time. Today, the only places that have a resemblance to the original plotlands are buildings down Pound Lane and nearby side roads.

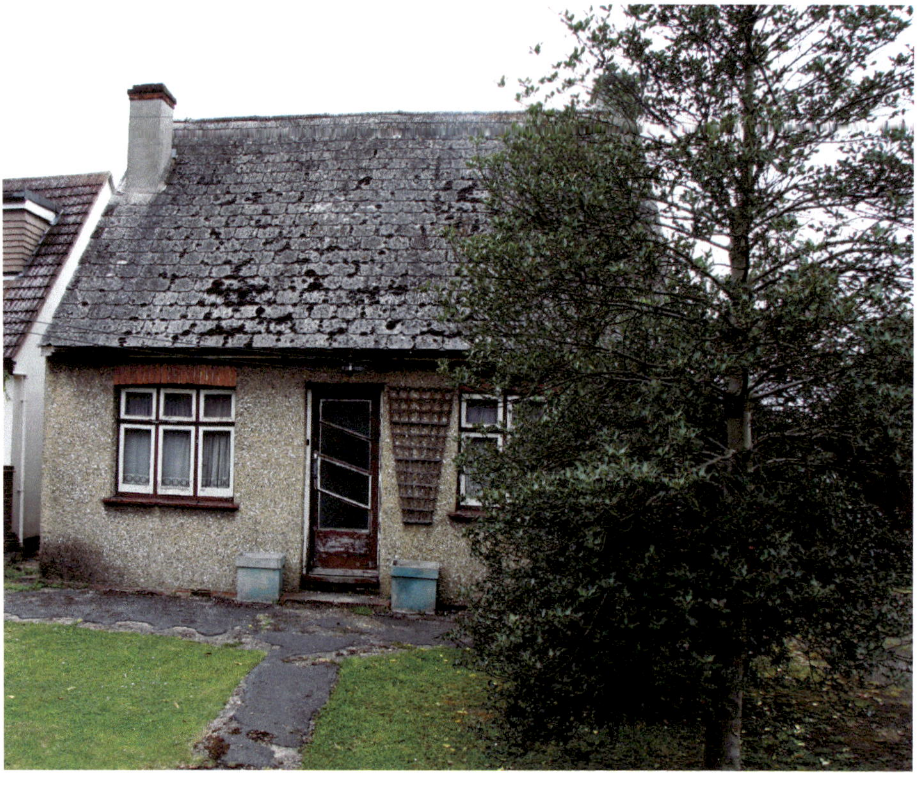

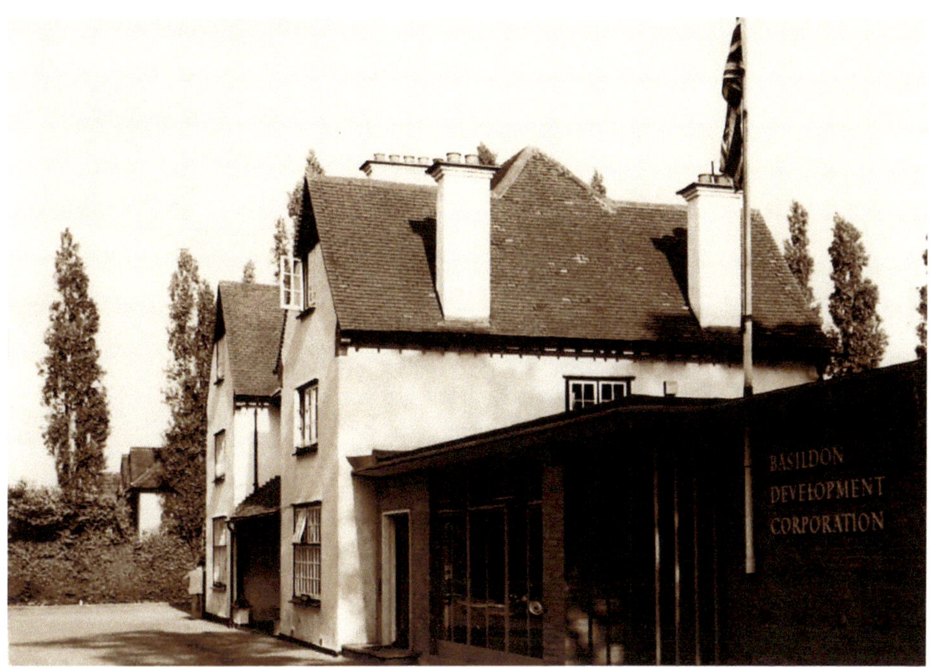

Bowers Gifford – Gifford House

It seemed that the Basildon Development Corporation chose this building in London Road, Bowers Gifford, as it was quite distant from the designated area of the New Town. It was used for administration and planning. Previously, the War Office had used it as a medical centre in the Second World War, but it was originally built in 1924 for the rector of Bowers Gifford to use as a college. In 2006 a new building took its place, called Gifford House Care Home, which was run by AMS Care Ltd.

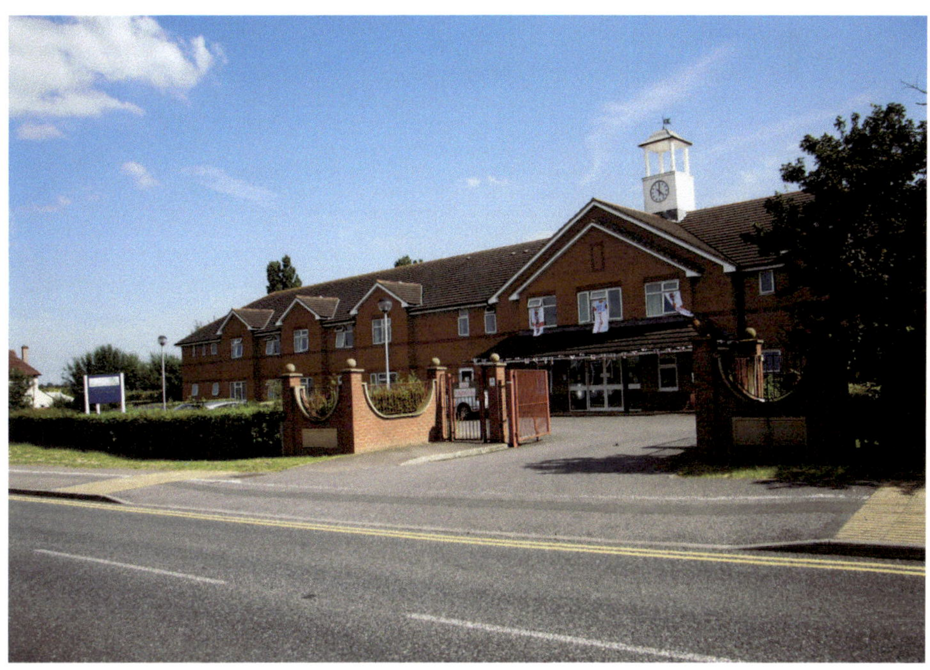

Acknowledgements

My sincere gratitude to the following for allowing me to reproduce photographs in this book: Basildon Borough Heritage Group, who have supplied all the old pictures from their extensive collection, apart from ones by:

Michael Marchant: pages 14 (*top*), 32 (*top*), 34 (*top*), 36 (*top*).

Tim Williams: page 75 (*top*), and for supplying Robin Woosey's picture: page 56 (*inset*).

Michelle Jeakins: page 27 (*inset, top and bottom*).

Marilyn DeBattista from St Luke's Hospice: page 66 (*bottom*).

Photographer, Peter Reynolds, who took the stunning photographs of Basildon Town and around: pages 45 (*bottom*), 50 (*bottom*), 53 (*bottom*), 54 (*inset*), 54 (*bottom*), 57 (*inset*), 60 (*bottom*), 64 (*bottom*), 65 (*bottom*), 67 (*bottom*).

I'd also like to thank Lisa Ford for allowing me to take pictures of: pages 36 (*bottom*), 37 (*top*), 37 (*bottom*).

The other modern-day photographs were taken by the author. I would like to express my gratitude to Vin Harrop, Founder and Director of the Basildon Heritage Trail, for past and recent support. Thank you to the following for sharing their memories: Ann Rugg (nee Bullimore), Peter Robinson and Nina Humphrey – Laindon. Michael Marchant – Radion Cinema, Laindon, Langdon Hills. Michelle Jeakins for writing about D. C. Jeakins. Co. Ltd, Laindon. Penny Betteridge and Amanda Farley – Laindon and Langdon Hills. Lisa Ford – West Ham Sanatorium, Langdon Hills. Gary Clark – Laindon and Basildon, Wendy King – Basildon. Gary Stolworthy – Basildon Bus Station, Andrew Adams from Johnson Tiles – Basildon Bus Station. Marilyn Battista – St Luke's Hospice, Basildon. Tim Williams – Depeche Mode, Vange.

I'd like to thank my family for their patience and feedback. I'd also like to thank Emily Tinker and my publisher, Amberley Publishing, for their assistance in producing this book.